THE ENGLISH FAMILIAR ESSAY IN THE EARLY NINETEENTH CENTURY

THE ENGLISH FAMILIAR ESSAY IN THE EARLY NINETEENTH CENTURY

THE ELEMENTS OLD AND NEW WHICH WENT INTO ITS MAKING AS EXEMPLIFIED IN THE WRITINGS OF HUNT, HAZLITT AND LAMB

MARIE HAMILTON LAW

NEW YORK

RUSSELL & RUSSELL · INC

1965

FIRST PUBLISHED IN 1934
REISSUED, 1965, BY RUSSELL & RUSSELL, INC.
BY ARRANGEMENT WITH MARIE HAMILTON LAW
L. C. CATALOG CARD NO: 65-17906

PRINTED IN THE UNITED STATES OF AMERICA

PREFACE

This study is based upon an examination of the familiar essays of Hunt, Lamb and Hazlitt with the purpose of determining the elements old and new which went into the making of the familiar essay in the early nineteenth century. In the absence of a definitive edition of the essays of Leigh Hunt, it has been impossible to make a thorough study of this essayist. The majority of Hunt's familiar essays appeared in his own periodicals, now difficult of access. The collections which have been made of his essays are far from inclusive; and a goodly number of his familiar papers still await an editor. Those which have been reprinted have in many instances suffered from extensive cutting, so that a study of them is necessarily incomplete.

I should like to take this opportunity to express my appreciation and indebtedness to Professor Percy Van Dyke Shelly for his direction of this study, which owes its completion to his guidance, encouragement and unfailing interest. I count it a great privilege to have had the inspiration afforded by his scholarship. I also wish to express my appreciation to the members of the English Department under whom I have studied for their kindness, and the vision they have given me of a scholarly and human approach to literature.

I am deeply indebted to Mrs. Anne Wallace Howland, Librarian of the Drexel Institute, Mr. Seymour Thompson, Librarian of the University of Pennsylvania, and Mr. E. R. B. Willis, Associate Librarian of Cornell University, and to the Staffs of these libraries for their courtesy and helpfulness in making the materials of this study available to me.

M. H. L.

Philadelphia, May, 1932.

CONTENTS

THE PERIODICAL ESSAY IN THE EIGHTEENTH CENTURY: THE *TATLER,* THE *SPECTATOR,* AND THEIR SUCCESSORS

The term "essay" continues to baffle and confound the makers of definitions, and its use in English for writings of many different kinds can but embarrass the sensitive critical conscience. Such widely varying types as Montaigne's essay *On Gardening,* Bacon's aphoristic essays, Locke's *Essay on the Human Understanding,* the periodical essays of Addison and Steele, the critical, biographical and historical papers of Macaulay, the scientific essays of Huxley, the versified philosophy of Pope's *Essay on Man*—have all been termed essays. A definition which should embrace such a variety of compositions would necessarily be so loose as to be no definition at all. One writer speaks of the essay as "a tempting label for any piece of writing which does not easily come within any of the better defined categories." [1] But this is merely to empty the word of all critical value, and to divorce it from its proper literary association. Certainly, for critical purposes, we must distinguish between writings which possess some distinction of thought and manner and certain qualities of permanence and those that are merely topical, ephemeral, journalistic, or technical—in other words between essays on the one hand and all those articles, "papers," and treatises which burden our current periodicals, both popular and learned, and which flourish today and tomorrow are cast into the oven. The term "essay" must be kept true to its high lineage and long and distinguished tradition, at least by the critic and the literary historian. Even in this sense the word is a broad one, including essays of different kinds; and these the critic must be careful to distinguish. But the highest type of all, the one that is most certainly to be classed as pure literature and ranked among the

---

[1] Jacob Zeitlin, ed. *Seventeenth Century Essays,* N. Y., 1926, Introduction, p. v.

fine arts is the personal or familiar essay, which Alexander Smith called "the lyric of prose," and which emerged in the work of Montaigne.

The most distinguishing mark of the familiar essay is its subjectivity; personality is its keynote. "It is not my acts that I write," said Montaigne, "it is I, it is my essence." The familiar essay conveys the moods, the fantasies and whims, the chance reflections and random observations of the essayist, and it has been excellently defined as "a short prose composition in which the author, writing of himself or of something that is near to his heart, discloses his personality to the reader in an intimate and familiar way." [2] Introduced into England in the seventeenth century, the *Essays* of Montaigne in the translations of John Florio (1603), and Charles Cotton (1685) soon attained a vogue, and this type of personal essay struck roots in English soil in the work of Sir William Cornwallis, Sir Thomas Browne, Abraham Cowley, and Sir William Temple—in these much more than in the essays of Bacon.

At the beginning of the eighteenth century a kind of essay appeared, known as the periodical essay, which held the attention of the English public throughout the century, and which although it has certain characteristics of the familiar essay, is to be distinguished from it. It contains description, narration and informal discussion, and treats trivial material in a whimsical manner. It is written for the most part in the first person, is conversational in tone, addresses the reader in friendly fashion, taking him into the writer's confidence, is witty, humorous and brief. Therefore in many essentials it is closely allied to the familiar or personal essay. Moreover, the periodical essayist sometimes introduces autobiographic elements into his writing, and expresses his opinion on many subjects, but he is not self-revealing in the manner of the familiar essayist. He does not show the innermost working of his heart but conceals himself behind a fictitious figure such as Isaac Bickerstaff, or the Spectator. Also the periodical essayist has an ulterior purpose: to report the news "foreign and domestic," to

---

[2] Prof. P. V. D. Shelly, "The Familiar Essay," *University of Pennsylvania Public Lectures*, 1916-17. Phila., 1917, p. 227 f., where will be found also a differentiation between the familiar essay and other related but different types.

afford entertainment, and to bring about reform in morals, manners and taste. To these ends he makes use of various kinds of writing, short stories, literary criticism, anecdotes, character sketches, letters and satire. His writing is more objective than subjective and his aim is never lost sight of. Thus in several essentials the periodical essay differs from the familiar essay, and between the seventeenth century personal essay and the eighteenth century periodical essay there is a real distinction. At the same time there are in the familiar essays of later development, especially in the early nineteenth century, many elements from former times, and the nineteenth century familiar essay could not have taken the form it did, had it not been for eighteenth century developments. To trace the elements old and new which went into the making of the familiar essays of Hunt, Lamb and Hazlitt is the purpose of this study. In these three writers the familiar essay reached its period of greatest development in England, and this sudden outburst and flowering of so important a literary *genre* is a phenomenon that demands explanation.

In the work of Hunt, Lamb and Hazlitt the familiar essay preserved all of its earlier characteristics but became so infused with the romantic spirit that it took on new colors and tendencies in a degree to distinguish it from the essays which had preceded it. True to its kind it followed no plan and had no purpose moral or didactic. Its charm consisted in its numerous digressions, its flavor of good conversation, the warmth of its imaginative fancy, and the self-revelation of the writer. The subject matter, grave, gay, humorous, witty, depending upon the mood of the essayist, displayed infinite variety: "On Going a Journey," "The Fear of Death," "The East Wind," "Bad Weather," "A Day by the Fire," —such papers revealed in prose a romantic spirit which found its counterpart in the poetry of the period. The essay partook of the prevailing romanticism in its return to the past, both in the impassioned recollection of past events, and in the charm with which the ancient and enduring is invested; in the poetic descriptions of nature which discover man's kinship to the natural world about him; in the sympathetic portrayal of humble life, in the melancholy sentiment which tinges many of the themes, and in the grotesque features introduced which add the element of strangeness.

The perfect freedom of the familiar essayist to wander whither his fancy led, to range over all time, and to employ any theme, to begin where he pleased and to stop when he wished afforded an aesthetic delight which had been wanting in the more limited range of subject matter, and in the realistic treatment characteristic of the periodical essay in the eighteenth century. The length of the familiar essay was likewise subject to the whim of the essayist; he might write briefly or at length, create a finished whole within a few pages or continue his paper serially. The familiar essayist, unlike the periodical essayist, wrote for no special coterie or group, nor did he make use of any set devices. He was free to use any literary form he desired; the narrative, the epistle, the dialogue, the "confession," the reverie, the impassioned recollection—all might be employed by him in turn. His style had a flavor, it bore the imprint of his mind and personality; it was in short the man. Such a style, self-revelatory, highly flexible, adapting itself to the theme without losing its individuality was essentially "literary" as distinguished from journalistic.

But though imbued to such an extent with the new spirit, the familiar essay in the nineteenth century gathered to itself elements characteristic of the periodical essays of Addison and Steele. It adapted to its use the letter, the character-sketch and the travel sketch, stamping these forms with its own familiar spirit. Thus the familiar essay as developed by Hunt, Lamb and Hazlitt carries on the tradition of Montaigne in that it is familiar in style, in subject matter, and in its revelation of the author's personality. It takes over certain characteristics of the periodical essay, and acquires a new interest through its romantic coloring.

In tracing the development of the familiar essay in the nineteenth century the outstanding topics which deserve consideration are its divergence as a literary form from the periodical essay which preceded it; the spirit of the age which fostered it; the periodicals in which it first emerged; the intellectual currents, old and new, which affected it, and the individual genius of the writers who early brought it to full flower.

The tone and temper of the eighteenth century were so unlike that of the nineteenth that it has become a commonplace to say that the latter represents a revolt from the former. The love of form, of ordered beauty, of the classical unities, which impressed their stamp upon the eighteenth century, in the succeeding age gave way to intellectual experimentation, to a seeking after new forms of expression, and to a play of imagination which in its exuberance looks back to the Elizabethans. This desire to break away from old forms and stereotyped ideas is apparent in the essay no less than in other imaginative literature. The familiar essays of Hunt, Lamb and Hazlitt are in marked contrast to the periodical essays of the *Tatler, Spectator, Rambler* and other literary magazines of the period. The transition, however, from one age to another, no matter how apparent, never constitutes a definite "break." The signs of coming change may be perceived afar off; and the new age builds upon the old, appropriating what it finds good and discarding the rest. So it was in those centuries which we commonly label with the respective tags, "classical" and "romantic." Pulsations of the romantic revival could be felt throughout the eighteenth century, and when this movement finally had gained sufficient strength to be perceived as such, it represented a fusion of the old and the new.

The work of Steele and Addison in the *Tatler* and the *Spectator* is typical and will serve to illustrate the characteristics of the eighteenth century essay in general. Charles Lamb said that it was impossible to pick up Montaigne without starting up a *Spectator* or a *Rambler* and this is true not only of many of the subjects chosen for discussion and of the manner in which classical writing is ransacked to provide illustration or to make some point complete, but also of the way in which the reader is taken into the writer's confidence. But whereas Montaigne confided his thoughts to paper chiefly for his own satisfaction and the diversion of his friends, Steele and Addison aimed to reach a wider audience. The Town in the age of Anne was in need of reform, and this the periodical essayist undertook, not in a dogmatic fashion but with the avowed purpose "to trace human life through all its mazes and recesses, and show much shorter methods than men ordinarily practice, to be happy, agreeable and great."

In the beginning the contents of the *Tatler* showed the influences of earlier publications such as Defoe's "Mercure Scandale; or

Advice from the Scandalous Club" (1704-05)[3]; the *Gentleman's Journal* (1692-94) ; and the *Monthly Miscellany* (1707-08). News, foreign and domestic, miscellaneous entertainment of all kinds, including poetry, music, translations, "novels," essays, fables, book notices, questions and answers which took the form of letters, were the stock-in-trade of these early periodicals. Their characteristic features were the natural outgrowth of the society for which they were written. It was in the London coffee houses that such papers as the *Tatler* found their widest circulation. Here the representatives of the aristocratic and middle classes came together, and over the steaming cups read and commented upon the news. The topics of conversation were not confined to politics and business but reflected the varied interests of city life, including its pastimes, follies and scandals.

Although the *Tatler* followed at first the general plan of the earlier journals in the selection of "news," Steele made two important contributions: he introduced a literary quality into his paper, thereby, as Professor Graham has pointed out, combining for the first time journalism and literature.[4] He also devised the plan of dating his news from various places, and it was to this latter "discovery" that the periodical essay owes its development, for it was from that section of the *Tatler,* purporting to be written "From My Own Apartment" that the essay serial gradually achieved its form. Steele originally planned to date "accounts of gallantry, pleasure and entertainment" from White's Chocolate House, poetry from Will's Coffee House, learning from the Grecian, foreign and domestic news from St. James's, and other material on a variety of subjects from "My Own Apartment." He, however, did not confine his letters to the subjects assigned to the various coffeehouses, and all departments were not represented in each number of the *Tatler.* Professor Greenough[5] has called attention to the fact that out of a total of four hundred and fifty-six papers in the *Tatler,* two hundred and five are dated "From My Own Apart-

---

[3] A department of Defoe's *Weekly Review.*

[4] Prof. Walter Graham, *English Literary Periodicals,* N. Y., 1930, p. 70.

[5] Prof. C. N. Greenough, "The Development of the *Tatler* Particularly in Regard to News." *Pub. Mod. Lang. Assn.* (1916), xxxi, p. 633 f.

ment." After the hundredth number, the *Tatler* consisted usually of one essay. For the departmentalized periodical covering a number of topics was substituted a single paper, which, like the drama, held the mirror up to nature. Contemporary life is pictured in all its phases, and so excellent is the characterization and the lively narration of incident that the novel is all but discovered. The material is presented in a realistic and usually objective manner.

This realistic tendency in the eighteenth century essay is especially manifested in the interest shown in the minute details of daily life, which is reflected in the *Tatler* in the topics chosen for discussion and in its description of type figures familiar to the London world. The beau, the dandy, the rake, the woman of fashion, the demimondaine, the merchant, the professional man are drawn to the life. The pages of the *Tatler* reveal London as a "Main Street" wherein the social world is exposed with satirical realism. The characters are often labeled with names familiar in romance, and they are sometimes enveloped in a cloak of fable, but the essential truth of the picture is not blurred, but rather etched with cameo clearness. The writer allows himself no digression, he has a point to make, an object in view and he holds steadily to his purpose. He addresses his audience in a spirit of friendliness; he takes them into his confidence, but he is not in "undress and slippers." He moralizes, but he scarcely presents a philosophy of life. The periodical essayist keeps his feet firmly upon the ground, he records the life about him, and a large part of the entertainment he afforded was owing to the truth of his pictures. Men liked to see the life of the town reflected, to hear topics discussed which were familiar. This type of writing set a pattern which held its audience until the end of the century—sufficient proof, if any were needed, of its popularity.

That the reader might still further be brought under the spell of realism, numerous devices were adopted to hold his interest. The dating of news from the various coffee-houses, the employment of a mouthpiece who had the all-seeing eye of one intimately acquainted with the London scene, and the many "clubs" which appear in the pages of the *Tatler* helped to create an atmosphere of reality and to give to the pictures of town life an added verisimilitude. The publishing of letters from supposed correspondents, and the reported conversations which took place in the clubs and coffeehouses were added realistic features.

The *Spectator* carried on the features of the earlier paper, and at the same time gave added emphasis to the realistic elements. Its varied literary fare included letters, stories, moral essays, allegories, fables, poetry and literary criticism. Like the *Tatler*, it aimed to enliven "morality with wit and to temper wit with morality." Isaac Bickerstaff was replaced by Mr. Spectator, who carried on the spirit of reform in a daily essay which treated of manners and morals in an entertaining fashion. The "club" feature was given added prominence by the creation of Sir Roger de Coverley and his friends, who typified well-known figures in English life. Sir Roger marks a great advance in realistic character-drawing in the essay. The characters in the *Tatler* illustrate certain moral attributes, but they are types, who never attain full-length portraiture. Sir Roger de Coverley is at once a type and an individual. Gradually the *Spectator* papers unfold the story of his life until he emerges a creation of flesh and blood. The portraiture is more complete than that of the earlier character-sketches, and is achieved by a wealth of realistic detail, characteristic of biography or of the novel. Realism in the *Spectator* is not confined to character delineation but infuses description of whatever kind.

The critical essays of the *Tatler* and *Spectator* do not claim our attention in this study, but they are interesting for two reasons: first because the eighteenth century critical audience was becoming an ever wider one owing to the rise of a middle class financially able to enjoy the products of the arts; and second, because of the association in the same periodical of essays devoted to criticism and essays dealing with manners, morals, politics and a wide variety of subjects. The result of this association is to be seen in the nineteenth century in the periodicals of Leigh Hunt, and in such magazines as the *London,* which in their contents carried on the idea of the miscellany. Lamb, Hazlitt and Hunt were all critical essayists of ability, turning their pens at will to criticism or to the writing of familiar essays. In their versatility they followed in the footsteps of Addison and Steele, just as the periodicals for which they wrote reflected features of the eighteenth century. Moreover, there could have been no such audience for the work of the early nineteenth century essayists, had the taste for such periodical literature not been slowly developing.

The *Tatler* and *Spectator* papers undoubtedly had more influence upon the familiar essay than did other periodicals of the eighteenth century, but other works of the same type are not without interest in tracing the transition in the essay form from the eighteenth to the nineteenth century.

In the first half of the eighteenth century over seventy new periodicals were published, many of which were but weak imitations of the *Tatler* and *Spectator*. The periodical essay which had put down such vigorous roots in the early part of the century seemed destined to extinction in journals which dealt in trivialities and lacked originality. In the second half of the century however, the periodical essay flourished anew in the work of Dr. Johnson, Goldsmith, and writers of lesser note who infused new vitality into the form. Periodicals appearing in the latter half of the century which deserve mention are the *Covent Garden Journal,* the *Rambler,* the *Idler,* the *Adventurer,* the *Connoisseur,* the *Bee,* the *Lounger,* and the *Mirror.* Of interest also are Goldsmith's "Citizen of the World" papers which appeared in the *Public Ledger.*

Not until the publication of Goldsmith's *Bee* (1759) did the periodical essay exhibit a romantic tendency,[6] but prior to this a more serious moral note, a less restricted outlook upon life, and a distinct literary quality is to be noted in several essay periodicals. The realistic tendency in some instances deepened, and excellent character-drawing and a conversational flavor continued to be characteristic of the periodical essay. Henry Fielding's essays in the *Covent Garden Journal* (January 4-November 25, 1752) deserve mention because of their literary quality, and also because of certain parallelisms which may be drawn between them and the work of the early nineteenth century familiar essayists. Fielding retained the literary devices of Addison and Steele, and like them essayed reform by satirizing the follies of London society. He

---

[6] This does not refer to critical essays, notably, those of Addison "On the Pleasures of the Imagination" (*Spectator,* Nos. 411-21), which show an appreciation of elements commonly associated with romanticism, such as wonder, strangeness, etc.

shows the same realism, gusto, sane outlook upon life, and sympathy for his fellow men in his essays as in his novels. Of the familiar essayists, Lamb in his zest for life, his healthy optimism and deep sympathy is most like Fielding. A close parallel may be drawn between Fielding and Hunt, Lamb and Hazlitt in the manner in which they decorate their essays with mottoes, quotations and literary paraphrase drawn from their intimate knowledge of books. In the manner too in which Fielding laughs *with* rather than *at* humanity, in his conversational style, and the way in which he takes the reader into his confidence may be seen his affinity to the early nineteenth century familiar essayists.

The realistic qualities which characterized the *Tatler* and *Spectator* are likewise marked in the *Rambler,* the *Adventurer* and the *Idler,* in all of which Dr. Johnson was either a leading or a guiding spirit.[7] The Rambler (March 20, 1750-March 14, 1752) struck a deeper moral note and indulged in even fewer flights of imagination than had its predecessors. "As it has been my principal design," said Dr. Johnson, "to inculcate wisdom or piety, I have allotted few papers to the idle sports of imagination."[8] He discarded to a large extent the paraphernalia of clubs and coffee-houses, and while he employed the traditional mouthpiece, it is almost without characterization. It has been remarked that Johnson, although by no means ignorant of life and manners, "could not descend to familiarities with tuckers and commodes, with fans and hoop-petticoats,"[9] and this is in general true, although upon occasion, he too concerned himself with feminine foibles. In the *Adventurer* (November 7, 1752-March 9, 1754), and the *Idler* (1758-1760), an effort was made to afford more entertainment, and

---

[7] The exact share Dr. Johnson had in the writing of the *Adventurer* has been the subject of discussion. It seems clear that Dr. Hawkesworth was the originator of the periodical, and perhaps its leading spirit. Dr. Johnson is credited by Chalmers with having written twenty-nine of the total of one hundred and forty papers. Marr is less definite, asserting that "Johnson, in addition to his assistance at the outset, wrote a good deal for the *Adventurer."* *British Essayists,* ed. by A. Chalmers, Lond. 1817, Vol. 19, p. xxxvi; George S. Marr. *Periodical Essayists of the Eighteenth Century,* N. Y., 1924, p. 137.

[8] *The Rambler,* No. 208.

[9] *The Rambler,* Historical and Biographical Preface by A. Chalmers, p. xlii. (The British Essayists.) Lond. 1823.

the excellent character sketches of well-known London types add humor and a more jovial spirit to the otherwise serious material. Dr. Johnson was a close student of human nature, and many of his sketches of people, are so detailed that they seem to have been drawn from life. In minuteness and truth of observation, his character portrayal is similar to that in the essays of Hunt, Hazlitt, and Lamb. Dr. Johnson complains that whereas his predecessors "had the whole field of life before them, untrodden and unsurveyed," he is "forced to peep into neglected corners, to note the casual varieties of the same species" and by minute industry to make distinctions "too subtle for common eyes." [10] In this respect also the early nineteenth century familiar essayists followed Dr. Johnson's lead by peeping into "neglected corners" and noting "casual varieties." Hunt describes his fellow-travellers in a stage-coach, and sailors and kitchen-maids; Lamb writes on chimney sweepers and the street beggars of London, Hazlitt delineates footmen and the character of country people. The theme of Dr. Johnson's essay "A Journey in a Stage Coach" [11] was later used to excellent advantage by Hunt and DeQuincey. Dr. Johnson's contributions to the *Rambler, Adventurer* and *Idler* are notable in that they enlarged the scope of the periodical essay in their deeper moral note, in their wider outlook upon society as a whole, and in their comparative freedom from the many literary devices of the *Tatler* and the *Spectator*.

If Dr. Johnson's essay periodicals at times struck too serious a vein, the reading public found a ready antidote in *The World* (January 4, 1753-December 30, 1756), a weekly essay journal edited by Edward Moore under the patronage of Horace Walpole and the Earl of Chesterfield. The light and entertaining tone of this periodical is forecast in the design of its editor which was "to ridicule, with novelty and good-humour, the fashions, follies, vices, and absurdities of that part of the human species which calls itself The World, and to trace it through all its business, pleasures, and amusements." [12] Its mouthpiece, Adam Fitz-Adam, a world-wide

---

[10] *Idler*, No. 3.

[11] *Adventurer*, No. 84.

[12] *The World*, No. 1.

traveler, master of science and learned in all languages, proposed to cure "lying, cheating, swearing, drinking, gambling, avarice, and ambition in the men; and envy, slander, coquetry, prudery, vanity, wantonness, and inconstancy in the women." [13]   In general design, therefore, the *World* was of the Tatler-Spectator type.   It is important for the advance it marks toward the modern magazine in the variety of its subject matter.   It includes besides topics of perennial interest to the town such as dueling and gambling, more serious matter such as "The Composition of Letters" by Horace Walpole, Chesterfield's recommendation of Johnson's *Dictionary*, the transmigration of souls by Soames Jenyns, and the reformation of the calendar.

The *Connoisseur* (January 31, 1754-September 30, 1756), a six-page weekly serial, was published and chiefly written by George Colman and Bonnell Thornton, two young Oxford men.   In design the *Connoisseur* imitates the realistic features of the *Tatler* and *Spectator*, without arriving at their excellence.   Mr. Town, critic and Censor-General, the successor to Bickerstaff, undertakes to correct the vices and follies of society by ironical comment which seldom assumes a very deep or serious tone.   His censorship includes the country as well as the town, and it is his "chief ambition to instruct and please the ladies."   Most of the subjects treated are second-hand and the remarks commonplace, and often coarse. The *Connoisseur's* chief claims to attention are the essays contributed to it by Cowper, and its influence upon Leigh Hunt.   Cowper's essays: "On Keeping a Secret" (No. 119), a "Letter from Mr. Village" (No. 134), and "On Conversation" (No. 138)[14] in subject matter and treatment closely approximate the familiar essay.   Cowper writes in the first person in an easy conversational style, with a foretaste of that quality which later made his letters such pleasant reading.   Like the early nineteenth century essayists he has a seeing eye, and he develops his essays by means of an amplification of small details.   In his "Letter from Mr. Village," giving "an account of the present state of the country churches,

---

[13] Op. cit.

[14] Two other papers, Nos. 111 and 115, are assigned to Cowper on internal evidence. No. 111 is signed "W. C." A. Chalmers, *British Essayists*, vol. 30, pp. xxii-xxiii.

their clergy, and their congregations," he describes in detail the dress and manners of those assembled for worship. The picture is a very amusing, if not a pious, one. In the manner in which Cowper adorns his essays with brief character sketches, he also provides a tie between the periodical essayists of the eighteenth century, and the nineteenth century familiar essayists. His character sketches in their brevity are like those of the *Tatler*, but in the essay frame provided for them, he furnished an example to the familiar essayists. In his essay "On Conversation," for example, he draws an interesting comparison between the conversation of the French and English, and gives point to his remarks by briefly characterizing the various types of conversationalists: the Attitudinarians and Face-Makers, the Professed Speakers, the Tatlers, the Half-Swearers, the Phraseologists, the Silent Men. He follows the same method in his essay "On Keeping a Secret," where he draws in humorous fashion and with great accuracy of observation, the characters of men who are unable to keep the confidences entrusted to them.

The influence of the *Connoisseur* upon Leigh Hunt was a direct one. "The lively papers of the *Connoisseur*," he writes in his *Autobiography*, "gave me an entirely fresh and delightful sense of the merits of essay-writing. I began to think that when Boyer crumpled up and chucked away my "themes" in a passion, he had not done justice to the honest weariness of my anti-formalities, and to their occasional evidences of something better." [15] Hunt thought some of the papers of the *Connoisseur* equal in humor to those of Goldsmith; although he later decided that "they had no pretensions to the genius of the *Vicar of Wakefield*." [16] Immediately following Hunt's acquaintance with the *Connoisseur*, he wrote his first prose for publication, a series of papers called "The Traveller," which appeared in the evening paper of the same name (afterwards incorporated with the *Globe*). Hunt wrote under the signature of "Mr. Town, junior, Critic and Censor-general" in imitation of the "Mr. Town" of the *Connoisseur*. He relates how he offered his papers "with fear and trembling" to the editor of the *Traveller*, and "was

---

[15] Leigh Hunt, *Autobiography*, Lond. 1891, p. 124.
[16] Ibid., p. 126.

astonished at the gaiety with which he accepted them." [17] "Luck-
ily," Hunt says, "the essays were little read; they were not at all
noticed in public." [18]

Goldsmith's *Bee* (October 6-November 24, 1759) in its essay
material shows a closer approximation to the work of the nineteenth century familiar essayists than any of the periodicals which
had preceded it. In the introduction to the first number, Goldsmith
declares his intention of pursuing no fixed method in his periodical.
"Like the Bee," he says, "which I had taken for the title of my
paper, I would rove from flower to flower, with seeming inatten-
tion, but concealed choice, expatiate over all the beauties of the
season, and make my industry my amusement." [19]

The *Bee* did not differ in its range from preceding essay periodicals, but in its general tone, it is more modern. Between it and
Leigh Hunt's *Indicator*, for instance, there is no such gap as between the *Tatler* and the *Indicator*. In fact the *Bee* and the *Indicator* bear a close resemblance to each other, even in name, for
Hunt named his "after a bird which shows people where to find
wild honey." One of the chief distinctions between the *Bee* and
such an immediate predecessor as the *World* is in the absence of the
editorial devices which the *Tatler* and its imitators had employed.
The *Bee* has no "Isaac Bickerstaff," or any anonymous mouthpiece
between author and reader. Nor is the frame device of "clubs"
or coffee houses employed. Some of the essays are presented as
letters, but the correspondents' column on personal matters has
vanished. Although the *Bee* was advertised as "consisting of a
variety of essays on the amusements, follies and vices in fashion,
particularly the most recent topics of conversation," it is the latter
that is given emphasis. A little travel and biography, theatrical
criticism, translations, stories taken from various sources, and moral
dissertations on abstract topics—"On Justice and Generosity," "On
the Instability of Worldly Grandeur," etc.,—make up the bulk of the
contents. The fop, the beau, the cuckold, the roarer, the world of
London fashion and folly no longer parade so frequently across the

---

[17] Op. cit., p. 125.
[18] Ibid.
[19] *The Bee*, No. 1 (Oliver Goldsmith, *Miscellaneous Works*, with biographical introduction by Prof. Masson. Lond., 1928.)

pages. The horizon has widened; Goldsmith views the scene with a more philosophical detachment than his predecessors. His moral essays display at times the seriousness of Johnson. His remarks upon the follies of his day have none of the "sparkle" or smart satire which characterize those of the *World*. In the first number he assured his readers that neither war nor scandal should form a part of his paper, and to this policy he adheres. His essay "On Dress" is a lively and humorous account of feminine fashions, which shows keen powers of observation. His recollection in this essay of his walk in the park with his Cousin Hannah, is in the familiar vein of the nineteenth century essayists, and exhibits the ability to draw character, to report dialogue, to invest an incident with humor, and to flash the whole before the reader in a few sentences, a talent which Lamb possessed in high degree. It also is illustrative of the transparent wall which separates this type of essay writing from the relating of incident in the novel.

Goldsmith's familiar mood is to be seen in the following passage: "When I reflect on the unambitious retirement in which I passed the earlier part of my life in the country, I cannot avoid feeling some pain in thinking that those happy days are never to return. In that retreat all nature seemed capable of affording pleasure; I then made no refinements on happiness, but could be pleased with the most awkward efforts of rustic mirth; thought cross-purposes the highest stretch of human wit, and questions and commands the most rational amusement for spending the evening. Happy could so charming an illusion still continue! I find age and knowledge only contribute to sour our dispositions. My present enjoyments may be more refined, but they are infinitely less pleasing. The pleasure Garrick gives can no way compare to that I have received from a country wag, who imitated a Quaker's sermon. The music of Mattei [20] is dissonance to what I felt when our old dairymaid sang me into tears with Johnny Armstrong's Last Good Night, or the Cruelty of Barbara Allen." [21] This would be exactly the mood in which Lamb or Hazlitt wrote, if it were heightened a little, and the recollection made more impassioned. Hazlitt recalling Wem, and

---

[20] In the 1765 Edition "of Mattei" was altered to "of the finest singer."

[21] "Happiness In a Great Measure Dependent on Constitution," *The Bee*, No. 2.

Lamb musing on his childhood days at "Blakesmoor," are inspired with the same pleasurable sensations. The similarity is further emphasized by the fact that the recollection is truly autobiographic.[22]

"A City Night Piece" is also written in familiar vein, and Goldsmith's description of those "who make the streets their couch, and find a short repose from wretchedness at the doors of the opulent" [23] is in marked contrast to the picture of London life drawn by preceding eighteenth century essayists. Something of the music of poetry as well as a touch of rhetoric, is in Goldsmith's prose: "The clock has just struck two, the expiring taper rises and sinks in the socket, the watchman forgets the hour in slumber, the laborious and the happy are at rest, and nothing wakes but meditation, guilt, revelry, and despair. The drunkard once more fills the destroying bowl, the robber walks his midnight round, and the suicide lifts his guilty arm against his own sacred person. . . . What a gloom hangs all around! The dying lamp feebly emits a yellow gleam; no sound is heard but of the chiming clock, or the distant watch-dog."[24]

The varied styles in which Goldsmith wrote in the *Bee* are worthy of note. That he consciously altered his style to suit the subject matter, we know from the introduction to the first number, where he states that "there is a studied difference in subject and style." [25] But whether Goldsmith writes in the reasoned manner of his essay "On Education," or in the familiar style of the papers already quoted, indulges in "A Reverie," narrates the story of Hypatia, or with scientific exactness describes the life of a spider, his prose is clear, simple, flexible, and unmannered. It bears the stamp of no age, but is as fresh today as when it was written. There are indications that Goldsmith in the *Bee* and in his essays contributed to the *Busy Body*, the *British Magazine*, etc., was trying to appeal to a higher standard of taste than that catered to by the average magazine. His "Specimen of a Magazine in Miniature" is an excellent

---

[22] Goldsmith wrote Mr. Hodson, Dec. 27, 1757: "If I go to the opera where Signora Colomba pours out all the mazes of melody, I sit and sigh for Lissoy's fire-side, and Johnny Armstrong's Last Good Night from Peggy Golden." Oliver Goldsmith. *Works*, edited by Peter Cunningham, Lond., 1854, p. 31 (notes).

[23] *The Bee*, No. 4.

[24] Ibid.

[25] Ibid., No. 1.

satire on the contents of the average magazine of the time. In the *Bee* (No. 4, October 27, 1759) he comments upon its slow sale, and says: "perhaps I was mistaken in designing my paper as an agreeable relaxation to the studious, or an help to conversation among the gay; instead of addressing it to such, I should have written down to the taste and apprehension of the many, and sought for reputation on the broad road. Literary fame, I now find, like religious, generally begins among the vulgar." [26]

Goldsmith made a further contribution to the essay in his *Citizen of the World* papers which first appeared in the *Public Ledger*, 1760-61. This series of one hundred and twenty-three letters,[27] purporting to have been written by a Chinese living in England, appealed to the London public which had tired of the usual moral disquisition of the periodical essayists. In the learned Chinese critic, Lien Chi Altangi, Goldsmith found a means of criticising the English nation by comparing it with a foreign land. Instead of using the device of club and coffee-house, he bound his essays together by a "frame-tale" which supplied the amusement and love-interest. The large design is a moral one: to expose the follies of his generation, and to satirize "prevailing absurdities which commonly usurp the softer names of fashions." Unlike Johnson, he does not attempt to deal with vices common to all men.

The familiar style in which the *Citizen of the World* papers were written subjected Goldsmith to criticism since the pseudo-oriental works of the period were couched in grandiloquent and flowery language, supposed to be imitative of the Eastern manner. Goldsmith replied to his critics: "What is palmed upon you daily for an imitation of Eastern writing no way resembles their manner, either in sentiment or diction." [28] Also he pretended that his style was the result of translation: "The Editor on this, and every other occasion, has endeavored to translate the letter-writer in such a manner as he himself, had he perfectly understood English, would have written." [29] The conversational tone of Goldsmith's style, the

---

[26] *The Bee*, No. 4.
[27] In the original series in the *Public Ledger* there were one hundred and eighteen letters.
[28] *Public Ledger*, Letter XXXI. *Citizen of the World*, Letter 33.
[29] *Public Ledger*, Letter XXXII.

romantic mood of some of his essays, his excellent characterization, and keen power of observation all helped to point the way to the familiar essay of the next century.

Goldsmith's essays were favorites of Leigh Hunt. "Goldsmith enchanted me," he writes. "I knew no end of repeating passages out of the *Essays* and the *Citizen of the World*—such as the account of the Club, with its Babel of talk; of Beau Tibbs, with his dinner of ox-cheek, which 'his grace was so fond of'; and of the wooden-legged sailor. . . . Then there was his correct, sweet style; the village painting in his poems; . . . and above all, the *Vicar of Wakefield*—with Burchell, whom I adored." [30] Hunt in his zest for life, his "animal spirits," his optimism, his good nature, his sympathy and his unworldliness has much in common with Goldsmith, whom he also resembles in the simplicity and easy grace of his style, and in his ability to draw character touched with humor.

Hazlitt also was an admirer of Goldsmith. He thought him "more observing, more original, more natural and picturesque than Johnson," [31] and he considered Beau Tibbs "the best comic sketch since the time of Addison." [32]

Certain characteristics of the writing of the early nineteenth century familiar essayists are also to be found in two Scotch essay periodicals, the *Mirror* (1779-1780), and the *Lounger* (1785-1787). The *Mirror*, a single essay periodical, which made its first appearance January 23, 1779, was issued every Tuesday and Saturday by Henry Mackenzie, author of the *Man of Feeling*, assisted by a group of friends, none of whom had previously written for publication. The aim of the paper as stated in the first number, was "to hold, as it were, the Mirror up to Nature, to show Virtue her own features, Vice her own image, and the very age and body of the Time his form and pressure." The intention was not only "to show the world what it is," but "to point out what it should be." [33] The difficulties of the periodical writer are set forth at some length, and are of interest as showing the attitude of the

---

[30] *Autobiography*, pp. 126-27.
[31] "On the Periodical Essayists," *Collected Works of William Hazlitt*, ed. by A. R. Waller and Arnold Glover, Lond. 1903, v. 8, p. 104.
[32] Ibid., p. 105.
[33] *Mirror*, No. 1.

public at this time toward the essay periodical. "An anonymous periodical writer, when he first gives his work to the public, is pretty much in the situation of the stranger. If he endeavour to amuse the young and the lively, by the sprightliness of his wit, or the sallies of his imagination, the grave and the serious throw aside his works as trifling and contemptible. The reader of romance and sentiment finds no pleasure but in some eventful story, suited to his taste and disposition; while with him who aims at instruction in politics, religion, or morality, nothing is relished that has not a relation to the object he pursues. But no sooner is the public informed that this unknown author has already figured in the world as a poet, historian, or essayist; that his writings are read and admired by the Shaftesburies, the Addisons, and the Chesterfields of the age; than beauties are discovered in every line; he is extolled as a man of universal talents, who can laugh with the merry, and be serious with the grave; who, at one time, can animate his reader with the glowing sentiments of virtue and compassion, and, at another, carry him through the calm disquisitions of science and philosophy." [34]

The usual subjects common to the essay periodical are found in the *Mirror*. Theatrical and literary criticism, education, duelling, the character of a man of fashion, "female manners," national character of France and England, modern good-breeding compared with the ancient, dreams, superstition and the fear of death, calamities incident to extreme old age, a dangerous species of coquette, are among the topics discussed, an assortment which in its range suggests nothing new. The importance of the *Mirror* in the development of the essay is its attitude toward nature, which is "romantic" as compared with the traditional attitude of Addison and Johnson. The effect of nature upon man, the feelings of sadness it inspires and the recollections it awakens form the theme of the essay "Of Spring" (*Mirror*, No. 16), written by Mackenzie. An extract will serve to illustrate its romantic vein:

"Amidst the returning verdure of the earth, the mildness of the air, and the serenity of the sky, I have found a still and quiet melancholy take possession of my soul, which the beauty of the

---

[34] Op. cit.

landscape and the melody of the birds rather soothed than over-came. . . . Spring, as the renewal of verdure and of vegetation, becomes naturally the season of remembrance. We are surrounded with objects new only in their revival, but which we acknowledge as our acquaintances in the years that are past. Winter, which stopped the progression of nature, removed them from us for a while, and we meet, like friends long parted, with emotions rather of tenderness than of gaiety..

"This train of ideas once awakened, memory follows over a very extensive field. And, in such a disposition of mind, objects of cheerfulness and delight are, from those very qualities, the most adapted to inspire that milder sort of sadness which, in the language of our native bard, is 'pleasant and mournful to the soul.' They will inspire this, not only from the recollection of the past, but from the prospect of the future. . . ." [35]

A romantic tendency is also evident in the description of natural scenery in the paper entitled "Effects of Excessive Delicacy and Refinement" (Mirror No. 10), written by W. W. Craig, a lawyer. Its sentiment is worthy of the author of the *Man of Feeling:* "Our road lay through a *glen*, romantic and picturesque, which we reach-ed soon after sun-set, in a mild and still evening. On each side were stupendous mountains; their height; the rude and projecting rocks, of which some of them were composed; the gloomy caverns they seemed to contain; and the appearance of devastation, occa-sioned by traces of cataracts falling from their tops, presented to our view a scene truly sublime. Mr. *Fleetwood* felt an unusual elevation of spirit. His soul rose within him, and was swelled with that silent awe, so well suited to his contemplative mind. In the words of the poet, he could have said,

> —"Welcome, kindred glooms,
> Congenial horrors, hail!
> —Be these my theme,
> These that exalt the soul to solemn thought,
> And Heavenly musing!" [36]

The literary criticism of the *Mirror* also exhibits a romantic attitude. In the paper entitled: "Advantage which the Artist in

---

[35] *Mirror*, No. 16.
[36] Ibid., No. 10.

the Fine Arts has over Nature in the Assemblage and Arrangement of Objects; exemplified in Milton's Allegro and Penseroso," the following passage occurs: "Verses may be polished, and may glow with excellent imagery; but unless, like the poems of Parnel, or the lesser poems of Milton, they please by their enchanting influence on the heart, and, by exciting feelings that are consistent, or of a similar tendency, they are never truly delightful." [37]

The *Mirror* was discontinued Saturday, May 27, 1780. Its demise was credited among other things, to Edinburgh's not having the same attraction for the reader as London. That this drawback was not a serious one is proved by the fact that five years later the same group of writers started the *Lounger* (February 5, 1785-January 6, 1787) which like the *Mirror* is a single essay periodical. In the first number, Mackenzie takes the reader into his confidence: "A Lounger of the sort I could wish to be thought, is one who, even amidst a certain intercourse with mankind, preserves a constant intimacy with himself; it is not, therefore, to be wondered at, if he should sometimes, if I may be allowed the expression, correspond with himself, and write down, if he can write at all, what he wishes this favourite companion more particularly to remark. Exactly of this sort are the notes and memorandums I have sometimes been tempted to make: transcripts of what I have felt or thought, or little records of what I have heard or read, set down without any other arrangement than what the disposition of the time might prompt. These little papers formed a kind of new society, which I could command at any time, without stirring from my fireside." [38]

The *Lounger*, like the *Tatler* and *Spectator*, deals with the lesser moralities: "The creed of custom is not always that of right; and it is the privilege of such a work, as well as one of its chief uses, to attack the intrenchments of fashion, whenever she is at war with modesty or virtue." [39]   Present-day manners are contrasted with those of a former age by the clever fiction of the return of its

---

[37] *Mirror*, No. 24.
[38] *Lounger*, No. 1.
[39] Ibid., No. 2.

eidolon, Colonel Caustic, to society after a period of retirement, caused by an unhappy love affair. Such a person "is somewhat in the situation of the foreigner. Like him, he is apt to be misled by prejudices; but like him, too, he remarks many things which escape the observation of those whose sensations are blunted by habit, and whose attention is less awake to the objects around them." [40] Thus the device of the foreign spectator or critic is combined with that of the native countryman, by the simple expedient of making the *eidolon* a kind of Rip Van Winkle. Also, as in the earlier periodicals, special attention is given to the interests of its feminine readers. Mackenzie throws down his gauntlet, so to speak, and declares that "Every periodical writer, like every knight-errant of old, in assuming his office, is understood to swear fealty to the Ladies." [41] The character sketches in the *Lounger* are particularly well done. The art of drawing character seems to have especially interested Mackenzie and his fellow-workers, judging from an essay in the *Mirror*,[42] which carefully analyzes the different kinds of character-writing and points out the faults of each. Leigh Hunt in his *A Book for a Corner* quotes two character-sketches from the *Lounger*—those of the old lady and the old gentleman. Hunt's own sketches, on the same themes, were undoubtedly influenced by those in the *Lounger*.

The century closed without producing any periodicals which in content, style or form bring us closer to those of the nineteenth century. Imitations of the *Tatler* and *Spectator* continued to appear, but the material was becoming outworn. A contributor to the *Monthly Mirror* (1795) complains: "Periodical publications are daily coming into disgrace. The moral and intellectual world were never so enlightened and improved as when Addison, Steele, and others gave their lucubrations to the public. The form, the method, the system remained, but the animation, the genius, the soul were fled." [43]

---

[40] *Lounger*, No. 14.

[41] Ibid., No. 22.

[42] "Of the Art of Drawing Characters in Writing," *Mirror*, No. 31.

[43] Quoted from G. S. Marr, *Periodical Essayists of the Eighteenth Century*, p. 247.

Another writer, Vicesimus Knox, who published a collection of forty essays: *Winter Evenings, or Lucubrations on Life and Letters* in the last decade of the century, likewise notes the decline of periodical essays: "Diaries of belles and beaus, extraordinary intelligence, cross readings of newspapers, are now worn thread-bare. Indeed, every mode of humour, which the *Spectator* adopted, has been imitated so often as to have lost something of its grace." [44]

Toward the latter part of the century the essay serial appeared less and less as a separate publication, and by the beginning of the nineteenth century had virtually disappeared. The only important exception is Leigh Hunt's *Reflector* (1810-1811). The essay was taken over by the magazines and newspapers, which continued to increase in number if not in importance. Also, the rise of the novel, in the latter half of the eighteenth century, absorbed much of the attention of the reading public. Fiction was no longer regarded as fit only for entertainment, but was looked upon as a serious form of literature with a moral purpose. And the criticism of the novel in reviews and magazines called popular attention to this new literary form.

From this review of the essay in certain outstanding periodicals of the eighteenth century, it is apparent that all the forms which it took were developed in the *Tatler* and the *Spectator*. Moral, critical, "character," anecdotal, epistolary, autobiographic, and narrative essays, allegories, dreams, Oriental fantasies, "little novels"—had all made their appearance in the first quarter of the century. After that, the most significant contributions made to the essay in the course of the century consisted not in the development of new types, but in the romantic spirit which infused some of the papers, notably those of Goldsmith, Mackenzie and his circle, and in the effort to introduce a more serious note into the essay, to divorce it from the doings of the town, to widen the scope of its subject matter, and to get rid of the many stereotyped devices and "frames" which imitation rendered outworn. The failure to achieve entire success in freeing the essay in the latter half of the century from imitation of earlier models is somewhat difficult to understand, but may be partially accounted for by the fact that the reading

---

[44] "On Some Peculiarities in Periodical Essays," *Winter Evenings*, Lond., 1823, vol. I, p. 22.

public had acquired a taste for the essay periodical of the *Tatler* and *Spectator* type, and were dissatisfied when such writers as Johnson and Goldsmith made an effort to break away from the old devices.

Particularly important in its effect upon later essayists was the literary style of the periodical essay. Simplicity, urbanity, grace, intimacy may be said to characterize much of the essay-writing of the period. The clear style, which adapted itself to the subject in hand, the intimate relations established between essayist and reader, the wit and humor, the variety of subject matter, the excellent delineation of types, the concreteness lent by "characters," the use of quotations to adorn and enforce—these characteristics carried over into the familiar essay of the nineteenth century.

CHAPTER II

THE TURN OF THE CENTURY: THE NEW PERIODICALS AND THEIR RELATION TO THE ESSAY

The essay in the eighteenth century had not only become established as one of the leading literary forms, but it had proved adaptable to practically all kinds of subject matter. Therefore the nineteenth century found at hand a form which admirably suited its needs. The spirit of the age demanded expression; many leavens had been at work since Addison's lucubrations upon Queen Anne society. Two great forces: the French and the Industrial Revolutions had stirred England politically, economically, socially and spiritually. She had witnessed the mighty spectacle of a nation no farther distant than the width of the Channel, shaking off the fetters of Church and State, and proclaiming a new freedom, whose contagion had spread with fire-like rapidity. In England the virus was all the more effective because of its native origin in the theories of Locke, Hobbes and Hume. Reinforced by the doctrines of Rousseau, Helvetius, Montesquieu and Diderot, the new freedom had been given added momentum by the cataclysm of revolution. Rousseau in his *Social Contract* had broken the idol of the divine right of kings, and set on foot educational reform through his *Emile*. Helvetius' theories reappeared in the utilitarianism of Jeremy Bentham and his disciples, and gave impetus to needed social reforms. Holbach's doctrine of Necessity, the philosophical ideas flowing into England from Germany, the many questions raised by the French Encyclopedists, and new discoveries in science quickened men's minds and produced an intellectual ferment which sought satisfaction in reading and discussion. The application of machinery to industrial processes gave rise to new social and economic problems, and created a feeling of sympathy for the common man, caught in the maelstrom of conditions, with which he had no power to cope. The eighteenth century had wit-

31

nessed the rise of the middle class to a position of political and financial importance—the nineteenth century became "class conscious" of the laboring man, of whom Crabbe and Burns had sung, and whose tragic lot was poignantly expressed by Wordsworth. The dignity and worth of man as man asserted itself in the form of a strong individualism which became one of the dominant elements in the Romantic Revival. Poetry as well as prose was enlisted in the cause of liberty and justice. Wordsworth, hailed the French Revolution as the deliverer of mankind, and wrote an ode in which he declared carnage was God's daughter[1]; Shelley, in his political allegory, *The Revolt of Islam,* "sought to enlist the harmony of metrical language . . . in the cause of a liberal and comprehensive morality," and to kindle in the hearts of his readers "a virtuous enthusiasm for . . . doctrines of liberty and justice." [2]   Byron likewise turned his pen to the defense of liberty. Literature reflected current questions, and there was a rapidly forming reading public interested in these questions.

The multiplication of newspapers, magazines and reviews in the early part of the century was in answer to a direct demand on the part of the reading public. Hazlitt well suggests this when he says: "Knowledge is no longer confined to the few: the object therefore is, to make it accessible and attractive to the many. . . . We can no longer be churls of knowledge, ascetics in pretension. We must yield to the spirit of change (whether for the better or worse); and 'to beguile the time, look like the time.'" [3]   Besides the desire of people to keep informed on current questions, two other factors were responsible for the increase in the reading public: the extension of public education, and the improved methods used in printing and distributing newspapers, periodicals and books. The educational movement was greatly accelerated in the first half of the century. Half a million pupils were attending day schools in 1818, and by 1833 the number had doubled, the ratio being one day student to every eleven persons.[4] The "school master was abroad,"

---

1 *Ode* No. XLV, *Poems dedicated to National Independence and Liberty,* ed. by Hutchinson, Oxford, 1895.

2 Percy Bysshe Shelley. *Complete Poetical Works,* Bost., 1901, p. 45.

3 "The Periodical Press," *Works,* vol. x, p. 210.

4 A. H. Thorndike, *Literature in a Changing Age,* N. Y., 1920, pp. 23-24.

as Lord Brougham declared. His "Society for the Diffusion of Useful Knowledge," founded in 1827, was one of several which by means of low cost publications sought to make reading matter accessible to the masses. The Sunday school movement was another means by which popular education was promoted.

Coincident with the increased facilities for education was the use of steam power for printing. September 28, 1814, marks a new era in journalism for on that date the London *Times* was first printed on presses operated by steam, making it possible to produce eleven hundred impressions per hour. The result was the increase of the printed word at a rate which in some quarters was viewed with alarm. Hazlitt complains that "modern authorship is become a species of stenography: we contrive even to read by proxy. We skim the cream of prose without any trouble; we get at the quintessence of poetry without loss of time. The staple commodity, the coarse, heavy, dirty, unwieldly bullion of books is driven out of the market of learning, and the intercourse of the literary world is carried on, and the credit of great capitalists sustained by the flimsy circulating medium of magazines and reviews." [5]

Lamb also notes the change that the increase in magazines and reviews brought about: "Times are altered now. We are all readers; our young men are split up into so many book-clubs, knots of literati; we criticise; we read the *Quarterly* and *Edinburgh* . . . and instead of the old, honest, unpretending illiterature so becoming to our profession—we read and *judge* of everything. . . . We read to say that we have read." [6]

The early nineteenth century was an age of paradoxes. Amid the welter of politics, false philosophies, economic experiments and governmental evils, there was produced some of the finest imaginative literature in the English tongue. The familiar essay came to its perfection in journals given largely to political and personal animosities—and in the same person we find the urbane, graceful and self-revealing familiar essayist, and the political partisan who dipped his pen in acid when he wrote of his enemies.

We have already seen how the eighteenth century essay was

---

[5] "Lectures on the Age of Elizabeth," *Works*, v. 5, p. 319.

[6] "Readers against the Grain," *The Works of Charles and Mary Lamb*, ed. by E. V. Lucas, Lond., 1905, vol. I, p. 273.

shaped by the social conditions of its time and by the periodicals in which it appeared. The same is true of the familiar essay in the succeeding century; it was a product of the spirit of the age, and of the printed mediums which sponsored it.

The nineteenth century literary periodicals were one of the main influences in the development of the familiar essay. Among the factors which affected this development may be mentioned: (1) the additional space afforded. The earlier news sheets by their size limited the length to which the essay might run; the *Rambler* essays, for example, occupied regularly six folio pages. The *Tatler* and *Spectator* papers were limited by the folio half sheet upon which they were printed. The older magazines such as the *Gentleman's,* which carried over into the new century, were so crowded with miscellaneous information that little space was left for literary features. The periodicals of the nineteenth century that took literature for their province devoted a large proportion of their space, varying from a few pages to as many as twenty-two, to their essay features, thus enabling the essayist to expand his ideas. (2) The new literary periodicals reached a wider and more cosmopolitan reading public than had their predecessors. In the eighteenth century the essay serials had addressed themselves, as we have already noted, to a limited audience. In the next century, increased educational advantages enabled more men to read than ever before, and this enlarged the scope of the essay in theme and treatment. This was particularly true of the familiar essay, which directed its attention to no particular class or party, but ranging over a multiplicity of themes, appealed to the abiding interests of mankind. (3) The literary periodicals of the nineteenth century put greater emphasis upon literature, drama, the fine arts and criticism than had been possible in the narrow confines of the so-called "literary" periodicals of the preceding age. They set a high standard of excellence in writing, attracted to their pages the best literary talent of the time, and proved an inspirational force in developing authors who with the decline of literary patronage might otherwise have failed to find a hearing. They acted as a "proving ground" where a literary work might be tried out upon the public before its appearance in book form. This was particularly the case with regard to the familiar essay. The majority of the essays of Lamb,

Hazlitt and Hunt appeared first in periodicals, and one of the "Imaginary Conversations" of Landor had its initial publication in the *London Magazine* to guage its appeal to the public. Another stimulus was provided by the rivalry which sometimes existed among the contributors to the same or rival periodicals. Editors were urged to their best efforts by keen competition, and the essay achieved new standards in style and content.

The nineteenth century literary periodicals trace their family tree back to the seventeenth and eighteenth centuries, but in form and content they differed from their predecessors in a degree to warrant description, particularly those in which the familiar essay appeared. The work of the familiar essayists was confined to no one type of literary periodical, but appeared in reviews, magazines, and weekly journals of belles-lettres, in successors to the essay periodical such as Leigh Hunt's *Reflector,* and sometimes in newspapers. The form and content of these periodicals are interesting in relation to the essay types which they contained. The following comments make no attempt to group the periodicals by type, but rather to follow chronologically the development of the familiar essay in their pages.

The establishment of the *Edinburgh Review* and the *Quarterly Review,* in 1802 and 1809 respectively was a notable event in literary history, but it had no immediate effect upon the development of the familiar essay. Indirectly, however, it pointed the way to the establishment of a distinctly literary periodical, the *Reflector,* which first appeared in October, 1810. Its founder was Leigh Hunt, who was not only instrumental in developing the familiar essay, but provided the early vehicles for it. Hunt, who had for some time been associated with his brother John as editor of the *Examiner,* a weekly free lance political organ, now turned his journalistic ability to the conduct of a two-hundred page quarterly devoted to philosophy, politics and the liberal arts. Among the contributors were George Dyer, Barron Field, Dr. John Aikin, O. G. Gilchrist, Thomas Barnes and Charles Lamb, most of whom had been at Christ's Hospital where Leigh Hunt was educated. In a Prospectus Hunt announced that the *Reflector* was needed because "reform of periodical writing is as much wanted in Magazines as it was formerly in Reviews, and still is in Newspapers."

The old magazines were "notoriously in their dotage," and the new ones "returned to the infancy of their species—to pattern-drawing, doll-dressing, and a song about Phillis." He sums up the contents of these "flimsy publications" as "a little fashionable biography; some remarks at length on eating, drinking or dressing; an anecdote or two; a design or two for handkerchiefs and settees; a country-dance; a touch of botany; a touch of politics; a touch of criticism, a faux pas; and a story *to be continued,* like those of the Improvissatori, who throw down their hats at an interesting point and must be paid more to proceed." Hunt's first aim in the *Reflector,* he declares, will be to avoid the grosser faults of magazines, and to write "a Chronicle for posterity." Politics will be included because *"they are now, in their turn, exhibiting their re-action upon literature, as literature in the preceding age exhibited its action upon them."* Dramatic criticism and the fine arts are not to be neglected, but the principal feature of the *Reflector* is to be *"Miscellaneous Literature,* consisting of Essays on Men and Manners, Enquiries into past and present Literature, and all subjects relative to Wit, Morals, and a true Refinement. There will be no direct Review of Books, but new works, as far as they regard the character of the times, will meet with passing notice; and occasional articles will be written to shew the peculiar faults or beauties, injuriousness or utility, of such as have strongly attracted the public attention." [7]

Hunt epitomized the purpose of the *Reflector* when he said it was to reveal "the mind" of the times. It succeeded in giving a lively survey of metropolitan movements, but its crowning achievement was the essays of Charles Lamb. As Mr. Blunden has observed, Lamb was given a latitude in the *Reflector* which did not consist in liberality of space alone.[8] Here for the first time, if we are to judge from his previous discouragements, Lamb had opportunity to exercise his talent not only in criticism, but in the form with which he was experimenting—the familiar essay. "The *Reflector,"* says Mr. Lucas, "gave Lamb his first encouragement to spread his

---

7 The *Reflector,* a quarterly magazine on subjects of philosophy, politics and the liberal arts; conducted by the ed. of the *Examiner,* v. I, Oct., 1810 to Dec., 1811. Lond., 1811, pref. pp. iii-ix.

8 Edmund Blunden, *Leigh Hunt and His Circle,* N. Y., 1930, p. 60.

wings with some of the freedom that an essayist demands. . . .
It is not too much to say that had he lacked the preliminary training
which his *Reflector* exercises gave him his *Elia* essays would have
been the poorer." [9]

Lamb contributed fifteen papers to the *Reflector,* the last number of which contained seven of his essays. These *Reflector* papers
are particularly interesting because of the progress they indicate in
Lamb's development as a critical and a familiar essayist. "On the
Character and Genius of Hogarth," "On Garrick and Acting; and
the Plays of Shakespeare considered with reference to their Fitness
for Stage Presentation" are conceded to be among Lamb's best
work. These essays, aside from their remarkable critical faculty,
are evidence that he had already achieved a distinguished, highly
personal and flexible style, obedient to every turn of his thought.
In these critical essays he also reveals a faculty which later was to
make his familiar essays so delightful—the ability to let his mind
play over a subject, and illuminate it in unexpected ways, as when
he says of Hogarth: "Other pictures we look at, his prints we
read." Lamb's essays in familiar vein contributed to the *Reflector*
include "A Bachelor's Complaint of the Behaviour of Married
People," "Edax on Appetite," "*Hospita* on the Immoderate Indulgence of the Pleasures of the Palate," "The Good Clerk, a Character," "On Burial Societies; and the Character of an Undertaker,"
and "On the Inconveniences Resulting from being Hanged." These
papers show a close affinity to those of the *Spectator,* in their use
of the letter form and the "character." In interest and power of
expression, they are inferior to Lamb's critical essays, but they are
of exceeding value in a study of the development of the familiar
essay. They are proof that Lamb did not immediately strike the
rich vein of his style as a familiar essayist, although in "Rosamund
Gray" and in "The Londoner" he had given promise of the style
which he was later to develop. That Lamb for his essay form
should have gone back to Steele and Addison is the more interesting
since he was under no restrictions in writing for the *Reflector*.[10]

It was in the *Reflector* that Hunt first showed his ability as a
familiar essayist in his "A Day by the Fire." Here are pictured

---

[9] E. V. Lucas, *The Life of Charles Lamb,* N. Y., 1905, vol. I, p. 373.
[10] For further discussion of Lamb's *Reflector* essays see pp. 68-70.

the joys of the fireside at all hours of the day. The continual play of ideas upon the same theme, the many angles from which the writer views his subject, and the sustained fancy prove not the amateur trying his hand, but the finished essayist. Not only the essayist but the poet speaks, even though the medium is prose. The "charming current of personal sensation and thought," the self-revealing mood of the essayist, is what lends the essay its chief distinction. Hunt's other contributions to the *Reflector* likewise display a mastery of prose style, and a freedom and originality in critical opinion which was of inestimable value in an age when criticism was infused with personal and political animosity.

In December, 1811, with the publication of the fourth number, the *Reflector* was discontinued owing chiefly to lack of funds, but it had achieved a result greater than any its founder could have foreseen. It had brought Leigh Hunt and Lamb together, it had served as the cradle of the familiar essay in the nineteenth century, and in the history of periodicals it marked the fusion of the essay serial and the new type of review. That Hunt was making a conscious effort to supplant the old type of "literary" periodical is evident from the Prospectus, which clearly indicates the low estate to which periodical writing had been brought, and the need for reform.

The *Examiner,* a sixteen-page weekly periodical, was begun by Hunt and his brother John in 1808 as a "Sunday Paper, on Politics, Domestic Economy and Theatricals." Although primarily devoted to politics, it dealt with philosophy, poetry, criticism, statesmanship, ethics and theology, which Hunt humorously remarks, "all took a final tone in my lips." [11] It had for its object, in addition to parliamentary reform, "liberality of opinion in general . . . and a fusion of literary taste into all subjects whatsoever." [12] The *Examiner* owed its name to the paper of Swift and his fellow Tories. "I did not think of their politics," Hunt says. "I thought only of their wit and fine writing, which, in my youthful confidence, I proposed to myself to emulate; and I could find no previous political journal qualified to be its godfather." [13]

[11] *Autobiography*, p. 155.
[12] Ibid., p. 156.
[13] Ibid., p. 155.

Lamb was represented in the pages of the *Examiner,* but not as a familiar essayist. Besides several poems and epigrams he supplied a number of short articles under the head of "Table Talk" (1813), and in 1814 a paper on a play by Kenney as well as a poem on Jordan's acting. Hazlitt was added to the list of contributors to the *Examiner,* in 1814, during which year appeared his essays "On Posthumous Fame," "On Hogarth's Marriage-a-la-Mode," his review of Wordsworth's "Excursion," and "On the Love of Nature," the mystical elements of which have been compared to Wordsworth's "Intimations of Immortality." Meanwhile Hunt was practically the chief contributor to the *Examiner,* for which, in addition to political articles and theatrical criticism, he wrote his suburban essays, a series of political satires in doggerel verse, and "Sonnets on Hampstead."

The most important contribution of the *Examiner* to the familiar essay was the establishment of its Round Table column in 1815. In the opening number of the series Hunt explained that the writers would not assume fictitious characters; that they were "literally speaking, a small party of friends, who meet once a week at a Round Table to discuss the merits of a leg of mutton and of the subjects upon which we are to write." He gives his reason for doing away with the *eidolons* of the periodical essayists: "A hundred years back, when the mode of living was different from what it is now, and taverns and coffee-houses made the persons of the wits familiar to every body, assumptions of this kind may have been necessary. *Captain* Steele, for instance, the gay fellow about town, might not always have been listened to with becoming attention, or even gravity, especially if he had been a little too inarticulate overnight;—he therefore put on the wrinkles and privileges of Isaac Bickerstaff, the old gentleman. . . . We have not the same occasion for disguise; and, therefore, as we prefer at all times a plain, straight-forward behaviour, and, in fact, choose to be as original as we can in our productions, we have avoided the trouble of adding assumed characters to our real ones; and shall talk, just as we think, walk and take dinner, in our own proper persons." [14]

---

[14] *The Round Table: A Collection of Essays on Literature, Men, and Manners,* by William Hazlitt, Edinburgh, 1817, vol. I, No. 1.

This decision to do away with a device which had long been a feature of the periodical essay, marks an important departure. The intimate relation between writer and reader was not only maintained, but was made a still closer one by the essayist speaking in his own person. In this same paper Hunt also speaks of the Round Table writers' intention "to avoid the solitary and dictatorial manner" of the periodical essayists, and "without any sort of formality" to let "the stream of conversation wander through any ground it pleases." [15] In the second paper of the series, Hunt again emphasizes the informal nature of the "Round Table." The "conversation" is to be "casual and unconstrained," and "sometimes of the character of table-talk." "The same article may contain a variety of subjects, and start off from one point to another with as unshackled and extemporaneous an enjoyment as one of Montaigne's." [16]

The "friends" who were to sit at the "Round Table" were Barnes, Hazlitt and Hunt himself, but Barnes was unable to carry his share in the enterprise. The subjects to be treated were "Manners, Morals and Taste," and it was hoped that something of the chivalric glory of King Arthur and his knights might be revived. In addition to the essays which deserve the appelation "familiar," the material of the "Round Table" covered such topics as classical education, the value of life, the unreasonableness of women, human caprice and melancholy, Steele's *Tatler,* a tribute to Milton, modernizing Chaucer, ridicule of Methodists, thoughts on death, the doctrine of eternal necessity, the Malthusian theory. It is interesting to note that the familiar essay in the nineteenth century was thus appearing in the midst of diverse material. Its importance as a new literary type was scarcely yet appreciated, and it was still engaged in the process of divorcing itself from earlier models.

In 1816 Hunt contributed to the "Round Table" three character sketches, two of which "The Old Lady" and "The Maid-Servant" are among his most popular essays. Others of his written in the familiar mood which appeared in the "Round Table" are "Washerwomen," "On the Night-mare," a dream fantasy, and "A Day by the Fire," which had previously been printed in the *Reflector.*

---

[15] Op. cit., vol. I, No. 1.
[16] Ibid., vol. I, No. 2.

Hazlitt in his Round Table papers wrote more frequently in a reasoned and critical manner, than in a familiar style. His first essay, for example, "On the Love of Life," argues that the strength of our attachment to human life "is a very fallacious test of its happiness." It is adorned with quotations from Addison, Jeremy Taylor, Milton and others. Antithesis so fancied by the older essayists, is used with telling effect, but the essay lacks imagination and self-revelation. The majority of these papers by Hazlitt enter "into the meaning and logic of things; into causes and results; into motives and indications of character," but it is possible to discern a romantic and impassioned feeling which was later to become characteristic of Hazlitt as a familiar essayist. For instance, "On the Love of the Country" contains passages in praise of nature written in a romantic manner. The "Round Table" is important, as marking the emergence of Hazlitt as a familiar, or miscellaneous essayist, for in spite of the fact that many of his contributions to it were critical papers, his other contributions mark a distinct departure from his earlier parliamentary, dramatic and critical writings in other periodicals.

Hazlitt's development as a familiar essayist was undoubtedly hastened by a series of events which threw the burden of writing the Round Table upon him. He himself tells us how he came to be the sole support of the project: "Our plan had been no sooner arranged and entered upon, than Buonaparte landed at Frejus, *et voilá la Table Ronde dissoute*. Our little congress was broken up as well as the great one: Politics called off the attention of the Editor from the Belles Lettres; and the task of continuing the work fell chiefly upon the person who was least able to give life and spirit to the original design." [17]   Leigh Hunt had been released from prison February 3, 1815; in the following month Napoleon returned from Elba. His landing at Frejus thus indirectly bears upon the development of the essay.

The "Round Table" terminated January 5, 1817. In the same year Hazlitt had reprinted in book form a collection of essays contributed to the Round Table column in the *Examiner,* and to other periodicals. In the preface he states that out of the fifty-

---

[17] "Advertisement" to *The Round Table,* vol. I.   Edinburgh, 1817.

two numbers only twelve are Hunt's and for the remainder he alone is responsible.

In December 1818 Hazlitt began to write for Constable's *Edinburgh Magazine*. Here appeared "On Nicknames"; "On Respectable People"; "On the Question Whether Pope was a Poet"; "Remarks on Mr. West's Picture of Death on the Pale Horse." Of Hazlitt's essays other than critical in the *Edinburgh Magazine,* that "On Fashion" (September, 1818) warrants attention. In theme it is an echo of a favorite topic with the periodical essayists. But there the likeness ends. One has only to read Steele on the same subject [18] to realize the distance the essay has traveled. Where, in the eighteenth century essay periodicals can such "lucubrations" on fashion as the following be found? "Fashion is the abortive issue of vain ostentation and exclusive egotism: it is haughty, trifling, affected, servile, despotic, mean, and ambitious, precise and fantastical, all in a breath—tied to no rule, and bound to conform to every whim of the minute. 'The fashion of an hour old mocks the wearer.' It is a sublimated essence of levity, caprice, vanity, extravagance, idleness, and selfishness. It thinks of nothing but not being contaminated by vulgar use, and winds and doubles like a hare, and betakes itself to the most paltry shifts to avoid being overtaken by the common hunt that are always in full chase after it. It contrives to keep up its fastidious pretensions, not by the difficulty of the attainment, but by the rapidity and evanescent nature of the changes." [19]

"On Nicknames" (*Edinburgh Magazine,* September, 1818) is too much heated by the ardour of reform to take its place among the familiar essays whose chief aim is to give pleasure, but it is an excellent example of the manner in which Hazlitt could play endless variations on the same theme, and reinforce his ideas by quotation and example drawn from literature and the fine arts. There is nothing quite like this ability in the periodical essayists. It was not simply the result of learning and wide reading; if so Addison and Johnson would have possessed it. Neither does the spirit of the age entirely account for it. It seems rather to have been a matter of individual genius.

---

[18] *Guardian,* No. 10.
[19] *Works,* vol. XI, p. 438.

Although Hunt was instrumental in fostering the literary genius of Hazlitt and Lamb, their most mature work, or much of it, appeared not in Hunt's periodicals, but in a literary miscellany, the *London Magazine,* which was founded in 1820 under the editorship of John Scott, a brilliant journalist. The *London* represented the best type of the modern literary periodical and under the guidance of Scott became one of the leading critical journals. It began as a hundred-and-eighteen page miscellany, issued monthly, and aimed to present "sound principles in questions of taste, morals and politics." It also aimed to express the new cosmopolitan spirit, and gave space to foreign criticism and literature, and to "the theories and progress of the fine arts in the various national schools of Europe." [20]

Brief as was the *London's* career, it has been adjudged in its early years "richer in good authors and enduring literature than any other English magazine has been before or since." [21] Its fame, if it had nothing else to assure it, would be handed down to posterity because of Lamb's "Essays of Elia," De Quincey's "Confessions of an Opium Eater" and some of Hazlitt's "Table Talk" which appeared in its pages. The *London* not only set a high standard of literary criticism, and contained some of the best writing of the period, but also proved a patron of new authors. It launched De Quincey and Tom Hood upon their literary careers, and undoubtedly played a very definite part in fostering Lamb's literary powers. Its contributors met together at intervals, and the resulting exchange of ideas must frequently have fired many latent sparks of genius. Hood in his *Literary Reminiscences* has given a delightful picture of the dinners of the *London* group which included besides himself,—Lamb, Hazlitt, De Quincey, Carlyle, Henry Francis Cary, the translator of Dante, B. W. Proctor, Allan Cunningham, Thomas Hood, George Darley, John Clare, the peasant poet of Northamptonshire, Hartley Coleridge, Thomas Noon Talfourd, Horace Smith, J. H. Reynolds and Bernard Barton, the Quaker poet.

---

[20] See Prospectus to the first number of the *London Magazine.*

[21] F. E. Pierce, *Currents and Eddies in the English Romantic Generation,* New Haven, 1918, p. 199.

Between his contributions to the *Reflector* in 1811 and his work for the *London,* Lamb produced little in the familiar essay *genre* worthy of note, but in his Elia essays many of which appeared in the *London Magazine* from August, 1820, to August, 1825, he did his greatest work. During this period he wrote but little for any other periodical, and after 1826 he practically ceased writing except for three or four papers which appeared in the *Englishman's Magazine* in 1831.

To the *London Magazine* Hazlitt contributed some of his most characteristic work as an essayist. He wrote for it regularly from June, 1820, to December, 1821, and his work and Lamb's often appeared in the same issue. Hazlitt had introduced Lamb to Scott and, according to Talfourd, Hazlitt prevailed on Lamb to enter into a friendly rivalry with him. Hazlitt's first essay "On the Qualifications Necessary to Success in Life" was printed in the June, 1820, issue, and Lamb's first Elia essay, "Recollections of the South Sea House" appeared two months later. Echoes of the essayists' "rivalry" have come down to us. In a letter from Hazlitt to Scott (dated by W. C. Hazlitt April 12, 1820) we read "Do you keep the Past and Future? You see Lamb argues the same view of the subject. That 'young master' will anticipate all my discoveries, if I don't mind." [22] It is fairly certain, as Mr. Bertram Dobell has pointed out,[23] that Hazlitt had Lamb's "New Year's Eve" in mind, for it contains lines of thought similar to "On the Past and Future," and also has the phrase "young master" in it. Lamb's essay, however, did not appear in the *London* until January, 1821, and Mr. E. V. Lucas is at a loss to account for the disparity in the date of Hazlitt's letter and that of publication of the essay, except by the supposition that the letter is undated or indistinctly dated, and that W. C. Hazlitt conjectured the date. It seems more than likely that Hazlitt had seen Lamb's essay in manuscript, a supposition which has been discredited because he was not on good terms with Lamb at the time. "On the Past and Future" appeared in *Table Talk* in 1821. Hazlitt's essay, "On the Fear of Death," published in *Table Talk,* vol. II, 1822, also

---

[22] W. C. Hazlitt, *Four Generations of a Literary Family,* Lond. and N. Y., 1897, vol. I, p. 140.

[23] Bertram Dobell. *Sidelights on Charles Lamb,* Lond., 1903, p. 213.

contains passages which bear close resemblance to those in "New Year's Eve." It is unwise in such a case to attempt to determine indebtedness. Coleridge thought Hazlitt was more indebted to Lamb for ideas that Lamb was to Hazlitt, but on the other hand Hazlitt anticipated Lamb's ideas on several occasions. The free exchange of thought between these two friends is more interesting than important in its effect. Two of the best of Hazlitt's familiar essays, "On the Conversation of Authors" and "On Reading Old Books" appeared in the *London Magazine,* September 1820, and February 1821, respectively. In February 1821, Scott was killed in a duel, the outcome of his remarks against *Blackwoods* in the *London Magazine.* Baldwin, publisher of the *London,* called upon Hazlitt's aid in the emergency, and he wrote the editorial notes for the April number and four articles for the May issue. In May, 1821, Hazlitt was offered the editorship of the *London* and declined it.[24] He continued however as a contributor, and during the fall of 1821 wrote "On a Landscape of Nicolas Poussin," "Why Distant Objects Please," and "On Coffee-House Politicians"; in 1822-23 he contributed several papers on picture galleries.

Hazlitt's essays in the *London,* such as "On Reading Old Books," "On the Conversation of Authors," and "On Coffee-House Politicians" show a familiar and self-revelatory quality that contrasts with the reasoned style of his earlier essays. It is true that he had indulged in the mood of impassioned recollection in some of his previous papers, but the familiar note was not long sustained. As in the essay on fashion, Hazlitt again makes use of a periodical essay theme in "On Coffee-House Politicians." Portions of it, however, might have been written by Lamb himself, particularly those "thumb-nail" sketches of eccentric characters: "there was old S——, tall and gaunt, with his couplet from Pope and case at Nisi Prius, M—— eyeing the ventilator and lying *perdu* for a moral, and H— — and A— — taking another friendly finishing glass! These and many more wind-falls of character he gave us in thought, word and action. . . . Oh! it was a rich treat to see him describe M-df-rd, him of the Courier, the Contemplative Man, who wrote an answer to Coelebs, coming into a room, folding up his

---

24 P. P. Howe, *Life of William Hazlitt,* Lond., n.d., p. 326.

great coat, taking out a little pocket volume, laying it down to think, rubbing the calf of his leg with grave self-complacency, and starting out of his reverie when spoken to with an inimitable vapid exclamation of 'Eh!' M-df-rd is like a man made of fleecy hosiery: R—— was lack and lean 'as is the ribbed seasand.' " [25]

If such a passage suggests the drawing of character in Lamb's "Old Benchers of the Inner Temple" [26] even more does Lamb's essay "Detached Thoughts on Books and Reading," which appeared in the *London Magazine,* July, 1822, remind us of Hazlitt's paper "On Reading Old Books," which had appeared in the previous year. Without doubt an added impetus was given to the development of the familiar essay by the association of Lamb and Hazlitt in the *London Magazine.*

Another magazine to which Hunt, Hazlitt and Lamb contributed was the *New Monthly.* Under the name of the *New Monthly Magazine and Universal Register* it had been founded by Henry Colburn in 1814, in opposition to the "Jacobinism" of the *Monthly Magazine and British Register* (1796-1843). The varied content of the one hundred and twenty pages, which constituted each issue, has been compared to such a miscellany as the *Gentleman's Magazine.* In 1820, under the editorship of Thomas Campbell, it became the *New Monthly Magazine and Literary Journal,* a change in name indicative of its more literary character. Campbell contributed to it his own poetical work, and attracted to its pages such well-known writers as Thomas Noon Talfourd, Douglas Jerrold and Bernard Barton.

Leigh Hunt began to contribute to the *New Monthly* in 1821. Under date of September 1, 1824, he wrote his sister-in-law, Elizabeth Kent: "I have had a fourth offer from Colburn to write for the *New Monthly Magazine,* which by the way looks well for my present standing with the public." [27] Among his contributions which extended over a number of years, were essays, poems, "conversations," and translations,—a variety similar to that of his own magazines. In 1825 he contributed a series of papers,

---

25 *Works,* vol. VI, pp. 195-96.

26 *London Magazine,* Sept., 1821.

27 *Correspondence of Leigh Hunt, ed. by his eldest son,* Lond., 1862, vol. I, p. 232.

"The Family Journal," which he signed "Will Honeycomb." The dialogue form in which the "Journal" is written may have been suggested by Landor's *Imaginary Conversations,* the first two volumes of which were published in 1824. Hunt seems to have been experimenting with the "conversation" or dialogue style of essay, for in 1825 he also contributed to the *New Monthly,* "Conversations of Pope," "The Conversation of Swift and Pope," and "The Dialogue with a Sportsman."

Lamb's first contribution to the *New Monthly* was "The Illustrious Defunct" (January, 1825). A year later on January first he began his "Popular Fallacies," which appeared regularly until September, 1826. With regard to the "Fallacies" Lamb wrote Bernard Barton (February, 1826) : "I poke out a monthly crudity for Colburn in his magazine, which I call 'Popular Fallacies,' and periodically crush a proverb or two, setting up my folly against the wisdom of nations." [28] The idea of this series of papers had been suggested to Lamb by the *Pseudodoxia Epidemica,* or *Discourse of Vulgar Errors* by Sir Thomas Browne, one of his favorite writers. Two of the "Popular Fallacies" were afterwards made into essays: "The Sanity of True Genius" and "The Genteel Style in Writing." Lamb's contributions to the *New Monthly,* like Hunt's, were not among his most distinctive work.

Hazlitt, on the other hand, wrote for the *New Monthly* one of his best familiar essays "On Going a Journey" [29] which appeared under the head *Table Talk.* Other essays of his under the same caption were : "On Great and Little Things" (No. II, 1822) and "On Sonnets" (No. III, 1822). From 1822 until his death in 1830, Hazlitt was a more or less regular contributor to the *New Monthly.* Like Hunt, he tried his hand at the "Conversation" and wrote a series of papers, "The Conversations of James Northcote" (I-VI) which were published from August, 1826, to March, 1827, in the *New Monthly* under the title of "Boswell Redivivus." They were accompanied by an explanatory note by Hazlitt, in which he acknowledges his debt to Leigh Hunt: "My Dialogues are done much upon the same principle as the *Family Journal:* I shall be

---

[28] *Works,* vol. VII, p. 699.

[29] *Table Talk,* No. I, *New Monthly Magazine,* vol. IV, 1822.

more than satisfied if they are thought to possess but half the spirit and verisimilitude." [30]

Two of Hazlitt's essays: "My First Acquaintance with Poets" and "Shakespear's Fools" appeared in Leigh Hunt's and Byron's *Liberal* (1822-23), issued under tragic auspices, for Shelley, who was to have been its guiding spirit, did not live to participate in it. It was "Printed by and for John Hunt," and ended with the fourth number, because of Byron's defection and its want of financial success. Its plan was disclosed by Leigh Hunt in the preface to the first number: "The object of our work is not political, except inasmuch as all writing now-a-days must involve something to that effect, the connexion between politics and all other subjects of interest to mankind having been discovered, never again to be done away. We wish to do our work quietly, if people will let us,—to contribute our liberalities in the shape of Poetry, Essays, Tales, Translations, and other amenities, of which kings themselves may read and profit, if they are not afraid of seeing their own faces in every species of inkstand. Italian Literature, in particular, will be a favourite subject with us; and so was German and Spanish to have been, till we lost the accomplished Scholar and Friend who was to share our task; but perhaps we may be able to get a supply of the scholarship, though not of the friendship. It may be our good fortune to have more than one foreign correspondent, who will be an acquisition to the reader. In the meantime, we must do our best by ourselves; and the reader may be assured he shall have all that is in us, clear and candid at all events, if nothing else; for

> We love to pour out all ourselves as plain
> As downright Shippen or as old Montaigne." [31]

Charles Brown, James Hogg, Mary Shelley, Horace Smith were among the contributors to the *Liberal,* but the greater part of it was written by Leigh Hunt. Unfortunately, Hunt, owing to ill health, and the grief occasioned by Shelley's death, was not at his best. He displayed his versatility, however, in the range of his contributions, which included essays, fables, translations from

---

[30] *Works,* vol. VI, p. 506 (notes).
[31] Preface to the *Liberal; Verse and Prose from the South.* 2 vols. Lond., 1822: Printed by and for John Hunt, 22 Old Bond Street. (p. vii)

Ariosto and other Italian poets, two long satirical poems, "The Dogs" and "The Book of Beginnings" in the style and meter of "Don Juan," "Letters from Abroad," giving his first impressions of Italy, and a paper "Rhyme and Reason" in which he contended that the "reason" of much modern poetry was contained wholly in its rhymes.

It is more interesting, perhaps, than important in the development of the essay, to find the work of Hazlitt and Hunt in conjunction with Byron's "Heaven and Earth," his "Vision of Judgment" which Hunt called "the best satire since the days of Pope," and Shelley's exquisite song "I Arise from Dreams of Thee," [32] his beautiful translation, the "May-Day Night" from Goethe, and his "Lines to a Critic."

The storm of criticism and invective which greeted the *Liberal* is indicative of the strong partisan feeling and animosity which permeated the periodical literature of the time.

Leigh Hunt is to be seen at his best as a familiar essayist in his contributions to the *Indicator* and its successor, *The Companion.* The *Indicator,* edited by Hunt, was begun on the 13th of October, 1819, and continued until March 21, 1821, when his connection with it ceased.[33]   This periodical was a weekly eight-page sheet issued on Thursdays, price twopence, and of it Hunt wrote to the Shelleys with his usual exuberance: "I have now a new periodical work in hand, in addition to the *Examiner.* . . . It is to be called the *Indicator,* after a bird of that name who shows people where to find wild honey; and will, in fact, be nothing but a collection of very short pieces of remark, biography, ancient fictions, &c.; in short, of any subjects that come to hand, and of which I shall endeavour to *extract the essence* for the reader.   It will have nothing temporary whatsoever in it, political or critical; and indeed will be as pleasant labour to me as I can have, poetry always excepted."   In the same letter Hunt asks Shelley to contribute a paragraph "now and then, as little startling at *first* as possible to vulgar prejudices." [34]

---

[32] "Song, Written for an Indian Air," *Liberal,* No. 2.
[33] A new series commenced on March 28, 1821, and ended on October 13, 1821.
[34] Letter from Leigh Hunt to P. B. and M. W. Shelley written Sept. 20, 1819.   In *Correspondence of Leigh Hunt,* vol. 1, p. 149.

The discontinuance of the *Indicator* in 1821 was due to Hunt's ill health. In the last number under his editorship (March 21, 1821 he wrote his "Farewell" in characteristic vein "He has generally had," he says, "to perform his task without books, often with little comfort but the performance, always in the midst of a struggle of some sort." There are further reflections of this struggle in Hunt's *Autobiography* where we learn that the *Indicator* papers and his translation of the *Aminta* of Tasso tided him over a financial crisis "caused by the falling off in the receipts of the *Examiner* . . . declining under the twofold vicissitude of triumphant ascendancy in the Tories, and the desertion of reform by the Whigs." [35]

It is cause for wonder that, beset by ill-health and financial distress, Hunt could have produced, while writing under continued pressure, essays of such high merit and urbanity of spirit as those of the *Indicator.* That these papers were favorites with Lamb, Hazlitt, Keats and Shelley, we know from his *Autobiography:* "Let me console myself a little by remembering how much Hazlitt and Lamb, and others, were pleased with the *Indicator.* . . . Hazlitt's favourite paper (for they liked it enough to have favourite papers) was the one on *Sleep* . . . Lamb preferred the paper on *Coaches and Their Horses,* that on the *Deaths of Little Children,* and (I think) the one entitled *Thoughts and Guesses on Human Nature.* Shelley took to the story of the *Fair Revenge;* and the paper that was most liked by Keats, if I remember, was the one on a hot summer's day, entitled *A Now.* He was with me while I was writing and reading it to him, and contributed one or two of the passages." [36]   Keats further assisted Hunt by contributing to the *Indicator* his "La Belle Dame sans Merci" (May 10, 1820), and the sonnet "A Dream after reading Dante's Episode of Paulo and Francesca" (June 28, 1820). That the intimacy between Hunt and Keats was a very close one at this time, is to be gathered from the fact that they lived together, in Mortimer Terrace, Kentish Town. Lamb is represented by three short articles in the *Indicator* (December 13, 1820), all of which had previously ap-

---

[35] *Autobiography,* p. 249.
[36] Ibid., pp. 249-50.

peared in the *Examiner:* "Books with one Idea in Them," "Gray's
Bard" and "Play-House Memoranda."

Hunt continued his essays [37] in the *Literary Examiner,* founded
by John Hunt, July 5, 1823. It was a sixteen-page periodical, published each Saturday, which consisted of an essay, book reviews,
poetry and other literary matter. For this work Hunt, in addition
to the essays he contributed, translated Redi's *Bacco in Toscano.*
Owing to his ill health, however, the *Literary Examiner* came to a
close with the twenty-sixth number dated December 27, 1823.

The real successor to the *Indicator* was Leigh Hunt's *Companion,*
which appeared weekly every Wednesday from January 9th to
July 23, 1828. Beginning with the fifth number it increased from
eight to sixteen pages, and became a close competitor of the
Athenaeum. It consisted of a series of essays by Hunt in the
manner of the *Indicator,* theatrical and literary criticism, and
notices of public events. In it appeared some of Hunt's most
charming familiar essays, including "An Earth Upon Heaven,"
and "Walks Home by Night."

Both the *Indicator* and the *Companion* were later reprinted with
some omissions in book form, with the sub-title "A Miscellany
for the Fields and the Fire-side."

The efforts made by John and Leigh Hunt to develop the
journal of belles-lettres are an interesting chapter both in the
history of the essay and in that of the periodical. As has already
been noted the nineteenth century periodicals reached a comparatively wide reading public. It was the desire of Leigh Hunt to
appeal to a still wider circle of readers in his journals. As he himself says, he wished "to extend an acquaintance with matters of
intellectual refinement among the uneducated." [38]   He disputes with
Mr. Robert Chambers, the editor of the *Edinburgh Journal,* Chambers' claim that he and his brother were the originators of cheap,
respectable literature, by reminding him that the appearance of the
Tatler (Leigh Hunt's) was antecedent to that of the *Edinburgh.*
The *Indicator,* the *Tatler,* and *Leigh Hunt's London Journal* were
all planned with the idea of appealing to those with little education,

----

[37] His essays in the *Literary Examiner* continued the consecutive number-
ing of those in the *Indicator.*

[38] *Leigh Hunt's London Journal and the Printing Machine,* Lond., 1834-35,
No. 4, vol. 1, p. 28. (Wed., April 23, 1834.)

but it is in the *London Journal* that Hunt most fully sets forth his purpose.

But before turning to the *London Journal,* it is worth while to note Hunt's *Tatler,* which is particularly interesting because it was a daily literary journal and thus a departure from the weekly type of belles-lettres periodicals, standardized by the *Examiner. The Tatler, a Daily Journal of Literature and the Stage* ran from September 4, 1830, to March 31, 1832, and was entirely the work of Leigh Hunt except when he was too ill to write for it. It consisted of four folio pages and cost twopence. It resembled the *Indicator* in part, but also had somewhat the character of a newspaper. Hunt displayed his critical ability in the "Play Goer" and the "Reader" departments which kept the public informed of the latest in plays and books. But the content of the paper was not purely literary. Hunt used it as a jousting field in which to meet his political enemies: "I . . . tilted against governments and aristocracies, and kings and princes in general. . . . I also got out of patience with my old antagonists the Tories, to whom I resolved to give as good as they brought; and I did so, and stopped every new assailant. A daily paper, however small, is a weapon that gives an immense advantage; you can make your attacks in it so often." [39] After 493 numbers, the *Tatler* was abandoned. Hunt was physically exhausted by his efforts to write the entire paper, and also to attend the plays he criticised and write the notice of them the same night. "The work, slight as it looked," he says, "nearly killed me." [40]

Although the *Tatler* might in some respects be accounted a failure, it made many friends for Hunt and pointed the way to a fresh literary venture in his *London Journal,* a sixteen-page folio, which in partnership with Charles Knight, Hunt published every Wednesday, beginning April 2, 1834. The purpose was clearly set forth after the title: *"Leigh Hunt's London Journal* to assist the enquiring, animate the struggling, and sympathize with all." The *Journal* was so named because it was intended to be an English counterpart of the *Edinburgh Journal.* Unlike the *Examiner* and the *Tatler* it was entirely divorced from politics. Of the plan

---

[39] *Autobiography,* p. 375.
[40] Ibid., p. 374.

of the *London Journal* Hunt in his "Address" in the first number writes: "It is proposed, as the general plan of the Journal . . . that it should consist of One Original Paper or Essay every week, from the pen of the Editor; of matter combining entertainment with information, selected by him in the course of his reading, both old and new; of a weekly Abstract of some popular or otherwise interesting book, the spirit of which will be given *entire,* after the fashion of the excellent abridgements in *Johnstone's Edinburgh Magazine;* and lastly, of a brief current notice of the Existing State of Poetry, Painting, and Music, and a general sprinkle of Notes, Verses, Miscellaneous Paragraphs, and other helps to pleasant and companionable perusal." [41]

This general plan was adhered to; each number as a rule opened with an essay from Hunt's pen, and many of his most charming familiar essays, some of which were reprints from his earlier periodicals, are to be found in its pages. Among those which reveal Hunt as a delightfully companionable essayist, talking of commonplace things in a manner to invest them with his own spontaneous and child-like delight, are: "Breakfast in Summer," "Windows," "Reminiscences of a Journey," "The Cat by the Fire," "Twelfth Night," "A Journey by Coach." Other of his essays, some of which were critical, covered a wide range of subject matter, as "The Present State of the Fine Arts in England," "Conversation of Swift and Pope," "Cleanliness, Air, Exercise and Diet."

Leigh Hunt's London Journal has been called an epitome of Hunt himself.[42] He composed all of the original matter in it (not reprinted from elsewhere) and on almost every page his benevolent philosophy shines forth. It is the effort of a mature man who has suffered much and reflected on life, to pass along to his fellow men the fruits of his experience with the idea of giving them "pleasure." The spirit of the familiar essayist pervades the entire periodical. Hunt takes his readers into his confidence, addresses them in the most friendly and intimate manner, and even abolishes the advertisements in order that he may chat more freely with his correspondents.

Leigh Hunt's London Journal reveals perhaps even better than

---

[41] *Leigh Hunt's London Journal,* No. 1, vol. I, p. 1. (Wed., April 2, 1834.)
[42] Launcelot Cross, *Characteristics of Leigh Hunt.* Lond., 1878.

his *Autobiography* what manner of man Hunt was: his moods, his opinions upon all manner of subjects, extracts from his favorite works, the things he delighted in upon his walks, details of his home surroundings, glimpses of his family life, what he liked to eat, crowd the pages of his journal, and express his personality, and his taste, and above all his desire to share his experiences and pleasures with mankind. That this was a sincere desire no one can question, who reads his declarations to this effect so often expressed in his *Journal*. "We wished," he says, "to create one corner and field of periodical literature, in which men might be sure of hope and cheerfulness, and of the cultivation of peaceful and flowery thoughts, without the accompaniment of anything inconsistent with them; we knew that there was a desire at the bottom of every human heart to retain a faith in such thoughts, and to see others believe in the religion and recommend it; and heartily have anxious as well as happy readers in this green and beautiful England responded to our belief. . . . The *London Journal* is a sort of park for rich and poor, for the reflecting and well-intentioned of all sorts; where every one can be alone, or in company, as he thinks fit, and see, with his mind's eye, a succession of Elysian sights, ancient and modern, and as many familiar objects to boot, or hear nothing but birds and waterfalls, or the comforted beatings of his own heart,—all effected for him by no greater magician than Good Faith and a little reading." [43]

It is pleasant to think that a periodical so redolent of the spirit of the familiar essay also contained the work of Hunt's friends and fellow-essayists Hazlitt and Lamb. Hazlitt is represented by his "Characters of Shakespeare's Plays," which being out of print, Hunt reprinted each week in the later issues of the *London Journal*. Another interesting work of Hazlitt's which Hunt reprinted (Saturday, October 17, 1835, No. 81) was the "First production of Mr. Hazlitt, written when he was thirteen years of age," and addressed to the editor of the *Shrewsbury Chronicle* at the time of the Birmingham riots. The article is a defense of Dr. Priestley's character, and is evidence of Hazlitt's ability to write reasoned and clearly argued prose at an early age.[44]

---

[43] *Leigh Hunt's London Journal*, No. 23, vol. I, p. 177. (Wed., Sept. 3, 1834.)

[44] Hunt copied this article from the current number of the *Monthly Repository*.

In volume two of the *Journal appeared* "Specimens of the Wit, Humour, and Criticism of Charles Lamb." These extracts culled from Lamb's *Works* continued for four numbers. Hunt's memoir of Charles Lamb which had originally been printed in the *Athenaeum* appeared in the *Journal* for Wednesday, January 21, 1835.

After sixty-two numbers, *Leigh Hunt's London Journal* united (May 27, 1835) with *Knight's Printing Machine,* and henceforth until it ceased publication, in December, 1835, was issued on Saturdays instead of Wednesdays. In explaining its demise, Hunt says: "The note which it had struck was of too aesthetical a nature for cheap readers in those days." [45] Thornton Hunt attributed the *Journal's* failure not only to his father's "speciality (sic) of idea and expression," which limited his circle of readers, but to "the expenditure in time, exertion, and health" in editing such a periodical, an expenditure constantly in excess of the returns.[46] Although the *London Journal* had a comparatively short life,[47] it is of particular importance among periodicals, because Hunt's personality lives in its pages, and also because it contains much material that he later used in some of his most popular books, notably *The Seer* (1840-41) ; *Imagination and Fancy* (1844) ; *Wit and Humour* (1846) ; and *The Town* (1848). The latter work appeared in the supplement to the *Journal, Part 1,* under the title, "The Streets of the Metropolis ; their Memories and Great Men."

This brief survey of the periodicals in which the most important of the familiar essays of Lamb, Hunt and Hazlitt appeared, reveals the following facts : First, the familiar essay was the product of the magazines rather than of the reviews ; the magazines were in the nature of miscellanies, containing material on a wide range of topics, and including usually literary criticism as well as that of the drama and the fine arts. The variety of subject matter was in direct response to the varied interests of the time and made an appeal to men of many activities and tastes. Second, the literary

---

[45] *Autobiography*, p. 381.
[46] *Correspondence of Leigh Hunt*, vol. 1, p. 267.
[47] An attempt was made by Leigh Hunt to revive the *London Journal* in 1850, but it ran for seventeen numbers only (December 7 to March 29) and then failed for lack of funds. It was likewise a sixteen-page, penny-and-a-half paper, and bore the title "Leigh Hunt's Journal—a miscellany for the cultivation of the memorable, the progressive and the beautiful" (Nos. 1-17, London, 1850-51).

standard of many of the contributors was high and indeed reached a surprising level when the haste with which much of the work was produced is considered. Third, a definite effort was made to be cosmopolitan. Criticism, translations and extracts from foreign literature are a feature of most of the magazines. Fictional tales, oriental in character or origin, appear frequently in Leigh Hunt's periodicals. Fourth, the same essayists were writing critical and familiar essays, and publishing them in the same magazines. The critical essays cover a wide variety of themes, and an even greater range of subject matter is displayed in the familiar essays which, like those of Montaigne, take man for their province. Many of the papers would fit into neither of these classifications, but are character sketches, dream fantasies, reported conversations, "reasoned" discussions of abstract topics, etc. Fifth, Leigh Hunt by opening the pages of the *Examiner* and *Reflector* to Lamb and Hazlitt, and by the many literary periodicals of high standard which he fostered was largely responsible for the nurture of the nineteenth century familiar essay.

The literary quality of the periodicals in the early nineteenth century is of particular importance in the development of the familiar essay. The magazines and reviews were edited for the most part by men of learning and culture, who set and maintained a high standard of literary workmanship. There is abundant evidence that colloquial or careless writing was not tolerated, and that an author not only had to have something to say, but know how to say it. In reading the magazines of the period, one is impressed by the clear, forceful, pointed style of the prose. And not a little of this care for style was due to the exactions of all-powerful editors. The familiar essayists necessarily shared the prevailing concern for style, and the fact that their work had to vie with so much other excellent prose-writing undoubtedly gave them added incentive to put forth their best efforts. Also it was a critical age, and the great outpouring of criticism in the periodicals directed men's attention to *form* as well as *content*. The perfection which the familiar essay attained at this time, seems to have been not only the result of individual genius, but genius directed and fostered by periodicals of high literary standard.

CHAPTER III

SEVENTEENTH AND EIGHTEENTH CENTURY INFLU-ENCES IN THE ESSAYS OF HUNT, LAMB AND HAZLITT

(1) In General

The influence of the seventeenth century is more marked in Lamb than in either Hunt or Hazlitt. Lamb's delight in Robert Burton, Sir Thomas Browne, Jeremy Taylor, and other "worthies" is well known. His humor expresses itself in whimsies and quaint conceits closely akin to those of the seventeenth century writers; and his personal oddities and his mirth and melancholy proclaim his affinity with them. "Out-of-the-way humours and opinions—heads with some diverting twist in them—the oddities of author-ship" [1] he says pleased him most. Such he found in the *Anatomy of Melancholy*, over which he would muse "for the thousandth time." His affection for his own copy of this old book in its ancient dress with its quaint frontispiece, made intolerable to him the thought that the work should ever be modernized or issued in new binding. "What hapless stationer," he says, "could dream of Burton ever becoming popular?" [2]

The idea of writing in the manner of Burton was first suggested to Lamb by Coleridge, and resulted in his "forgery" of a manuscript of Burton: "Curious Fragments, extracted from a commonplace book, which belonged to Robert Burton, the famous author of *The Anatomy of Melancholy*." The "Fragments" purporting to be taken from Burton's diaries, were published in 1801 with *John Woodvil*. The manner in which Lamb here reveals Burton in different moods, writes in his style, and transmits his flavor, shows how thoroughly he had made the *Anatomy* his own. Burton's influence upon Lamb has already been so thoroughly treated [3]

---

[1] "Mackery End, in Hertfordshire," *Works*, vol. II, p. 75.
[2] "Detached Thoughts on Books and Reading," *Works*, vol. II, p. 174.
[3] Bernard Lake. *A general introduction to Charles Lamb. Together with a special study of his relation to Robert Burton.* Leipzig, 1903. (Doctoral dissertation.)

that further discussion of it here is unnecessary. It should be remarked however that two important characteristics of Lamb's work owe their origin in part at least to Burton's influence: the fantastic element seen so strongly for instance in Lamb's "Anatomy of Tailors," and "A Chapter on Ears," and his use of quotation to give added point and flavor to his essays. The most definite effect of Burton may be traced in Lamb's work previous to the *Essays of Elia,* when he consciously imitated the *Anatomy.* The Elia essays frequently give us " 'sweet assurance' that they are descended from the race of Burton," but direct influence is not evident.

Sir Thomas Browne was also a favorite of Lamb's, and one of the two authors chosen from the whole range of English literature whom he would like to have met. The *Urn Burial* was among his own prized volumes, and in "The Two Races of Men" he laments its loss from his shelves, and hints that Coleridge is the culprit. "C. will hardly allege that he knows more about that treatise than I do, who introduced it to him, and was indeed the first (of the moderns) to discover its beauties—but so have I known a foolish lover to praise his mistress in the presence of a rival more qualified to carry her off than himself." [4] The *Religio Medici* (1642) and *Pseudodoxia Epidemica,* or *Discourse of Vulgar Errors* (1646) he read thoroughly, and their influence upon his essays may be clearly seen. He begins "Imperfect Sympathies" by quoting a passage from the *Religio Medici:* "I am of a constitution so general that it consorts and sympathizeth with all things; I have no antipathy, or rather idiosyncracy in anything. Those national repugnances do not touch me, nor do I behold with prejudice the French, Italian, Spaniard, or Dutch." [5] Lamb then proceeds to disagree with Browne and although he no longer quotes from the *Religio Medici,* his essay is a refutation of some of the ideas expressed there. For example Browne distinguishes the "Essences of Being" : "There is but one first cause, and four second causes of all things. Some are without efficient, as God; others without matter, as Angels; some without form as the first matter: but every Essence, created or uncreated, hath its final cause, and some positive end both of its Essence and Operation. This is the

---

4 "The Two Races of Men," *Works,* vol. II, p. 25.
5 *Religio Medici,* pt. 2, sec. 1.

cause I grope after in the works of Nature; on this hangs the
Providence of God." [6] Lamb in the first part of his essay doubtless refers to this passage, and gives us something of the flavor of
Browne by imitating his Latinized and periodic style: "That the
author of the Religio Medici, mounted upon the airy stilts of
abstraction, conversant about notional and conjectural essences; in
whose categories of Being the possible took the upper hand of the
actual; should have overlooked the impertinent individualities of
such poor concretions as mankind, is not much to be admired." [7]

In his essay "On Burial Societies" Lamb quotes from *Urn
Burial* the passage "Man is a noble animal, splendid in ashes, and
pompous in the grave," [8] and humorously comments upon the
"appetite in the species" for things funereal. In this essay however, Lamb makes no effort to write in the manner of Browne.
He refers indirectly to *Urn Burial* in "The Old and New School-
master," when he says: "Had he asked of me what song the Syrens
sang, or what name Achilles assumed when he hid himself among
women, I might, with Sir Thomas Browne, have hazarded a 'wide
solution.'" Lamb doubtless had in mind the following passage of
Urn Burial: "What Song the Syrens sang, or what name Achilles
assumed when he hid himself among women, though puzzling questions, are not beyond all conjecture. What time the person of
these Ossuaries entered the famous Nations of the dead, and slept
with Princes and Counsellors, might admit a wide solution." [9]

In "My Relations" Lamb quotes from Browne's *Christian
Morals* (1716)[10] to give added emphasis to his own opinion.

Lamb's "Popular Fallacies," which originally appeared in the
New Monthly Magazine, January to September, 1826, were suggested to him by Browne's *Pseudodoxia Epidemica,* or *Discourse
of Vulgar Errors.* Lamb's themes as well as his style and diction
are in many instances reminiscent of the earlier writer. "That we
Should Rise with the Lark" (No. XIV) for example is not only

---

[6] *Religio Medici*, pt. 1, sec. 14.

[7] "Imperfect Sympathies," *Works*, vol. II, p. 58.

[8] *Urn Burial*, a Brief Discourse of the Sepulchral Urns lately found in
Norfolk, chapter V.

[9] Ibid.

[10] The book was left unfinished by Sir Thomas Browne's death and was
not published until this date.

written upon dreams, a favorite theme of Browne's, but has the flavor of his "discourse." "Some people have no good of their dreams," Lamb says. "We love to chew the cud of a foregone vision: to collect the scattered rays of a brighter phantasm, or act over again, with firmer nerves, the sadder nocturnal tragedies; to drag into day-light a struggling and half-vanishing night-mare; to handle and examine the terrors, or the airy solaces. . . . The abstracted media of dreams seem no ill introduction to that spiritual presence, upon which, in no long time, we expect to be thrown. . . . Therefore, we cherish dreams. . . . We feel attenuated into their meagre essences, and have given the hand of half-way approach to incorporeal being." [11]

Lamb's style invites comparison with that of Sir Thomas Browne in its bold use of metaphor, balance and antithesis of sentence structure, its fanciful conceits and its musical cadences. Its charm and flavor doubtless owe much to his familiarity with the work of Browne and other seventeenth century writers. However, Lamb has so thoroughly stamped his style with his own individuality that it is not to be referred to any one writer.

In "The Genteel Style of Writing" Lamb comments upon another seventeenth century favorite, Sir William Temple, whose essays, in a collection called *Miscellania,* were published in 1780-92. Lamb contrasts Temple's style with that of Lord Shaftesbury, whose *Characteristics of Men, Manners, Opinions and Times* appeared in 1711. "It is an ordinary criticism," says Lamb, "that my Lord Shaftesbury, and Sir William Temple, are models of the genteel style in writing. We should prefer saying of the lordly, and the gentlemanly. Nothing can be more unlike than the inflated finical rhapsodies of Shaftesbury, and the plain natural chit-chat of Temple. . . . The peer seems to have written with his coronet on, and his Earl's mantle before him; the commoner in his elbow chair and undress. What can be more pleasant than the way in which the retired statesman peeps out in the essays, penned by the latter in his delightful retreat at Shene?" After quoting from Temple's "sweet Garden Essay," Lamb continues: "The writings of Temple are, in general, after this easy copy. On one

---

[11] *Works*, vol. II, pp. 270-71.

occasion, indeed, his wit, which was mostly subordinate to nature and tenderness, has seduced him into a string of felicitous antitheses, which . . . have been a model to Addison and succeeding essayists." This critical opinion of Lamb's has been quoted at length because it so clearly shows his preference for a familiar and simple style in writing. Even though he himself sometimes chose to write in an antithetical and figurative fashion, it was not the style he most admired. That he realized its dangers we know from a letter to Coleridge (August 14, 1800) in which he writes: "To tell the truth, I began to scent that I was getting into that sort of style which Longinus and Dionysius Halicarnassus aptly call 'the affected.' " [12]

Other seventeenth century writers whom Lamb has singled out for comment are Margaret Cavendish, Duchess of Newcastle, whom he calls "the thrice, noble, chaste, and virtuous,—but . . . somewhat fantastical, and original-brain'd, generous Margaret Newcastle." [13] "Such a book . . . as the Life of the Duke of Newcastle, by his Duchess," says Lamb, "no casket is rich enough, no casing sufficiently durable, to honour and keep safe. . . . " [14]

He also held in high regard Jeremy Taylor, whose *Holy Living* and *Holy Dying* (1650-51) he particularly admired. He refers to Taylor in his article "Guy Faux," and wrote at length in apprecia-tion of him to Robert Lloyd (April 6, 1801). "Coleridge," Lamb says, "was the man who first solemnly exhorted me to 'study' the works of Dr. Jeremy Taylor, and I have had reason to bless the hour in which he did it." Lamb preferred the *Holy Dying* to the *Holy Living*. In the former he particularly admired the many similes, and the fancy and humour of the *Story of the Ephesian Matron*. Taylor he considers "has more delicacy and sweetness than any mortal, the 'gentle' Shakespeare hardly excepted—his similes and allusions are taken, as the bees take honey, from all the youngest, greenest, exquisitest parts of nature . . . —his imagina-tion was a spacious Garden, where no vile insects could crawl in; his apprehension a 'Court' where no foul thoughts kept 'leets and

---

[12] *Life, Letters and Writings of Charles Lamb*, ed. by Percy Fitzgerald, Lond., 1886, vol. I, p. 403.

[13] "Mackery End, in Hertfordshire," *Works*, vol. II, p. 76.

[14] "Detached Thoughts on Books and Reading," Ibid., p. 174.

holydays.'" Lamb also in this letter calls attention to the fact that Taylor wrote for different classes of people; that in his devotional works he contrives his conceits, allusions and analogies to appeal to the fancy of women and young people, whereas his *Liberty of Prophecy* is "fitted to great Clerks and learned Fathers, with no more of Fancy than is subordinate and ornamental." [15]

In his *Specimens from the Writings of Fuller, the Church Historian,* which appeared in the *Reflector* (No. 4) 1812,[16] Lamb has singled out for quotation those passages which best illustrate Fuller's figurative language and the use of conceits, which Lamb notes are "oftentimes deeply steeped in human feeling and passion."

In general, it may be said that Lamb was particularly interested in those seventeenth century writers, whose work exhibited familiar elements, was rich in fancy and well chosen conceits, and whose style was individual and exhibited odd and fantastic turns of thought.

Hunt and Hazlitt were less influenced by the seventeenth century than was Lamb, yet their interest in these writers is worthy of note. It appears partly in critical comment, some of it unfavorable, and partly in their use of quotations and their choice of themes. In his *Lectures on the Age of Elizabeth,* Hazlitt criticizes Browne at length and clothes his criticism in a wealth of figurative language which Browne himself might have envied: "His is the sublime of indifference; a passion for the abstruse and imaginary. He turns the world round for his amusement, as if it was a globe of paste-board. He looks down on sublunary affairs as if he had taken his station in one of the planets. The Antipodes are next-door neighbours to him, and Dooms-day is not far off. With a thought he embraces both the poles; the march of his pen is over the great divisions of geography and chronology. . . . The great Platonic year revolves in one of his periods. Nature is too little for the grasp of his style. He scoops an antithesis out of fabulous antiquity, and rakes up an epithet from the sweepings of Chaos. . . . He stands on the edge of the world of sense and reason, and gains a vertigo by looking down at impossibilities and

---

[15] *Charles Lamb and the Lloyds,* ed. by E. V. Lucas, Phila., 1898, p. 147 f.
[16] *Works,* vol. I, p. 112 f.

chimeras." [17] Hazlitt's criticism shows close study of Browne as a writer; and his impatience with Browne's abstractions. He sums up Browne's characteristics with the cogent comment that "he only existed at the circumference of his nature." Of his style Hazlitt says that he decks out his "contradictions and non-entities" "in the pride and pedantry of words as if they were the attire of his proper person: the categories hang about his neck like the gold chain of knighthood, and he 'walks gowned' in the intricate folds and swelling drapery of dark sayings and impenetrable riddles!" [18] The "one gorgeous passage" quoted by Hazlitt as illustrative of Browne's writing begins "What song the Syrens sang." Lamb's reference to the same passage in one of his essays has already been referred to.

Hazlitt contrasts Jeremy Taylor with Sir Thomas Browne, and it is plain that he reserves his enthusiasm for Taylor. He calls his *Holy Living* and *Holy Dying* "a divine pastoral." "His style," he says, "is prismatic. It unfolds the colours of the rainbow; it floats like the bubble through the air; it is like innumerable dew-drops that glitter on the face of the morning and tremble as they glitter." [19] Hazlitt also observes that Taylor's "writings are more like fine poetry than any other prose whatever; they are a choral song in praise of virtue, a hymn to the Spirit of the Universe." [20] He sums up the difference between Browne and Taylor: "The one shews that things are nothing out of themselves, or in relation to the whole: the one, what they are in themselves, and in relation to us." [21]

Hazlitt concludes his essay "On the Prose-Style of Poets" by remarking "that some of the old English prose-writers (who were not poets) are the best, and, at the same time, the most *poetical* in the favourable sense. Among these we may reckon some of the old divines, and Jeremy Taylor at the head of them. There is a flush like the dawn over his writings; the sweetness of the rose, the freshness of the morning-dew. There is a softness in his style,

---

[17] *Works*, vol. V, pp. 333-34.
[18] Ibid., p. 335.
[19] "Lectures on the Age of Elizabeth," Ibid., pp. 341-42.
[20] Ibid., p. 342.
[21] Ibid., p. 343.

proceeding from the tenderness of his heart; but his head is firm, and his hand is free. His materials are as finely wrought up as they are original and attractive in themselves." [22] Hazlitt's critical comments on Browne and Taylor show his preference for a prose style which is individual, poetic, colorful, and not over-decorated.

Although Hazlitt had appreciation and praise for the seventeenth century essayists, he did not care to model his style after them. "A sprinkling of archaisms is not amiss;" he believes, "but a tissue of obsolete expressions is more fit *for keep than wear*. I do not say I would not use any phrase that had been brought into fashion before the middle or the end of the last century; but I should be shy of using any that had not been employed by any approved author during the whole of that time. Words, like clothes, get old-fashioned, or mean and ridiculous, when they have been for some time laid aside." [23] Lamb is the only imitator of 'old English' style, Hazlitt says, that he can read with pleasure, and he attributes this to the fact that Lamb "is so thoroughly imbued with the spirit of his authors, that the idea of imitation is almost done away with. There is an inward unction, a marrowy vein both in the thought and feeling, an intuition, deep and lively, of his subject, that carries off any quaintness or awkwardness arising from an antiquated style and dress." [24]

Although no direct influence of the seventeenth century essayists is to be found in Hazlitt's work, he follows their example in the use of metaphor, simile and fanciful figures of speech, and in the decoration of his essays with quotations. He also quotes occasionally from them, and writes upon similar themes. In his essay "On the Love of Life," for example, he quotes from *Holy Dying*, in support of his statement that 'the love of life is, in general, the effect not of our enjoyments, but of our passions." [25]

Hunt was not influenced in style by the seventeenth century esayists, but his knowledge of their work is evident from his references to it in his essays. In "Poetical Anomolies of Shape," he

---

[22] *Works*, vol. VII, p. 17.
[23] "On Familiar Style," Ibid., vol. VI, p. 245.
[24] Ibid., p. 245.
[25] Ibid., vol. I, p. 1.

says: "When Sir Thomas Browne, in the infinite range of his meta-physical optics, turned his glass, as he no doubt often did towards the inhabitants of other worlds, the stories of angels and Centaurs would help his imaginative good-nature to a more willing concep-tion of creatures in other planets unlike those on earth; to other 'lords of creation'; and other, and perhaps nobler humanities." [26] He again refers to Browne in his essay, "Bees, Butterflies, etc.": "Sir Thomas Browne would not have thought it beneath him to ask what all those innumerable little gentry (we mean the insects) are about, between our breakfast and dinner; how the time passes in the solitudes of America, or the depths of the Persian Gulf; or what they are doing even, towards three in the afternoon, in the planet Mercury." [27] In "Of Dreams," Hunt quotes from Browne (*Inner Temple Mask*) and calls him "Spenser's follower." [28] Bur-ton's *Anatomy of Melancholy* furnishes a quotation for Hunt's "Treatise on Devils"; and frequent references to melancholy in Hunt's essays reflect his interest in the subject.

Such themes as death, melancholy, witchcraft, devils, angels, dreams were favorites with the seventeenth century essayists, and the familiar essayists likewise have made interesting use of these subjects. Hazlitt writes on "The Fear of Death," [29] and Hunt devotes three essays to the subject: "On Death and Burial";[30] "Life after Death—Belief in Spirits" [31] and "Deaths of Little Children." [32] Lamb gives a new turn to the same theme in "On Burial Societies." [33] Hunt treats Burton's favorite topic in his "Advice to the Melancholy." [34] Lamb's "On the Melancholy of Tailors," [35] and his "Curious Fragments" [36] have previously been

[26] *Indicator; A Miscellany for the Fields and the Fireside.* By Leigh Hunt, N. Y., 1845, pt. 1, p. 187-88.

[27] Ibid., pt. 2, p. 153.

[28] Ibid., pt. 2, p. 96.

[29] Works, vol. VI, p. 321 f.

[30] Leigh Hunt. *The Seer, or Commonplaces Refreshed.* Bost., 1864, vol. II, p. 148 f.

[31] Ibid., p. 140 f.

[32] *Indicator*, pt. I, p. 182 f.

[33] *Works*, vol. I, p. 92.

[34] *Indicator*, pt. I, p. 23 f.

[35] *Works*, vol. I, p. 172 f.

[36] *Ibid.*, p. 31 f.

mentioned. His "Witches and Other Night-Fears" [37] carries on the traditional theme, and a closely allied subject forms the theme of Hunt's essay "A Treatise on Devils." [38] Hunt and Lamb write on the heavenly hierarchy in "A Few Words on Angels";[39] and "The Child Angel; a Dream," [40] and dreams are the subject of essays by Hunt [41] and Hazlitt.[42]

When we turn to the eighteenth century we find the periodical essay exercising a more general influence upon Hunt, Lamb and Hazlitt than does the work of seventeenth century writers. As has already been noted, the *Tatler* and *Spectator* in particular, affected the nineteenth century familiar essay. Long after they ceased publication, the *Tatler* and *Spectator* were prized volumes in many households. That they provided models for school compositions we know from Leigh Hunt, who has left an amusing picture of his early efforts, when at Christ's Hospital, to abridge papers from the *Spectator*. One of the favorite essays with the boys, because it was considered one of the easiest, began: "I have always preferred cheerfulness to mirth." "I had heard this paper so often," Hunt says, "and was so tired with it, that it gave me a great inclination to prefer mirth to cheerfulness." [43] Thus Hunt early made the acquaintance of the *Spectator* essays, and must have absorbed much of their style, even though their worldly wisdom seemed to him then "very difficult and perplexing." Years later he received as a gift, a copy of the original number of Steele's *Tatler,* and in a letter of thanks expresses his delight: "I have been carrying it about the house with me, like a child who has had a picture-book given it; and have put it among some favourite books on a shelf, just before the table at which I write, that it may help to give me pleasant thoughts. I persuade myself that Steele may have had this identical copy in his hand, perhaps Pope, perhaps my Lady Suffolk." [44]

---

[37] *Works*, vol. II, p. 65 f.
[38] Leigh Hunt. *Wishing-Cap Papers*, Bost., 1888. p. 160 f.
[39] Ibid., p. 184 f.
[40] *Works*, vol. II, p. 244 f.
[41] "Of Dreams," *Indicator*, pt. II, p. 93 f.
[42] "On Dreams," *Works*, vol. VII, p. 17 f.
[43] *Autobiography*, p. 71.
[44] To J. F., June 20, 1831, *Correspondence of Leigh Hunt*, vol. 1, p. 263.

Hunt shows his familiarity with the material in the *Spectator* and *Tatler* by references to it scattered through his essays, and on more than one occasion he uses the same poetical quotations as Steele had used in the *Tatler*. In his collection *A Book for a Corner* he includes stories which had been published in the *Tatler*. In his essay, "A Word Upon Indexes" he recalls the indexes to the *Tatler* and the *Spectator*, and says let anyone read them and "then call an index a dry thing if he can. . . . But as grapes, ready to burst with wine, issue out of most stony places, like jolly fellows bringing Burgundy out of a cellar; so an index, like the Tatler's, often gives us a taste of the quintessence of his humour." [45] Hunt's interest in the periodical essayists is still further shown by his naming one of his own papers *The Tatler,* and also by the fact that the Round Table in the *Examiner* as originally planned, was to have been patterned after the *Tatler* and *Spectator*.

Hazlitt also, when a boy, made the acquaintance of the *Tatler*. In *English Comic Writers* he pays homage to Steele: "I owed this acknowledgement to a writer who has so often put me in good humour with myself, and everything about me, when few things else could, and when the tomes of casuistry and ecclesiastical history, with which the little duodecimo volumes of the *Tatler* were overwhelmed and surrounded, in the only library to which I had access when a boy, had tried their tranquillising effects upon me in vain." [46] His boyhood liking was confirmed by his mature judgment; he always preferred the *Tatler* to the *Spectator* and thought Steele a less artificial and more original writer than Addison. His Round Table paper No. 3 is devoted to the *Tatler*. "Of all our periodical Essayists, he says, "the *Tatler* (sic) . . . has always appeared to me the most amusing and agreeable." [47]   In the same essay Hazlitt expresses his admiration for certain characteristics of Steele's writing, viz: the power of keen observation and the ability to record truthfully, which he refers to as "the freshness and stamp of nature"; "the indications of character and strokes of humour"; "the reflections" which "arise from the occasion . . . more like the remarks which occur in sensible conversa-

---

[45] *Indicator*, pt. II, pp. 88-89.
[46] "On the Periodical Essayists," *Works*, vol. VIII, p. 99.
[47] Ibid., p. 95.

tion, and less like a lecture"; and the descriptions which "resemble loose sketches or fragments of a comedy." [48]   It is Steele's understanding of the fundamental qualities of human nature that particularly attracts Hazlitt: "Systems and opinions change but nature is always true."   Therefore he prefers the *Tatler* with its "first sprightly runnings" to the "moral dissertations and critical reasonings" of the *Spectator*.   It is to be noted that the qualities which Hazlitt most appreciated in the *Tatler* essays are those which carried over into the familiar essay: truth of observation, humor, the flavor of good conversation, the ability to describe with dramatic terseness so that a scene is flashed upon the mind or a character is "indicated."

Hazlitt however is not unappreciative of Addison.   He finds some of his moral essays "exquisitely beautiful and quite happy" —"the perfection of elegant sermonizing." [49]   "I am far from wishing to depreciate Addison's talents," he says, "but I am anxious to do justice to Steele, who was, I think, upon the whole, a less artificial and more original writer." [50]

Leigh Hunt also was attracted by Addison's moral essays: "But what grace, ease, wit, and sense in his writings; and how much good they did to private life, and what gratitude we owe him to this hour in consequence!   No man can be sure, that a good part of the decency and amenity of intercourse which he enjoys in his own house at this moment, is not owing to the lessons of Addison." [51]   As we shall try to show later, Hunt was probably influenced in his philosophy of life by Addison.

Lamb was likewise familiar with the essays of Addison and Steele.   His own library contained volumes of the *Spectator* and the *Guardian*.   Some of his early contributions to the *Reflector* (1810-12), "Edax on Appetite," "On Hissing at the Theatre," "On Burial Societies," clearly show the influence of the *Spectator*.   He preferred however the graceful rambling of Cowley's essays to

---

[48] Ibid, p. 97.

[49] "On the Periodical Essayists," *Works*, vol. VIII, p. 99.

[50] Ibid, p. 97.

[51] "Second Week in May," *Leigh Hunt's London Journal*, No. 6, p. 42. (Wednesday, May 7, 1834.)

"the courtly elegance and ease of Addison; abstracting . . . the latter's exquisite humour." [52]

Lamb's essays in the *Reflector* are doubly interesting in that they show the influence of the periodical essay, and mark a transition stage in the familiar essay when it had not entirely freed itself from eighteenth century models. We have only to compare his *Reflector* papers with his Elia essays to realize the difference in treatment. They lack the play of fancy, the self-revelation, and the originality which distinguish the writings of Elia. Their affinity to the *Spectator* essays is to be seen in their style, and in the manner in which they make us of the letter and the character. "Edax on Appetite" is illustrative of the type. It begins: "Mr. Reflector,—I am going to lay before you a case of the most iniquitous persecution that ever poor devil suffered" and concludes: "Some of my acquaintance, who may read my case in your pages under a borrowed name, may be induced to give it a more humane consideration than I could ever yet obtain from them under my own. Make them, if possible, to *reflect,* that an original peculiarity of constitution is no crime; that not that which goes into the mouth desecrates a man, but that which comes out of it,—such as sarcasm, bitter jests, mocks and taunts, and ill-natured observations; and let them consider, if there be such things (which we have all heard of) as Pious Treachery, Innocent Adultery, &c. whether there may not be also such a thing as Innocent Gluttony.

I shall only subscribe myself,
Your afflicted servant, Edax." [53]

Addison himself might be speaking, but the sly humor is Lamb's own. The manner in which Lamb reproduces the style and tone of the "moral" essays of the *Spectator* is proof that he absorbed the style of what he read. He shows the same facility in giving the very flavor and essence of Burton, and yet what a distance in style separates the *Anatomy of Melancholy* from the *Spectator.*

Lamb's use of the "character" in his *Reflector* papers may have been suggested by the "characters" in the *Tatler.* The many

---

[52] *Life, Letters and Writings of Charles Lamb,* ed. by Percy Fitzgerald, vol. 1, p. 363.
[53] *Works,* vol. I, pp. 118, 124.

character-sketches in the Elia essays also invite comparison with those of the Sir Roger de Coverley papers in the *Spectator*. In two of the *Reflector* papers: "On the Danger of Confounding Moral with Personal Deformity," and "On Burial Societies," Lamb uses the device of a handbill, about whose contents he weaves his essay. The handbills are in the nature of advertisements, and again, Lamb may have derived this idea for his papers from the humorous "Advertisements" of the *Spectator*. Likewise Lamb's club for authors who have been fairly damned may have been suggested by the club device of the periodical essayists.

That Lamb for his essay form should have gone back to Steele and Addison is the more interesting when we recall that he had already written more in the vein of the familiar essayist in his "Londoner," which he had contributed to the *Morning Post* in 1802. That he was not following the example of Leigh Hunt is evident from Hunt's *Reflector* essay, "A Day by the Fire," which displays the characteristics of the familiar essay at its best. Likenesses to the *Spectator* may be noted in Hunt's essay in only minor respects, notably in his use of quotation to adorn and give point to his remarks, and in the easy chair drawn up to the fire. But here we find none of the well known "devices" set up between author and reader. Hunt speaks directly in his own person. "I must request the reader to go with me through a day's enjoyments by the fireside. It is part of my business as a Reflector, to look about for helps to reflection; and, for this reason, among many others, I indulge myself in keeping a good fire from morning till night. I have also a reflective turn for an easy chair, and a very thinking attachment to comfort in general." [54]

In the literary department of the *Examiner* which Hunt set up in 1815 under the title of the "Round Table," we see again the influence of the periodical essayists. Hunt proposed to publish a series of papers in the manner of the *Spectator* and *Tatler,* which were to be contributed by various persons on a variety of subjects, Hunt himself being responsible for the dramatic criticism. The "club" idea was retained, but with the difference that its members would assume no fictitious characters, but talk undisguisedly, as

---

[54] *Reflector,* No. 4.

the natural beings they were. Politics somewhat disrupted the plan, and the essays did not adhere as closely to their Queen Anne models as was to have been expected. However, in the range of their interests, "Manners, Morals and Taste," they followed their models. The first essay contributed by Hazlitt to the "Round Table," "On the Love of Life," in its gravity of tone and in its conclusion that the strength of our attachment to life "is a very fallacious test of its happiness" has all the moral earnestness of Addison, but the style is Hazlitt's. Addison is among the authors whom Hazlitt draws upon for quotations to adorn his essay. The subjects considered in the "Round Table," to which attention has already been called, reflect the interests of the nineteenth century no less than the *Tatler* and *Spectator* had mirrored those of the eighteenth. In its general plan if not in its style the "Round Table" partook of the nature of the essay periodical.

One of the most delightful of Hunt's essays, "Coffee Houses and Smoking" takes us into the haunts of the Queen Anne essayists and their readers. Hunt imagines himself back in the eighteenth century, sitting in one of the coffee houses talking to Will Honeycomb. He arrives there by way of Gliddon's snuff and tobacco shop in King Street: "Ay, here, said I, is wherewithal to fill the boxes of the Steeles and Congreves, and the pipes of the Aldriches and Sir Roger de Coverleys. But where is the room in which we can fancy them? Where is the coffee house to match? Where the union of a certain domestic comfort with publicity,—journals of literature as well as news,—a fire visible to all,—cups without inebriety,—smoking without vulgarity?" [55]

Like the periodical essayists, Hunt aimed to improve society through his journals. In his early career as a journalist, he sought the reform of politics and the evils arising from public life; in his later years he turned to the "Christianizing of public manners," but that he meant this in no narrow sense the following passage from his *London Journal* shows: "It is our ambition to be one of the sowers of a good seed in places where it is not common but would be most profitable, to be one of those who should try to render a sort of public loving-kindness, a grace of common-life, a conventional, and for that very reason, in the higher sense of the

----

[55] *Wishing-Cap Papers*, p. 252.

word, a social and universal elegance. . . . We would fain do something, however small and light, towards Christianizing public manners." [56]   Earlier in the same paper Hunt speaks of "love enshrined as the only final teacher of all knowledge and advancement." "No new religion, truly," he remarks, but "too sacred and wonderful to have justice done it in these small chapels built for conventional persuasion." [57]

Hunt, then, if we interpret him aright, would use his paper as a pulpit, and would preach to mankind the fundamental doctrine of Christianity: love. Through the dissemination of loving-kindness he would teach men a better way of life, and would enable them to find pleasure in simple things. His audience was wide and he aimed at fundamentals. His purpose like that of the *Tatler* and *Spectator* was a moral one but the difference is one in outlook of the two centuries.

In the following number of his *Journal* Hunt set forth his "credo" of cheerfulness, which resembles that of Addison. In two papers of the *Spectator* (Nos. 381, 387) Addison treats of cheerfulness, first as a moral habit of mind, and second in its natural state. In the first paper Addison remarks: "A cheerful mind is not only disposed to be affable and obliging, but raises the same good-humour in those who come within its influence. A man finds himself pleased, he does not know why, with the cheerfulness of his companion. It is like a sudden sunshine that awakes a secret delight in the mind, without her attending to it. The heart rejoices of its own accord, and naturally flows out into friendship and benevolence towards the person who has so kindly an effect upon it." [58]

Hunt in his *Journal* [59] writes: "Our object was to put more sunshine into the feelings of our countrymen, more good will and good humour, a greater *habit* of being pleased with one another and with everything, and therefore a greater power of dispensing with uneasy sources of satisfaction. We wished to create one

---

[56] *Leigh Hunt's London Journal*, No. 22, vol. I, p. 176 (Wed., Aug. 27, 1834).
[57] Ibid.
[58] *Spectator*, No. 381.
[59] No. 23, vol. I, p. 177 (Wed., Sept. 3, 1834).

corner and field of periodical literature, in which men might be sure of hope and cheerfulness, and of the cultivation of peaceful and flowery thoughts, without the accompaniment of anything inconsistent with them."

In Addison's second essay on cheerfulness,[60] there is this passage: "Cheerfulness bears the same friendly regard to the mind as to the body. It vanishes all anxious care and discontent, sooths (sic) and composes the passions, and keeps the soul in a perpetual calm. But having already touched on this last consideration, I shall here take notice, that *the world in which we are placed is filled with innumerable objects that are proper to raise and keep alive this happy temper of mind."* [61]

It is interesting to compare the italicized portion of the passage above, with the following one from Hunt: "If we end in doing nothing but extending a faith in capabilities of any sort, and showing some thousands of our fellow-creatures *that sources of amusement and instruction await but a touch in the objects around them,* to start up like magic, and enrich the meanest hut, perhaps the most satiated ennui, we shall have done something not unworthy to receive the countenance of their unanimity." [62]

Not only did Hunt in his *Journals* advocate cheerfulness and contentment with the simple things of life, but he practiced what he preached. His faith in the essential goodness of man, his own cheerfulness in spite of trials and discouragements, his almost childish delight in ordinary things are expressed continually in his later writing. It is this benevolent attitude carried to the extreme which accounts for much of his sentimentality.

In his introduction to the *Indicator* and *Companion* written in 1833, when they were published in book form, Hunt says: "Both the works were written with the same view of inculcating a love of nature and imagination, and of furnishing a sample of the enjoyment which they afford; and he [the author] cannot give a better proof of that enjoyment, as far as he was capable of it, than by stating, that both were written during times of great trouble with

---

[60] *Spectator,* No. 387.

[61] Italics by the present writer.

[62] *Leigh Hunt's London Journal,* No. 22, vol. I, p. 176 (Wed., Aug. 27, 1834). Italics by the present writer.

him, and both helped him to see much of that fair play between his own anxieties and his natural cheerfulness, of which an indestructible belief in the good and the beautiful has rendered him perhaps not undeserving." [63]

This "philosophy" of cheerfulness also expresses itself in Hunt's attitude toward nature. In all the myriad manifestations of nature, particularly in the seasons, and in the beauty of field and wood and growing things, Hunt would find a solace for man from the cares of the world, a fount of that cheerfulness which in man is but an expression of his faith in a higher Being. Addison gives succinct expression to this idea: "The creation is a perpetual feast to the mind of a good man; every thing he sees cheers and delights him. Providence has imprinted so many smiles on nature, that it is impossible for a mind which is not sunk in more gross and sensual delights, to take a survey of them without several secret sensations of pleasure." [64]

This of course is no new thought; it was expressed by the Psalmist David, but since Hunt seems to have absorbed other ideas of Addison's with regard to "cheerfulness," there is reason to believe that the idea of nature as a source of man's cheer might have received emphasis from the same source. But it should be noted that however much Hunt may have felt the moral import of this truth, his treatment of it is more frequently romantic than didactic; and in his descriptions of nature there is much of the exuberance which marked the Romantic Revival.

(2) THE "CHARACTER" AND THE CHARACTER-SKETCH

One of the seventeenth and eighteenth century influences which may be traced in the essays of Hunt, Lamb and Hazlitt is that of the character-writers. The many character sketches which adorn the pages of these essayists, owe their origin not to the full-length character delineations of the novel, but to those briefer, more concise presentations of personal or type traits which are called "characters." Character-writing underwent certain developments

---

[63] Introduction: *The Indicator, and the Companion; A Miscellany for the Fields and the Fire-side.* By Leigh Hunt. In Two Parts. Part I. Lond., 1840.

[64] *Spectator,* No. 393.

in the seventeenth century which made possible the many individualized descriptions of type characteristic of the *Tatler* and *Spectator* and other eighteenth century periodicals, and these influenced the character-sketches of the early nineteenth century essayists.

The "character" has been defined as "a short account, usually in prose, of the properties, qualities, or peculiarities which serve to individualize a type." [65]   The character-writer is concerned with features common to the type he is describing, rather than with the peculiar qualities which individualize the person or thing.   The "character" has been likened to a kind of prose sonnet which is limited as to range of subject, since there are few individual types of character and these change but little from century to century. A distinguishing mark of the "character" is its form; short balanced sentences are usually employed, which lend it conciseness and emphasize its brevity.   The opening sentence is frequently a definition and is followed by a detailing of the characteristic traits of the type described.   The ending may be epigrammatic, or in the form of a conceit.   The motive is usually didactic or satirical.

The vogue of character-writing in England in the seventeenth century may be traced to a French translation of the *Ethical Characters* of Theophrastus, made by Casaubon, a French scholar in 1592.   The early seventeenth century character-writers took Theophrastus for their model and their work exhibits many of his outstanding qualities, such as classic economy of form, conciseness and precision of expression.   Character-writing, it is true, had been practiced in England before the seventeenth century, but it had appeared in some other form, such as poetry and the drama, and it was not until Hall, Overbury and Earle produced their "characters," that the "character" was isolated from other literary *genres*.   While the work of the English character-writers of the seventeenth century shows the influence of Theophrastus, it also exhibits individual characteristics.

For example, Joseph Hall, whose *Characters of Virtues and Vices* appeared in 1608, while closely following the Greek model in describing the traits proper to a character, added his own com-

---

[65] Edward Chauncey Baldwin. "The Relation of the Seventeenth Century Character to the Periodical Essay." *P.M.L.A.*, No. XIX, 1904, p. 75.

ments in euphuistic style, thus introducing into English character-writing the fashion for conceits and epigrammatic expressions. He made some attempt to analyse the motives which actuated his characters, but he failed to lend life to his sketches. He further developed the "character" by describing those who are types not only by virtue of particular moral qualities, but because of certain attributes peculiar to their position or office. His "Character of a Good Magistrate" furnished the pattern for a succession of character descriptions of this type, which continued into the nineteenth century and is well illustrated by Lamb's "Character of an Undertaker."

Sir Thomas Overbury also advanced the art of character-writing through his collection of *Characters*, published in 1614, entitled: *A Wife . . . Whereunto are added many witty Characters and conceited Newes, written by himself and other learned Gentlemen his friends.* His use of conceits and antithesis carried on the tradition of euphuistic character-writing, but he proved himself an originator in his sketches describing the character of places, and in his description of national types, such as the "Braggadocio Welshman," which may be considered the prototype of Lamb's "true Caledonian" in his essay, "Imperfect Sympathies," and of Hazlitt's delineation of national traits in his paper "On the Scotch Character." Mr. Baldwin [66] has called attention to the fact that Overbury also anticipated the use of the "character" as a form of political satire, for instance in his pictures of "A Jesuit," "A Puritan," and "A Precisian." Thus he pointed the way for the many campaign tracts written in the form of "characters," and for such final developments of the form as Hazlitt's "Character of Mr. Pitt." Even more important was Overbury's picturing of contemporary manners through the "character," and his portrayal of external peculiarities, which made it possible to visualize the type described. His "Character of a Fine Gentleman" undoubtedly furnished a model to the periodical essayists, when they pointed their morals with character sketches of figures in the world of London fashion, and gave their sketches a humorous turn by describing outward peculiarities.

---

[66] Op. cit., p. 107.

The "character" thus developed from a number of moral attributes defining a type toward a more concrete picture, which suggested, if it did not delineate, an individual. Still further development of the form is to be found in John Earle's *Microcosmography, or Piece of the World discovered in Essays and Characters* (1628). His analysis of character, prompted by a desire to account for the traits exhibited by the type, marks another step in character portrayal, which was advancing steadily toward the portrait of the individual who would at the same time be representative of the type. Such character drawing led to the creation of Sir Roger de Coverley, who while individualized also represents a distinct type, and is the forerunner of portrait-types in the novel as well as the essay.

The "character" became divorced from its stereotyped form in the work of Thomas Fuller, whose *Holy and Profane States* appeared in 1642. For the usual balanced, concise, antithetical style is substituted a highly individual style. Anecdotes, witticisms and doggerel verses are introduced. By putting himself into his writing Fuller gave a more subjective treatment to his character-sketches, and lent them a charm and human quality which those of his predecessors had lacked. He expands and embellishes his "characters" by means of concrete illustrations drawn from the fund of stories which he had at his command. "His way of telling a story," says Lamb, "for its eager liveliness, and the perpetual running commentary of the narrator happily blended with the narration, is perhaps unequalled." [67] Fuller's wit and natural aptitude for conceits also contributed to his success as a character-writer. Coleridge says that his wit "in quantity, quality and perpetuity, surpassed that of the wittiest in a witty age." It is perhaps significant that Lamb's "character," "The Good Clerk," should have appeared in the same number of the *Reflector* with his "Specimens" from Fuller.

Another seventeenth century character-writer who deserves mention for having exerted an influence upon the familiar essay is Nicholas Breton, whose *Fantasticks* (1626) is chiefly interesting for its characterization of the seasons, which displays a keen

---

[67] "Specimens from the Writings of Fuller, the Church Historian," *Works*, v. I, p. 112.

observation of nature and a poetic vein new to the "character."
Breton is of particular importance for his influence upon Leigh
Hunt. The affinity between Hunt's essay "A Now" descriptive
of "a hot day" and Breton's description of June is a marked one.
Breton writes: "It is now June, and the Hay-makers are mustered
to make an army for the field where not alwayes in order, they
march under the Bagge, and the Bottle, when betwixt the Forke
and the Rake, there is seene great force of armes. Now doth the
broad Oke comfort the weary Laborer, while under his shady
Boughes he sits singing to his bread and cheese: the Hay-cocke
is the Poore mans Lodging, and the fresh River is his gracious
Neighbour." [68] Hunt says: "Now the mower begins to make his
sweeping cuts more slowly, and resorts oftener to the beer. Now
the carter sleeps a-top of his load of hay, or plods with double
slouch of shoulder, looking out with eyes winking under his shad-
ing hat, and with a hitch upward of one side of his mouth. . . .
Now laborers look well resting in their white shirts at the doors
of rural ale-houses. Now an elm is fine there, with a seat
under it. . . . " [69]

The English "character" by the beginning of the eighteenth
century had achieved variety in both theme and treatment. The
objective setting forth of the qualities representative of a type of
person, the pattern for which had been established by Theophrastus, was succeeded by the application of the "character" to various
themes such as modes of life, occupations, the animal and vegetable
kingdom, the elements, the seasons, and places. As the subject
matter for "characters" became still further exhausted, the form
was employed for a great variety of miscellaneous themes. In
treatment the "character" tended to become less objective and
euphuistic in style. A further development was in the allying of
the "character" with the essay, as in *The Good Schoolmaster,* in
which Fuller took for the topic sentence of each paragraph some
attribute of character descriptive of a school-master, and developed
the paragraphs in essay style. [70]

---

[68] Nicholas Breton, "June," *Fantasticks*, p. 9. In his *Works in Verse and Prose*, vol. 2, Edinburgh, 1879.
[69] *Indicator*, pt. 2, p. 17.
[70] The close union between the two forms is also recognized by Nicholas Breton in the Dedication of his *Characters upon Essays Moral and Divine* (1615).

In tracing the effect of the seventeenth century character-writers upon later essayists, no account can afford to omit Jean de La Bruyère, the most widely known of French character-writers, who indirectly represents English influence. Character-writing in France owed its inspiration largely to England, and especially to Bishop Hall's *Characters* published in a French translation in 1619. La Bruyère published in 1688 his *Les Caractères de Theophraste traduits du grec; avec les Caractères, et les Moeurs de ce Siècle.* He successfully accomplished what the English writers had worked toward, but had not achieved, that is the drawing of individual character in such a manner that the individual became representative of a class. His English predecessors had created types which by means of much witty ingenuity, they endowed with attributes which enabled an individual to recognize himself in the type, but La Bruyère made his readers believe in the individuality of the characters he typified. He effected this by means of minute personal details introduced into his description of a type. These details were apparently drawn from his circle of acquaintances, and with such verisimilitude as to warrant the publication of various "keys" to the identification of the originals. A further contribution made by La Bruyère was his union of the familiar essay with the "character." Hitherto the "character" had been allied with the Baconian type of essay. La Bruyère also lent interest to his "characters" by the addition of epigrammatic reflections which had the flavor of the maxims and *pensées* of La Rochefaucauld and Pascal. The effect of La Bruyère in England is to be particularly noted in the periodical essayists. Steele under guise of Isaac Bickerstaff freely acknowledges his debt to La Bruyère in the *Tatler* (No. 9): "I shall take all the privileges I may as an Englishman, and will lay hold of the late act of naturalization to introduce what I shall think fit from France. The use of that law may, I hope, be extended to people the polite world with new characters, as well as the kingdom itself with new subjects. Therefore an author of that nation, called La Bruyere, I shall make bold with on such occasions."

The "character," freed of euphuism, and sympathetically and humorously drawn, had reached a stage of development early in the eighteenth century which made it a ready medium for the periodical essayists. In the *Tatler* and *Spectator* the character-sketch proved an admirable means of lending concreteness to the general observations of the essayist, of emphasizing the moral he wished to bring home, and of providing the wit and humor necessary to hold the reader's attention. About one-sixth of the essays in the *Tatler* are "character" papers, varied in content, as for example: "Character of Sir Timothy Tittle" (No. 165), "Characters of a Prude and Coquette" (No. 126), "Characters of the Members of the Club at the Trumpet" (No. 132), "Characters of an Affectionate Couple" (No. 150), "Characters of Impudence and Absurdity" (No. 168), "Characters in a Stage-Coach" (No. 192). There is no attempt made in these sketches to keep the traditional form of the "character": the short balanced sentence, the opening definition of type, the epigrammatic ending. On the contrary the utmost freedom of form is displayed, so that these sketches should be considered as representing a transitional stage when the "character" had been freed from the early limitations displayed by the imitators of Theophrastus, but had not yet attained the detailed analysis of the character-sketch found later in the novel. Take for example the "Character of an Upholsterer" (*Tatler, No. 155*) whose original was said to have been Mr. Arne, an upholsterer in Covent Garden. The sketch is a clever take-off of a man who is a "newsmonger," so interested in reading and detailing the daily news that he neglects his family and business. Mr. Bickerstaff represents himself as carrying on a conversation with this "very grave person" who "looked extremely thin in a dearth of news, and never enjoyed himself in a westerly wind." The man's pet foible is revealed through what he says. His outward appearance is minutely described: "I saw," says Mr. Bickerstaff, "he was reduced to extreme poverty, by certain shabby superfluities in his dress: for, notwithstanding that it was a very sultry day for the time of the year, he wore a loose great coat and a *muff, with a long campaign wig* out of curl, to which he added the ornament of a pair of *black garters buckled under the knee."* Two points are worthy of note in this sketch as marking progress toward more fully developed character portrayal: the revelation of character through the conversation of the person depicted, and the emphasis upon oddities in appearance and manner.

Group-description in the *Tatler* and *Spectator* is of particular interest because of its effect upon the nineteenth century essayists. Such description consists of sketches of individuals who constitute a group, as members of a club, fellow-travelers in a stage-coach, etc. Not only the individuals, but their setting is clearly delineated. The characters frequently reveal themselves through conversation or dialogue and the whole is told in the familiar manner of one intimately associated with the group. The readers' interest is heightened by the odd contrasts presented, the individual eccentricities, and the strokes of character-drawing which show certain traits as typical. In *Tatler* No. 132, the members of the club at the Trumpet are characterized in humorous fashion, and well-known types in London clubdom are drawn in a few bold strokes, such as Major Matchlock "who served in the last civil wars, and has all the battles by heart," honest old Dick Reptile who speaks little himself but laughs at the jokes of others, and Sir Jeoffery Notch who calls every thriving man a pitiful upstart. Such brief sketches were the forerunners of the more extended character portrayals, describing members of a group, in the *Spectator*. In the sketches of Sir Roger de Coverley and his friends, there is no longer the attempt to condense portraiture in a single, brief paper, but the picture of the individual, as in the case of Sir Roger, slowly emerges from paper to paper. It would be impossible to separate it from the frame in which it appears and present it as a "character." The setting is elaborated as well as the individual.

The effect of such character delineation upon the familiar essayists of the early nineteenth century is to be seen in the humorous description of members of a group, in the self-revelation of the individual through conversation, and in the manner in which enough of the setting or background is introduced to give the sketch verisimilitude. The character-writing of Hunt, Lamb and Hazlitt displays great ingenuity and variety; usually in an essay frame, it shows the influence of both the seventeenth and the eighteenth century.

Lamb's experiments with the "character" detached from the essay, may be seen in his early writings. In his contributions to the *Reflector,* he treats the "character" (1) as an individual piece of writing and links it to the preceding essay by virtue of similarity in subject matter, as in "The Character of an Undertaker," which follows the essay on "Burial Societies." Here Lamb makes no effort to incorporate the "character" as part of his essay, but unites the two by means of the following paragraph:

"Looking over some papers lately that fell into my hands by chance, and appear to have been written about the beginning of the last century, I stumbled, among the rest, upon the following short Essay, which the writer calls *'The Character of an Undertaker.'* It is written with some stiffness and peculiarities of style, but some parts of it, I think, not unaptly characterize the profession to which Mr. Middleton has the honour to belong. The writer doubtless had in mind the entertaining character of *Sable,* in Steele's excellent comedy of the *Funeral.*" [71]

(2) As part of an essay, as in "The Good Clerk, a Character" which forms the entire first part of the essay of that name, the latter part of which is devoted to comment on Daniel Defoe's *The Complete English Tradesman.* As in "The Character of an Undertaker" there is a paragraph which serves to unite the "character" and the essay. In this instance Lamb has reversed the arrangement, placing the "character" first, and has unified his subject matter. This unity pertains not only to the theme, but to the satirical tone of the whole. Lamb does not draw upon dramatic portraiture for his "character," as in "The Undertaker," but upon his personal experience. For who can doubt that Lamb, with his tongue in his cheek, had in mind the requirements for clerks in a counting house such as the India House where he was employed, and not those maxims "inculcated and instilled into the breasts of the London Apprentices," the recollections of which he claims were responsible for this "character." It was sketched, he tells us, "in an interval of business, to divert some of the melancholy hours of a Counting House," and is "little a creature of fancy." [72] In these two "characters" Lamb reveals himself a master of the form. Like Overbury, whose *Characters* was among Lamb's favorite vol-

---

[71] *Works,* vol. I, p. 95.
[72] Ibid., p. 129.

umes, he allies the "character" with an occupation. In style Lamb's two "characters" differ. That of the "Undertaker" closely follows the traditional manner: short, balanced sentences object-ively setting forth the characteristics of the type. In the "Clerk" Lamb is obviously experimenting; he uses longer sentences and occasionally introduces comments of his own, thus giving the "character" a more familiar tone, as may be seen from the following:

"The Good Clerk.—He writeth a fair and swift hand, and is completely versed in the Four First Rules of Arithmetic, in the Rule of Three (which is sometimes called the Golden Rule) and in Practice. We mention these things, that we may leave no room for cavillers to say, that any thing essential hath been omitted in our definition; else to speak the truth, these are but ordinary ac-complishments, and such as every understrapper at a desk is com-monly furnished with. The character we treat of soareth higher." [73]

Lamb may have written these "characters" for the *Morning Post* and have found no opportunity to print them there. In a letter to Coleridge (October 11, 1802) he speaks of Bishop Hall's *Charac-ters*, which he says: "I know nothing about, having never seen them." In the same letter he writes: "I dare say I could find many things, of a light nature, to suit that paper." [*The Morning Post.*][74] The inference is that Coleridge suggested the "character" as a form upon which Lamb might try his pen.

There is a space of some years between Lamb's "characters" contributed to the *Reflector* and the character-sketches which form part of many of the Elia essays. We do not know whether in the interval Lamb continued to experiment with the form. After the *Reflector* papers he produced little for several years that added to his reputation as an essayist. Between the last *Reflector* paper in 1812, and the first Elia essay in 1820, his literary output with the exception of his first essay on Christ's Hospital (1813) and the "Confessions of a Drunkard" consisted mainly of brief para-

---

[73] Op. cit., p. 127.

[74] *Life, Letters and Writings of Charles Lamb,* ed. by Percy Fitzgerald, vol. I, p. 417.

graphs, reviews, dramatic criticism and epigrammatic verse, written for the most part at the instigation of Leigh Hunt.

In certain of the Elia essays Lamb employs the "character" in an essay framework, using it to give variety of style, and a pointed conciseness to his descriptions. The many ways in which he uses the form to portray what the person does, what he says and how he looks, show that he was continually experimenting. For example he introduces a "character" in the midst of an essay in such manner that it might be removed intact and remain a complete "character" as in "Imperfect Sympathies"; or he interrupts the "character" to interpolate other material, as in "The Old and New School-Master." He frequently interjects his own opinions, thereby giving a familiar tone to his character-writing. Unlike the seventeenth century writers he does not make use of far-fetched conceits, but his "characters" reflect his all-pervading humor and sympathy, be it a beggar he is describing, or his constitutional enemy, the "true Caledonian." Like the eighteenth century character-writers, Lamb pictures the individual through the type. Those "characters" in the Elia essays which most nearly preserve the traditional form will be discussed first.

In "A Complaint of the Decay of Beggars in the Metropolis" Lamb has drawn the "character" of a beggar who was a common figure in the London streets. He has epitomized the type with characteristic grace and sympathy, touched with humor: "Rags, which are the reproach of poverty, are the Beggar's robes, and graceful *insignia* of his profession, his tenure, his full dress, the suit in which he is expected to show himself in public. He is never out of the fashion, or limpeth awkwardly behind it. He is not required to put on court mourning. He weareth all colours, fearing none. His costume hath undergone less change than the Quaker's. He is the only man in the universe who is not obliged to study appearances." [75] This "character" in an essay frame adds variety and interest to the paper. Its rhythmic quality is marked, a feature likewise observable in Earle's "characters."

"Poor Relations" Lamb opens with an extended "character" describing a poor relation. Instead of a general definition of the

---

[75] *Works*, vol. II, p. 116.

type given in brief in the opening sentence, Lamb substitutes a number of whimsical metaphors, each humorously suggesting what this "most irrelevant thing in nature" is. It is the parody of a "character" tricked forth in the mannered prose of the seventeenth century. Having drawn the "character" in the abstract, Lamb then describes the poor relation concretely, still retaining the "character" form, and depicting the individual with such truth of observation that he becomes the embodiment of the type. "You are fond of having a character at your table," says Lamb, "and truly he is one."

In describing the patient in "The Convalescent," Lamb relates an experience he himself had undergone when ill of a nervous fever. The description takes the form of a "character" broken into short paragraphs, which compose the first half of the essay. A few sentences will suffice to show how closely the form is adhered to: "He has put on the strong armour of sickness, he is wrapped in the callous hide of suffering; he keeps his sympathy, like some curious vintage, under trusty lock and key, for his own use only. He lies pitying himself, honing and moaning to himself; . . . studying little stratagems and artificial alleviations." [76]

Lamb tells us that he tried all his life to like Scotchmen and was obliged to desist from the experiment in despair. His "character" of a "true Caledonian" in "Imperfect Sympathies" displays a wit which equals the seventeenth century character-writers at their best. Take for example the following: "His understanding is always at its meridian—you never see the first dawn, the early streaks"; "the twilight of dubiety never falls upon him"; "his morality never abates, he stops a metaphor like a suspected person in an enemy's country." This essay is a good example of Lamb's skill in incorporating the "character" with the essay so that no sudden transition in style is felt.

Lamb was also adept at drawing the members of a group in such manner that each one is sharply delineated. His skill in this type of character portrayal may best be compared to that of Steele and Addison in their sketches in the *Tatler* and *Spectator*. Sometimes it is the outward man who is pictured, or again it is the indi-

---

[76] Op. cit., p. 184.

vidual's pet foible that is chosen, and illustrated by some anecdote. Characteristic of Lamb's skill is his description in "The Old Benchers of the Inner Temple" of Thomas Coventry "whose person was a quadrate, his step massy and elephantine, his face square as the lion's, his gait peremptory and path-keeping indivertible from his way as a moving column, the scarecrow of his inferiors, the browbeaters of equals and superiors, who made a solitude of children wherever he came." Lamb interpolates his sketches with comments of his own made in the first person. In this and in the use of anecdote he is like Fuller. He shows his likeness to Addison and Steele in the manner in which his backgrounds serve not only for a setting, but assist in giving unification to the group. The "classic green recesses" of the Inner Temple for example, afford a unifying background for the old benchers. In his group-description Lamb does not use the short balanced sentence of the "character," and in this respect also his character-sketches resemble those of the *Tatler* and *Spectator*.

In "The South-Sea House" Lamb has written a number of brief character-sketches of his companions there. As in "The Old Benchers" he first draws the background for the individuals he is going to describe. The South-Sea House, like the Temple, is an oasis of quiet in the great throbbing city; it has "an indolence almost cloistral." The quiet, plodding workers going about their daily duties, may have had little to differentiate them as seen by a casual observer, but Lamb penetrates beneath the outer man, searches out his heart, and sympathetically reveals what sustains each one in his journey through life. There is Evans, the Cambro-Briton, a bachelor, who becomes expansive over his evening muffin recounting the glories of London; Thomas Taine, who has the "air and stoop of a nobleman" and is buoyed by the thought that his wife traces her lineage to a noble house; and John Tipp, who relieves his vacant hours with his fiddle, and who "thought an accountant the greatest character in the world, and himself the greatest accountant in it." Although these character sketches are of individuals, rather than types, when taken together they form a kind of composite picture which is typical.

Several of the Elia essays contain descriptions of people which are not "characters," but which clearly show the influence of the form. In "Mrs. Battle's Opinions on Whist" Lamb has drawn an unforgettable portrait of old Sarah Battle, "who next to her devotions, loved a good game of whist." The portraiture is as distinctive as that of Chaucer. Lamb is here representing not a type but an individual. He secures his effect by means of short sentences having parallelism of structure as in the "character." The following passage will serve to illustrate the method and its effectiveness:

"She took, and gave, no concessions. She hated favors. She never made a revoke, nor ever passed it over in her adversary without exacting the utmost forfeiture. She fought a good fight; cut and thrust. She held not her good sword (her cards) 'like a dancer.' She sat bolt upright; and neither showed you her cards, nor desired to see yours." [77]

Another portrait in Lamb's gallery which shows "character" influence is that of his brother John, who goes disguised as James Elia, a cousin, in "Poor Relations." Of him Lamb says: "The pen of Yorick and of none since his, could have drawn J. E. entire—those fine Shandian lights and shades, which make up his story. I must limp after in my poor antithetical manner, as the fates have given me grace and talent." [78] Elia's "antithetical manner" owes its inspiration to the "character." Lamb also employed the "character" form in his sketch of himself: "A Character of the Late Elia. By a Friend" which appeared in the *London Magazine,* 1823, and was later printed as the "Preface" to the *Last Essays.*

The preceding examples serve to show that Lamb derived his technique in character-writing from the seventeenth and eighteenth centuries. The secret of his success in character delineation however is not one of technique alone, but is owing to his sympathetic understanding of those with whom he came in contact, and his ability to discover those qualities in the ordinary man which lift him out of the commonplace and invest him with interest. Lamb's understanding of people reflects one of the strongest tendencies of the Romantic Revival,—that of sympathy with man.

Hazlitt's use of the "character" shows less variety than Lamb's. We seek vainly in Hazlitt for those oddities of style characteristic

---

[77] *Works,* vol. II, pp. 32-33.
[78] Ibid., p. 71.

of the seventeenth century writers. Unlike Lamb he had no
affinity with these writers, and expressed his preference for those
papers of Elia in which there is the least infusion of antiquated
language. This, however, does not imply that Hazlitt employed
the "character" less effectively than Lamb. The form lent itself
admirably to the ironic portrayal of those types of persons with
whom he had little sympathy or patience. He delights, for instance, in depicting the scholar with all his peculiarities. Midway
in his essay "On the Ignorance of the Learned" he draws an
extended "character" of a pedant. The form, by reason of its
conciseness, proved a ready medium for the heaped-up exaggeration of which Hazlitt was a master. The learned man is set before
us in his detachment from the ordinary things of life, and in his
preoccupation with learning for learning's sake: "He thinks and
cares nothing about his next-door neighbours, but he is deeply
read in the tribes and casts of the Hindoos and Calmuc Tartars.
He can hardly find his way into the next street, though he is
acquainted with the exact dimensions of Constantinople or Pekin.
He does not know whether his oldest acquaintance is a knave or a
fool, but he can pronounce a pompous lecture on all the principal
characters in history. . . . He cannot give a satisfactory answer
to the plainest question, nor is he ever in the right in any of his
opinions, upon any one matter of fact that really comes before him,
and yet he gives himself out for an infallible judge on all those
points, of which it is impossible that he or any other person living
should know anything but by conjecture." [79]   The exaggeration of
the qualities of the type in this description serves the same purpose
as caricature: it emphasizes the essential characteristics.

Hazlitt draws a more sympathetic picture of a learned man in
his essay "The Shyness of Scholars." [80]   He describes here not the
individual but the type, yet so true is the drawing to known facts
in Hazlitt's own life that the individual is pictured through the
type. The scholar is contrasted at length with the "mere man of
business or fashion"; his attributes are carefully set forth, his attitude toward society is minutely analyzed, until the reasons for his

[79] *Works*, vol. VI, p. 73.
[80] Ibid., vol. XII, p. 68 f.

shyness are all accounted for. After describing a scholar in the abstract, Hazlitt illustrates the type by means of two concrete examples: Gray and Porson. In this instance the "character" is completely identified with the essay, and it would be difficult to separate it from its context without violating unity.

In his second paper on "The Conversation of Authors" [81] Hazlitt contrasts the character of a scholar with that of a gentleman. The characterization is brief and might be removed from its essay frame and remain intact. The plan is again followed of first presenting abstractly the attributes of a scholar, and then illustrating these qualities by a concrete example, in this instance by a description of George Dyer, friend of both Hazlitt and Lamb. The use of simile in this sketch is particularly to be noted. Of George Dyer, Hazlitt says: "He hangs like a film and cobweb upon letters, or is like the dust upon the outside of knowledge, which should not be rudely brushed aside. He follows learning as its shadow; but as such, he is respectable. He browzes on the husk and leaves of books, as the young fawn browzes on the bark and leaves of trees. . . . He reads the world, like a favourite volume, only to find beauties in it, or like an edition of some old work which he is preparing for the press, only to make emendations in it, and to correct the errors that have inadvertently slipt in." [82]

Hazlitt sometimes employs contrast to make his "characters" more effective, as in his essay "On Effeminacy of Character." In this he develops three "characters": the effeminate character, and "another branch" of it,—the trifling or dilatory character, and the contrasting type, the firm or decisive character. Hazlitt's interest in analyzing character traits is here also apparent. In the effeminate, the want of energy "arises from the habitual and inveterate predominance of other feelings and motives"; in the dilatory it is "an inherent natural defect of vigour of nerve and voluntary power." [83] The decisive character is one "who knows his own mind and sticks to it; who sees at once what is to be done in given circumstances and does it." [84] In his intense preoccupation

---

[81] *Works*, vol. VII, p. 35.
[82] Ibid., pp. 43-44.
[83] Ibid., vol. VI, p. 252.
[84] Ibid., p. 253.

with probing beneath outward appearances to the underlying reality, and in his exaltation of the person who sees what is to be done and does it, Hazlitt is very like Carlyle.

Hazlitt also selects as the object of his scorn the good-natured man.[85] This type would seem to warrant praise rather than blame, but Hazlitt strips the character bare of its shallowness, and reveals the underlying selfishness. "A good-natured man is utterly unfit for any situation or office in life that requires integrity, fortitude or generosity,—any sacrifice except of opinion, or any exertion but to please. . . . He will not forego the smallest gratification to save the whole world. He makes his own convenience the standard of right and wrong. He avoids the feeling of pain in himself, and shuts his eyes to the suffering of others."[86] Hazlitt ends his essay with the "character" of an Irishman. The Irish too are "good-natured" and their virtues are those of the heart, not of the head.

Although Hazlitt selected for his character-studies those types with which he was not in sympathy, or who merited his just indignation, this does not argue lack of sympathy. His ability to penetrate beneath surface characteristics enabled him to reveal certain qualities which to the casual observer would remain hidden. "On Londoners and Country People," for example, contains the "character" of a true Cockney, described as one who "has never travelled beyond the purlieus of the Metropolis, either in the body or the spirit."[87] He is the embodiment of the city: "There is a glare, a perpetual hubbub, a noise, a crowd about him; he sees and hears a vast number of things and knows nothing. He is pert, raw, ignorant, conceited, ridiculous, shallow, contemptible."[88] But the x-ray of Hazlitt's observation reveals the true Cockney as something more than contemptible, for he is possessed of imagination, he "lives in a world of romance—a fairy-land of his own," which he creates from the gorgeous, busy, glowing scene around him. Hazlitt also humorously pictures the Cockney in the country, where "between sheepishness and conceit, he is in a very ludicrous situation."

---

[85] "On Good Nature," *Works*, vol. I, p. 100 f.
[86] Ibid., p. 103.
[87] Ibid., vol. VII, p. 66.
[88] Ibid., p. 67.

In contrast to the picture of the Cockney, is that of the rustic in Hazlitt's "Character of the Country People." Although not written in the form of a "character" the entire essay is an analysis of the characteristics of country people, whose narrowness, ignorance, rudeness, intolerance, conceit are set forth in detail. It is an uncompromising picture, and one which is not softened by the sympathetic attitude toward the humble man, characteristic of the Romantic Revival. Hazlitt finds in the rustic a very different person from the one Wordsworth pictures. " 'The spinsters and the knitters in the sun, and the free maids that weave their thread with bones,' " observes Hazlitt, "may indeed relieve the welcome pedlar of his wares, his laces, his true-love-knots, or penny-Ballads, but they will have nothing to say to the Lyrical Ballads, nor will the united counties of Westmorland, Cumberland, and Durham, subscribe to lighten the London warehouses of a single copy of the *Excursion*." [89]

This method of depicting type-characteristics is also to be found in Hazlitt's essay "On Corporate Bodies." Men in the aggregate are described, together with the attributes which distinguish the group. This is a different kind of group-description from that already referred to in connection with Lamb. Hazlitt does not sketch the individual members of a group, but details those attributes common to a group; he delineates a composite type and not an individual type. He makes this distinction clear: "Corporate bodies are more corrupt and profligate than individuals, because they have more power to do mischief, and are less amenable to disgrace or punishment. They feel neither shame, remorse, gratitude, nor good-will. The principle of private or natural conscience is extinguished in each individual . . . and nothing is considered but how the united efforts of the whole . . . may be best directed to the obtaining of political advantages and privileges to be shared as common spoil. . . . Public bodies are so far worse than the individuals composing them, because the *official* takes place of the *moral sense*." [90] In the same essay Hazlitt characterizes the individual requirements for admission to a corporate body. The person who would form part of such a body "must be a concen-

---

[89] *Works*, vol. XI, p. 311.
[90] Ibid., vol. VI, pp. 264, 265.

trated essence, a varnished, powdered, representative of the vices, absurdities, hypocrisy, jealousy, pride and pragmaticalness of his party."[91]   Such concise, figurative description is similar to that employed by Lamb in the opening paragraph of "Poor Relations."

In his essay "On Respectable People," Hazlitt again singles out a type which merits his scorn.   He defines respectability as meaning "a man's situation and success in life, not his character or conduct." He analyzes the qualities of the successful man, and illustrates them by citing certain characters from Fielding.   Again no attempt is made to follow the rhetorical form of the "character," but the abstract qualities differentiating the type are set forth in a manner which clearly indicates "character" influence.

Another of Hazlitt's essays which delineates a type is "On People with One Idea."   The man obsessed with a topic which he insists upon discussing in season and out of season is humorously portrayed.   Figurative language again lends force and vividness to the thought: "A topic of this sort, of which the person himself may be considered as almost sole proprietor and patentee, is an estate for life, free from all incumbrance of wit, thought, or study; you live upon it as a settled income; and others might as well think to eject you out of a capital freehold house and estate as think to drive you out of it into the wide world of common sense and argument."[92]   Anecdote is also freely employed to add interest to the essay.   In an easy, conversational manner, Hazlitt recalls stories of people with one idea, and his own evident enjoyment in the telling adds to that of the reader.

One of the most interesting uses which Hazlitt makes of the "character" is to personify an abstract quality, as in his essay "On Fashion."   Here he secures his effect by a multiplication of adjectives and substantives descriptive of the matter under consideration: "Fashion is the abortive issue of vain ostentation and exclusive egotism: it is haughty, trifling, affected, servile, despotic, mean, and ambitious, precise and fantastical, all in a breath—tied to no rule, and bound to conform to every whim of the minute. . . . It is a sublimated essence of levity, caprice, vanity, extravagance, idleness, and selfishness."[93]

---

[91] Op. cit., p. 267.
[92] Ibid., p. 61.
[93] Ibid., vol. XI, p. 438.

Hazlitt returns to the subject of fashion in his "character" of a man of fashion which forms part of his essay "On the Conversation of Lords." The use of simile is particularly effective in this "character." The man of fashion is compared to a child at a fair who "gets into a round-about of knowledge till his head becomes giddy, runs from sight to sight, from booth to booth, and like the child, goes home loaded with trinkets, gew-gaws and rattles." [94]

Hazlitt, like Lamb, describes himself in the form of a "character." His mood in this essay ("On Living to One's Self") is a lyrical one, and in giving expression to his own feeling, he is also voicing a mood characteristic of the familiar essayist. The love of contemplation, of nature and the changing seasons, of books and good conversation,—the sources from which the familiar essayist draws his inspiration, is sung by Hazlitt. He who lives wisely to himself does not want to mingle in the fray. "He reads the clouds, he looks at the stars, he watches the return of the seasons, the falling leaves of autumn, the perfumed breath of spring, starts with delight at the note of a thrush in a copse near him, sits by the fire, listens to the moaning of the wind, pores upon a book, or discourses the freezing hours away, or melts down hours to minutes in pleasing thought. . . . He hardly knows what he is capable of, and is not in the least concerned whether he shall ever make a figure in the world. . . . He is free as air, and independent as the wind." [95]

Hazlitt also possessed the art of drawing individuals as well as types. His early efforts as a portrait painter developed his powers of observation and his natural ability to read character, and to analyze individual traits. In his essay "On the Imitation of Nature," he has compared the art of the portrait painter and that of the biographer: "Portrait painting is the biography of the pencil, and he who gives most of the peculiarities and details, with most of the general character,—that is of *keeping*,—is the best biographer, and the best portrait-painter." [96] Hazlitt, like Lamb, was skilful in rapidly striking off the essential characteristics of

---

[94] *Works*, vol. XII, p. 49
[95] Ibid., vol. VI, pp. 91-92.
[96] Ibid., vol. XI, p. 221.

the individual members of a group. "On Coffee-House Politicians" contains several brief character-sketches, for example: E——, a Tory, always in the wrong, "an everlasting babbler on the stronger side of the question—querulous and dictatorial"; K—— the radical reformer and logician, who if there was but one side of a question would always be in the right; and M—, "that sturdy old English character, a lover of truth and justice." M—— is drawn at some length, and is a vivid figure as he sits with his glass in his hand, looking straight before him, an attitude significant of the candor and uprightness of his mind, "which can neither be wheedled nor brow-beat into unjustifiable complaisance." [97]

Such portraiture consists in selecting the essential characteristics of an individual, and describing them with the greatest economy. There is almost no attempt to picture the outward man. Details of dress and of manner are usually left to the imagination. The background is left hazy. Hazlitt is engaged in portraying the mental characteristics of the individual, the twists of his mind, his deep-rooted prejudices. He makes his sketch graphic by the use of figurative language, as when he says of the radical reformer: "He has the new light strong upon him, and he knocks other people down with its solid beams." [98]

Like La Bruyère, Hazlitt, through his individual portraits, is able to portray the type. Thus E—— is typical of the ingrained Tory, deriving all his opinions from custom and authority; K—— of the radical reformer and logician; M——, the "lover of truth and justice," liberal in opinion. Hazlitt frequently follows the delineation of a type by the sketch of an individual who is illustrative of the type. He makes use of this method in his essay "On Paradox and Commonplace." The followers of tradition and those who seize upon every new-fangled idea are characterized, and Shelley is described as representative of the latter type. Hazlitt again makes use of highly figurative language: "The author of the Prometheus Unbound . . . has a fire in his eye, a fever in his blood, a maggot in his brain, a hectic flutter in his speech, which mark out the philosophical fanatic. . . . His bending, flexible form

---

[97] *Works*, vol. VI, p. 199.
[98] Ibid., p. 198.

appears to take no strong hold of things, does not grapple with the world about him, but slides from it like a river—

> 'And in its liquid texture mortal wound
> Receives no more than can the fluid air.' " [99]

In "On the Conversation of Authors" Hazlitt has left delightful thumb-nail sketches of Hunt and Lamb. Hunt's portrait is admirably drawn in a single sentence, which Hazlitt concludes with the penetrating observation that if Hunt has a fault, it is that he "is fond of being looked up to, without considering by whom." [100]

Hazlitt had a peculiar genius for character-portrayal, whether he made use of the "character" to delineate a type, or whether he sketched an individual. In each instance his method is a concise one. His interest is in mental characteristics and in analyzing the causes of individual action. Although he frequently delineates types which are beyond the pale of his sympathy, his ability to render truthfully whatever he observed, makes his sketches noteworthy for accuracy of presentation, and freedom from individual bias. His use of the "character" is not as varied as that of Lamb, but by means of it, and the character-sketch, richly adorned with metaphor, simile and anecdote, he gives additional interest to his essays.

Leigh Hunt was interested in both the literary "portrait," and the "character." While in prison he read Bishop Earle's *Characters,* and thought them "sensible and witty, but too much sought out, like most of those things." [101] As early as 1815 he tried his hand at the literary portrait, and in his essay "On Washerwomen" makes some interesting comparisons between the portrait created by the writer and that of the artist. "Writers," he says, "might oftener indulge themselves . . . in detached sketches of men and things, which should be to *manners* what those of Theophrastus are to *character.*" [102] "Between the matter-of-fact works of the Dutch artists, and the subtle compositions of Hogarth, there seems to be a medium reserved only for the pen. The writer only can tell

---

[99] Op. cit., p. 148.
[100] Ibid., vol. VII, p. 38.
[101] *Correspondence of Leigh Hunt,* vol. 1, p. 80.
[102] *The Seer,* vol. II, p. 157.

you all he means—can let you into his whole mind and intention. The moral insinuations of the painter are, on the one hand, apt to be lost for want of distinctness; or tempted, on the other, by their visible nature, to put on too gross a shape." [103] "It is the writer only who, without hurting the most delicate propriety of the representation, can leave no doubt of all his intentions, who can insinuate his object, in two or three words, to the dullest conception; and, in conversing with the most foreign minds, take away all the awkwardness of interpretation." [104]

In searching for a model for such sketches, Hunt thought first of Sterne, then of Steele, "the greatest master of detached portraits," and of Shenstone, whose *School-Mistress* would seem to express best what Hunt had in mind, until he remembered Chaucer. "Alas!" he says, "we thought to be doing something a little original, and find it all existing already, and in unrivalled perfection, in his portraits of the Canterbury Pilgrims! We can only dilate, and vary upon his principle." [105] Like Chaucer, Hunt often turned to humble life; he describes the waiter, the maid-servant, washerwoman, etc. The similarity of Hunt's character sketches to those of Chaucer is also to be seen in their minute details. In "The Maid-Servant" [106] for example, the picture is drawn by means of a number of small details. First the maid's outward appearance is described, then her possessions, the interior of her room, what she does as she goes about her work, and finally her favorite amusements when she takes a holiday. "The Waiter" [107] might be called a companion piece to "The Maid-Servant." "We felt irresistibly impelled to sketch him," Hunt says, "like a portrait-painter who comes suddenly upon an old friend, or upon an old servant of the family. . . . We speak of the waiter properly and generally so called, —the representative of the whole, real, official race." [108] The sketch Hunt draws is that of an individual as well as a type. He describes the mannerisms and appearance of a particular waiter in

---

[103] Op. cit., p. 159.
[104] Ibid., pp. 159-160.
[105] Ibid., p. 160.
[106] The *Indicator*, pt. 2, p. 117 f.
[107] *The Seer*, vol. 1, p. 175 f.
[108] Ibid., p. 175.

a humorous and vivid manner. He again turns to humble life in his paper "The Butcher," [109] which has more of an essay frame than "The Maid-Servant" or "The Waiter." After philosophizing on the butcher's taking of animal life, and its analogy in nature, Hunt draws a brief picture of a butcher, which is more of a type description than the portraiture in the essays previously discussed. Hunt's sketches are seldom analytical like those of Hazlitt, nor have they the depth of sympathy characteristic of Lamb, but they are full of shrewd observation, are felicitously phrased and frequently humorous.

Hunt, like Lamb, was fascinated by the sights and sounds of London street life. He likes to describe the shop windows and the passing throngs, and to single out odd figures for comment. In his essay "Twelfth Night" he draws a "street portrait" of an urchin, which in its sympathetic understanding of boy life is a companion piece to Lamb's chimney-sweeper. He whimsically describes this child of the streets as "the nightingale of mud and cold;—one of those equivocal animal-spirits of the streets who come whistling along, you know not whether thief or errand-boy, sometimes with bundle and sometimes not, in corduroys, a jacket, and a cap, or bit of hat, with hair sticking through a hole in it."

A more extended sketch also drawn from common life, is that of "Seamen on Shore," [110] in which Hunt describes sailors as well as their officers. The source of the material for this essay we learn from Hunt's *Autobiography:* the sailor was a son of his nurse at Christ Hospital, and the officer a connection by marriage. [111] The seaman on shore is described in detail as to his appearance and the manner in which he spends his time. Hunt may have got the suggestion for his sketch from Chaucer's description of a "Shipman," in the Canterbury Tales, which Hunt quotes at the close of his essay, with the observation that Chaucer's shipman "is exactly of the same cast as the modern sailor,—the same robustness, courage, and rough-drawn virtue, doing its duty, without being very nice in helping itself to its recreations." [112]

---

[109] Op. cit., p. 180 f.
[110] *Indicator*, pt. 1, p. 164 f.
[111] *Autobiography*, p. 250.
[112] *Indicator*, pt. 1, p. 169.

Hunt, however, did not confine himself to low life in his character-sketches. In "The Old Lady," he has drawn a sympathetic and exquisite picture of an old gentlewoman. Particularly interesting is the manner in which he creates a background for his figure. He describes the two rooms which the old lady generally occupies, and in telling of the articles which adorn them, he contrives a perfect setting for their occupant. The Dresden shepherds and shepherdesses on the mantel-piece, the toilet-table with its snow-white drapery of muslin, the bits of ribbons and laces, and linen smelling of lavendar in the bureau are described in detail. Although Hunt probably had an actual person in mind, he delineates in the "old lady" a type, as true to life today as when written: "She thinks the young women of the present day too forward, and the men not respectful enough; but hopes her grandchildren will be better; though she differs with her daughter in several points respecting their management. She sets little value on the new accomplishments, is a great though delicate connoisseur in butcher's meat and all sorts of housewifery." [113]

Hunt reprints in his *A Book for a Corner,* a paper of Mackenzie's called "An Old Country House and an Old Lady" (*Lounger,* No. 87). In this essay a charming character-sketch is given of an old lady, mistress of an English country house. The attention paid to detail in describing the background of this "portrait," and the naming of books in the old lady's library are features which also characterize Hunt's sketch. It seems reasonable to suppose that Hunt, although in no sense imitative, followed the technique of Mackenzie, who also spoke of his sketch as "a portrait."

Hunt's "Old Gentleman" [114] is a worthy companion piece to the "Old Lady." The original of the portrait may have been Benjamin West, the painter, at whose home Hunt visited when a child. In his *Autobiography* Hunt recalls being greatly mortified in his youth when Mr. West offered him half-a-crown if he would solve the question of "Who was the father of Zebedee's children." In his essay Hunt says of the old gentleman: "He asks little boys in general who was the father of Zebedee's children." The method of portraiture is similar to that in the "Old Lady." The appear-

---

[113] *Indicator*, pt. 2, p. 123.
[114] Ibid. pt. 1, p. 138 f.

ance, the habits, the likes and dislikes of the old gentleman are described with an eye for small details which make a finished picture. The following description of the old gentleman will serve to illustrate Hunt's method.

"He is very clean and neat; and, in warm weather, is proud of opening his waistcoat half-way down and letting so much of his frill be seen, in order to show his hardiness as well as taste. His watch and shirt-buttons are of the best; and he does not care if he has two rings on a finger. . . . He has a small cocked hat for gala days, which he lifts higher from his head than the round one, when bowed to. In his pocket are two handkerchiefs (one for the neck at night-time), his spectacles and his pocket-book. The pocket-book, among other things, contains a receipt for a cough, and some verses cut out of an odd sheet of an old magazine, on the lovely Duchess of A." [115]

Hunt's character sketches in general show more the influence of the periodical essayists than of the seventeenth century "character" writers. Among his early papers, published originally in the *Reflector* (1811) is "Bad Temper and Other Disorders" which contains sketches in the manner of the *Tatler* and *Spectator* of the ill-tempered man, the envious man, and of the miser. Although he occasionally employs short balanced sentences in his descriptions, his sketches usually are not written in the form of "characters." Two of his essays, however, "A Now, Descriptive of a Hot Day," [116] and "A Now, Descriptive of a Cold Day" [117] show the influence of a seventeenth century character-writer, Nicholas Breton, who as has already been mentioned, introduced a novelty into character-writing by his characterization of the seasons. In both of these essays Hunt uses a balanced sentence structure, and secures emphasis and unity by the use of the word "now" to begin his sentences. Hunt says the use of "now" was suggested to him "by the striking convenience it affords descriptive writers, such as Thomson and others, who are fond of beginning their paragraphs with it, thereby saving themselves a world of trouble in bringing about a nicer conjunction of the vairous parts of their subject."

---

[115] Op. cit., p. 138.
[116] Ibid., pt. 2, p. 17 f.
[117] *The Seer*, vol. 2, p. 67 f.

For " 'A Now,' Descriptive of a Hot Day," Hunt got suggestions from Keats, the essay being written when the two friends were living together. In both of these papers, descriptive of the seasons, Hunt shows himself to have been as keen an observer of nature as he was of people.

In addition to his longer character-sketches, many of Hunt's essays contain brief descriptions of individuals or types, as that of the stage-coachman, which forms part of his paper, "Coaches," [118] and of washerwomen in "On Washerwomen." [119]

Hunt's interest was not in character analysis but in describing the individual or type as to outward appearance, setting, likes and dislikes, etc. He not only liked to describe people, but things, the seasons, the weather. He frequently delineates character, but the well-springs of individual acts are not sought, nor is there much probing beneath the surface. Hunt's particular skill consists in an enumeration of details often seemingly insignificant, whose total effect is to give a finished picture. This implies a seeing eye, and the ability to select what is most significant, as well as the talent to describe graphically. Hunt believed in the advantage of the writer over the painter to suggest by means of words what it is impossible to portray through line and color: "What painting gains in universality to the eye, it loses by an infinite proportion in power of suggestion to the understanding. . . . The beauty of this unlimited power of suggestion in writing is, that you may take up the driest and most commonplace of all possible subjects, and strike a light out of it to warm your intellect and your heart by." [120]

The "character" and the character-sketch not only add to the interest of the essays of Lamb, Hazlitt, and Hunt, but definitely contribute to the development of the essay. Although Hazlitt and Hunt make frequent use of the character-sketch, its most marked effect upon the development of the familiar essay is to be seen in Lamb's Elia papers. Of these fifty-one essays, about a third contain either "characters" or character-sketches, or both. In six of them: "Mrs. Battle's Opinions on Whist," "Captain Jackson," "My Relations," "Old China," "The Old Benchers of the Inner Temple,"

---

[118] *Indicator*, pt. 2, p. 32 f.
[119] *The Seer*, vol. 2, p. 157 f.
[120] "On Washerwomen," Ibid., pp. 160-61.

and "The South-Sea House," the character-sketch forms practically the entire essay. It is worthy of note that in all these instances the sketches are of actual people—relatives, friends or acquaintances of Lamb's. In other of his papers where the character-sketch forms only part of the essay, Lamb has also written of people he knew. In "Oxford in the Vacation," and "Amicus Redidivus" he writes of his friend, George Dyer; in "Two Races of Men," he describes John Fenwick under guise of Ralph Bigod; "Christ's Hospital" contains sketches of both masters and students whom Lamb knew in his school days; John Braham the great tenor is described in "Imperfect Sympathies"; an incident in the life of Fanny Kelly, the actress, is told in "Barbara S——"; Favell, a school-fellow of Lamb's, is sketched in "Poor Relations," and the "crew" is described in the "Old Margate Hoy." Six of the Elia essays contain "characters," which are of particular interest because of the skilful manner in which Lamb incorporates them into his essays, without a definite break in style. But these "characters" can scarcely be said to contribute to the essay's development to the degree that the character-sketches do. Like the eighteenth century essayists, Lamb understood the art of introducing conversation, incident and anecdote into his sketches of people, but he marks an advance over the periodical-essayists in his genius for searching out and reproducing the salient characteristics which distinguish personality, and in his genuinely sympathetic attitude toward his subject. His sketches probe deeper into human nature than those of the earlier essayists. By means of unexpected and frequently witty and humorous observations, Lamb lays bare the mind and heart of the person he is describing. He has the faculty of disclosing foibles and eccentricities which emphasize individuality of character, and at the same time reveal fundamental human qualities. Sympathy might be said to be the keynote of Lamb's character portrayal. He never shows his impatience with human nature as Hazlitt does, but discloses endearing qualities in men's weaknesses. He particularly displays his sympathetic penetration of character in his portraits of his sister Mary (Bridget Elia) and his brother John (James Elia). In "Mackery End, in Hertfordshire" and "Old China," he has drawn a most sympathetic and tender picture of Bridget Elia, his life-long companion. The turn of phrase, the

art with which neither too little nor too much is told, the natural
conversational tone of the whole renders the sketch one of the
most delightful in the language. The quiet humor which infuses it
gains in effect when we consider that it was probably written under
Bridget Elia's eye. "I must touch upon the foibles of my kins-
woman with a gentle hand," says Lamb, "for Bridget does not like
to be told of her faults. She hath an awkward trick (to say
no worse of it) of reading in company; at which time she will
answer *yes* or *no* to a question, without fully understanding its
purport—which is provoking, and derogatory in the highest degree
to the dignity of the putter of the said question." [121]   It is by
means of such observations that Lamb builds up his picture. What
light is thrown upon Bridget's tender sensibilities by the incident
of her bursting into tears, and complaining that her brother was
altered when he spoke to her in tones more kind than ordinary!
Lamb however does not confine himself to one method. In "Old
China" Bridget's character is revealed through her conversation
with her brother, in which she recalls the days when they were
very poor and every purchase beyond the necessities represented
an adventure. Not an incident is related in these sketches that
does not serve to illustrate some characteristic of Bridget Elia or
of Elia himself.

Lamb's skill in character-drawing is further shown in his description of his brother in "My Relations" and "Dream Children."
He develops the former essay by means of anecdote and incident
which throw into relief certain characteristics of James Elia, and
reveal his pet hobbies and idiosyncrasies. In a few sentences Lamb
creates a humorous picture of a non-conservative nature at odds
with itself : "The genuine child of impulse, the frigid philosopher
of prudence—the phlegm of my cousin's doctrine is invariably
at war with his temperament, which is high sanguine. With always
some fire-new project in his brain, J. E. is the systematic opponent
of innovation, and crier down of everything that has not stood the
test of age and experiment. With a hundred fine notions chasing
one another hourly in his fancy, he is startled at the least approach
to the romantic in others; and, determined by his own sense in

---

[121] "Mackery End, in Hertfordshire," *Works*, vol. II, p. 76.

everything, commends *you* to the guidance of common sense on all occasions. With a touch of the eccentric in all which he does, or says, he is only anxious that *you* should not commit yourself by doing any thing absurd or singular." [122] In "Dream Children" Lamb uses the reverie as a means of further adding to his sketch of his brother. He shows a varied technique in his character-portrayal, but in general he achieves his effect by carefully observing, selecting and recording the characteristics of his subject, giving point to his observations by means of anecdote, incident and related conversation. His method is indebted both to biography, and to character portrayal in the eighteenth century novel.

Character-drawing in the *Tatler* and *Spectator,* and other periodicals of their type, usually has some ulterior purpose, and as a rule more interest is shown in making the individual typical, than in revealing his personality. Lamb draws character in the spirit of the creative artist, and in so doing has enriched the essay with portraiture whose individuality and revelation of fundamental human qualities will endure.

(3) THE LETTER AND THE FAMILIAR ESSAY; THEIR LITERARY RELATIONSHIP

Another marked effect of the eighteenth century periodical essay upon the nineteenth century familiar essay is to be seen in the use of the letter. The introduction of letters into periodical essays is one of their most marked features. It is probable that this practice was an outgrowth of the question and answer column which formed a part of many seventeenth century periodicals. The transition from these columns may be seen in Defoe's *Little Review* where as Professor Graham has pointed out the queries became lengthened into letters and the answers into essays.[123] The letters were from correspondents, real or imaginary, who sought advice on a wide variety of subjects, particularly upon matters of social conduct and affairs of the heart. This feature therefore was already established in periodical writing when Steele

---

[122] "My Relations," *Works*, vol. II, p. 71.
[123] Walter Graham, *English Literary Periodicals,* p. 60.

undertook the *Tatler*. Moreover the familiar letter and the essay had long been closely affiliated, so there was literary warrant for combining the two forms. Like many innovations in literature, the familiar letter owes its origin to Latin literature, the debt in this instance being to Seneca's *Epistles to Lucillius,* which Bacon said "are but Essaies—that is dispersed Meditacons though conveyed in the form of Epistles." [124]

The letter was widely used as a literary form on the continent during the sixteenth and seventeenth centuries, and translations of letters into English, notably the *Epistolas Familiares* of Guevara (1575) and Jean Louis De Balzac's letters (published in France 1624), furnished the pattern for English familiar letter-writing. In the seventeenth century many collections of letters were published in England which were of conscious literary intent, and partook of the character of essays. Among these may be mentioned Bishop Hall's "Decades" of letters, the *Epistolae Ho-Elianae* of James Howell, Nicholas Breton's *Packet of Mad Lettres,* and the correspondence between Gabriel Harvey and Spenser. The word "letter" and "essay" in time came to be used interchangeably, for a short piece of writing which was familiar in tone.[125]

Thus the periodical essayist found ready at hand in the letter a form so familiar in tone that it was admirably fitted to establish a friendly relation between the author and his audience. This was what Steele and Addison aimed to do; also they wished to preserve anonymity and this too the letter effected, as well as lending verisimilitude to the contents of the paper. Moreover, variety was secured and interest sustained by letters from various correspondents. In the hands of Addison and Steele, the letter proved a medium for the discussion of various topics. Not only did they use it to satirize the vices and follies of society, but for theatrical and literary criticism, and for sermonizing. Much of the humor is provided through letters, some of which make no pretense at being authentic, as that from a lion, directed "From my Den in the Hay-market." [126]

---

[124] *Essays,* Dedication to Prince Henry, 1612 ed. (Arber).

[125] See Harold C. Binkley, "Essays and Letter-Writing," *P.M.L.A.*, vol. XLI, 1926, p. 342 f.

[126] *Spectator,* No. 14.

The letters in the *Tatler* and *Spectator* are introduced in various ways: by means of an introductory paragraph, followed by one or more letters illustrative of the theme, or the letters appear first, followed by comment upon their contents, or again the letter is inserted midway in the essay. Some of the papers are composed entirely of letters, with only a line or so of introduction. Frequently the paper is an answer to a letter, which has been received, but the contents of which are related, not reproduced.

Dr. Johnson also uses the letter form in the *Rambler,* the *Idler* and the *Adventurer,* to call attention to the follies of the age. He assumes a sprightlier tone in the letters than in his essays proper, especially those supposed to be written by women. Frequently the correspondence reveals the character of the writer, as in the letter from Zosima who tells of her experiences in seeking a place as lady's maid.[127]

Goldsmith's *Citizen of the World* papers, cast entirely in the form of letters, have already been mentioned; as well as their prototypes, *Lettres Persanes* of Montesquieu, translated into English in 1735, and Horace Walpole's *Letter from Xo Ho, a Chinese Philosopher at London, to his Friend Lien Chi at Peking,* published in 1757. In these works the letter form was used for essay material, and it is very difficult to draw any fine distinction between the two forms. This lack of clear definition is expressed by the Earl of Shaftesbury in his *Characteristicks:* [128] "When he (the author) has writ as many Pages as he likes, or as his Run of Fancy would permit, he then perhaps considers what *Name* he had best to give to his new Writing, whether he should call it Letter, Essay, Miscellany, or ought else. The Bookseller perhaps is to determine this at last, when all, besides the Preface, Epistle Dedicatory, and Title-page is dispatched."

Mr. Binkley in his study of the connection between the familiar letter and the familiar essay makes the following distinction: "The familiar letter, so to speak, is a primary form: that is, while it has antecedents, and shows at different periods of its development

---

[127] *Rambler*, No. 12.

[128] Anthony Ashley Cooper, third Earl of Shaftesbury, *Characteristicks of Men, Manners, Opinions, Times.* Miscellaneous Reflections, No. 1, Chap. III. Birmingham, 1773.

traces of extensive foreign influence, yet its definitive quality has never altered; it is not a thing of art, but rather personal and innate. Its fundamental quality is the first-person or lyrical mood. The essay, on the other hand, is artificial, a graceful medium of personal expression to a mildly sympathetic public. In it, too, the lyrical element predominates." [129] This view of the familiar letter is a narrow one, and fails to distinguish the letter as a literary form, and to recognize the very important element of art in the letter at its best. It can scarcely be said that letters which deserve to rank as literature are "innate." If by this term is meant "individual in expression," then so is the familiar essay "innate," and the distinction drawn is not a valid one. Another critic clearly distinguishes between the two forms as follows: "The letter, if it be truly a letter and not an essay in disguise, is written to a particular person. It is dual, not single; and the mood is shaped and determined as much perhaps by the recipient as by the writer. The essay is addressed to the impersonal, general reader and is meant to be read by many instead of one; it is public rather than private." [130] Professor MacDonald in his monograph on the English essay says that "to no particular *genre* does it [the letter] more closely ally itself than to the essay." The three chief elements of this union he considers are informality, spontaneity and egotism. [131]

It is obvious that the familiar letter and essay have many points in common, but the essay is addressed to a wider audience, and it does not depend for its effect upon the sympathetic mood of any one individual.

The numerous collections of letters published in the eighteenth century doubtless exerted an influence upon the early nineteenth century familiar essayists through the examples they afforded of a graceful, flexible style which was admirably fitted to the familiar and self-revelatory mood of the writer. They also helped to point

---

[129] Harold C. Binkley, "Essays and Letter-Writing," *P.M.L.A.*, vol. XLI, 1926, p. 350.

[130] Prof. P. V. D. Shelly. "The Familiar Essay." *University of Pennsylvania Public Lectures*, 1916-17, p. 238.

[131] W. L. MacDonald. "The Beginnings of the English Essay." *University of Toronto Studies*, No. 3, 1914, p. 87.

the way to the union of the essay with the autobiographic sketch and the travel sketch, for many familiar letters were closely allied to these forms, and the essayists could not fail to observe how perfectly the familiar mood could find expression in autobiography, and in personal impressions of places visited.

Chief among the collections which advanced letter-writing to an art are the letters of Horace Walpole, Lord Chesterfield, Swift, Pope, Bolingbroke, Lady Mary Wortley Montague, Cowper and Gray. Important also for their effect upon the style of the essay are the political letters of Swift, "Junius," Walpole, and Burke. The eighteenth century letter was a product of a cultured society, and implied a free interchange of ideas, a delight in social intercourse, and the art of polite conversation. Its adaptability to express mood, sentiment, and the innermost workings of the heart is seen in its use by Richardson in his novels.

In the development of the essay in the early nineteenth century, the letter was an important factor. It set the example for the use of an easy, distinctive style closely allied to good conversation, which could at pleasure be used to depict incident, to portray character, to describe natural objects, and most important of all, to reveal the mood of the writer. There is undoubtedly some inference to be drawn from the fact that Lamb was one of the century's greatest letter-writers as well as one of its greatest essayists. There is abundant evidence of the familiarity of Hazlitt, Lamb and Hunt with the work of the leading letter-writers. Hazlitt has expressed his appreciation of the letter as a literary form: "The letters of eminent men," he says, "make, to our taste, very choice and curious reading; and, except when their publication becomes a breach of honour or decorum, we are always rejoiced to meet with them in print. . . . Letters are certainly the honestest record of great minds, that we can become acquainted with; and we like them the more, for letting us into the follies and treacheries of high life, the secrets of the gay and the learned world and the mysteries of authorship. We are ushered, as it were, behind the scenes of life; and see gay ladies and learned men, the wise, the witty, and the ambitious, in all the nakedness, or undress at least, of their spirits." [132]

---

[132] "Letters of Horace Walpole," *Works*, vol. 10, p. 161.

Hazlitt's acquaintance with letter-writers ranged from Abelard and Eloise to his contemporaries. References to them are frequent in his essays. He alludes to the *Letters of Junius* no less than thirty-three times, and devotes an essay to the letters of Horace Walpole,[133] whom he calls "the very prince of gossips." His critical comments are pithy and interesting, as when he remarks that "Pope's letters, though extremely elegant, are failures as letters. He wrote them to the world, not to his friends; and they have therefore very much the air of universal secrets." [134] He praises Gray's letters for their observations on life, "full of sagacity and fine understanding" [135] and for their descriptions of natural scenery and Gothic antiquities. "Cowper," he says, "hath unwittingly beguiled us for many a long hour, by his letters to Lady Hesketh. . . . We are much more edified by one letter of Mr. Cowper, than we should be by a week's confinement and hard labour in the metaphysical Bridewell of Mr. Coleridge; and a single letter from the pen of Gray is worth all the pedlar-reasoning of Mr. Wordsworth's Eternal Recluse." [136] It was Burke's *Letter to a Noble Lord* which caused Hazlitt to become a convert to his style—"forked and playful as the lightning, crested like the serpent." [137]

Lamb was familiar with James Howell's *Epistolae Ho-Elianae* which may have suggested to him his sketches of London street figures. The letters of Margaret Cavendish, Duchess of Newcastle, were among his favorites, and four of his essays contain references to the "high fantastical Duchess." In "The Two Races of Men," Lamb humorously complains of the friendly theft from his library of "the Letters of that princely woman, the thrice noble Margaret Newcastle." [138] He also was familiar with the letters of Lady Mary Wortley Montague.[139]

Leigh Hunt was a close student of the eighteenth century letter-writers as may be seen from his essays on Lady Mary Wortley

---

133 "Letters of Horace Walpole," *Works*, vol. 10, p. 159 f.
134 Ibid., p. 161.
135 Ibid.
136 Ibid. p. 162.
137 "On Reading Old Books," Ibid., vol. 7, p. 228.
138 *Works*, vol. II, p. 26.
139 Ibid., p. 366 (notes).

Montague,[140] and Madame de Sévigné,[141] as well as from his appreciative comments on Gray and other letter-writers in his *A Book for a Corner*. Lady Montague's letters he characterizes as "admirable, better than acute, idiomatical, off-hand, conversational without inelegance, fresh as the laugh on the young cheek, and full of brain." [142] He admired Madame de Sévigné for her sincerity: "Truth, wit, and animal spirits compose the secret of her delightfulness; but truth above all, for it is that which shows all the rest to be true." [143] In *A Book for a Corner* Hunt includes five letters of Gray, which he prefaces by an appreciation: "Gray appears to us to be the best letter-writer in the language. Others equal him in particular qualities, and surpass him in amount of entertainment; but none are so nearly faultless." [144] He follows this with comment upon other letter-writers: Chesterfield, he considers "wants heart, and even his boasted 'delicacy'; Bolingbroke and Pope want simplicity; Cowper is more lively than strong; Shenstone reminds you of too many rainy days, Swift of too many things which he affected to despise; Gibbon too much of the formalist and the *littérateur*." [145] He thought Walpole and Lady Mary Wortley Montague the most amusing of all letter-writers.

Lamb made greater use of the letter in his essays than either Hazlitt or Hunt. His early essay "The Londoner," which first appeared in the *Morning Post* (February 1, 1802), is in the form of a letter addressed to "Mr. Reflector," and is signed "I am, sir, your faithful servant, A Londoner." Lamb was of course following a common practice in thus inditing his essay. It is interesting to compare it with his letter on a similar theme, to see how an idea expressed in a personal letter for an audience of one is metamorphized in style when a larger audience is addressed. A year before "The Londoner" appeared, Lamb in writing to Robert

---

[140] "Lady Mary Wortley Montague: an Account of Her Life and Writings." *Westminster Review*, 1837. Reprinted in *Men, Women, and Books*.
[141] "Life and Letters of Madame de Sévigné." *Edinburgh Review*, 1842. Reprinted in *Men, Women and Books*.
[142] Leigh Hunt. *Men, Women and Books, A Selection of Sketches, Essays and Critical Memoirs from His Uncollected Prose Writings*, Lond., 1891, p. 345.
[143] Ibid., p. 400.
[144] Leigh Hunt, *A Book for a Corner*, Second Series, N. Y., 1859, p. 115.
[145] Ibid., p. 115.

Lloyd (February 7, 1801) of his pleasure "in the multitudinous scenes of Life in the crowded streets of ever dear London" had used expressions almost identical with those of the essay.[146]   He wrote to Wordsworth (January 30, 1801) and to Manning (November 28, 1800, and early in 1801), in similar vein of the delights of London.   In his letter to Manning he lists the city sights which interest him in a manner reminiscent of Sir Thomas Browne: "Streets, streets, streets, markets, theatres, churches, Covent Gardens, shops sparkling with pretty faces of industrious milliners, neat sempstresses, ladies cheapening, gentlemen behind counters lying, authors in the street with spectacles, George Dyers (you may know them by their gait), lamps lit at night, pastry-cooks' and silversmiths' shops, beautiful Quakers of Pentonville, noise of coaches, drowsy cry of mechanic watchman at night, with bucks reeling home drunk; if you happen to wake at midnight, cries of Fire and Stop thief; inns of court, with their learned air, and halls, and butteries, just like Cambridge colleges; old book stalls, Jeremy Taylors, Burtons on Melancholy, and Religio Medicis on every stall.   These are thy pleasures, O London with-the-many-sins." [147]

 To Wordsworth, Lamb wrote much in the same vein: "I have passed all my days in London, until I have formed as many and intense local attachments, as any of you mountaineers can have done with dead nature.   The Lighted shops of the Strand and Fleet Street, the innumerable trades, tradesmen and customers, coaches, waggons, playhouses, all the bustle and wickedness round about Covent Garden, the very women of the Town, the Watchmen, drunken scenes, rattles,—life awake, if you awake, at all hours of the night, the impossibility of being dull in Fleet Street, the crowds, the very dirt and mud, the Sun shining upon houses and pavements, the print shops, the old book stalls, parsons cheap'ning books, coffee houses, steams of soups from kitchens, the pantomimes, London itself a pantomime and a masquerade,— all these things work themselves into my mind and feed me, without a power of satiating me.   The wonder of these sights impells me into night-walks about her crowded streets, and I often shed

---

[146] E. V. Lucas, ed. *Charles Lamb and the Lloyds*, pp. 144-45.
[147] *Works*, vol. VI, pp. 194-95.

tears in the motley Strand from fulness of joy at so much Life. All these emotions must be strange to you." [148]

When we turn to Lamb's essay, we find it similar in content to the letter, but addressed to a wider audience, and therefore less intimate in style. The mood of the writer however is unchanged; he is frankly and freely expressing his delight in the sights with which he has been familiar since childhood. The intimacy of conversation which carries over into the familiar letter, lends flavor to the essay:

"For my own part, now the *fit* is long past, I have no hesitation in declaring, that a mob of happy faces crouding up at the pit door of Drury-Lane Theatre just at the hour of five, give me ten thousand finer pleasures, than I ever received from all the flocks of *silly sheep,* that have whitened the plains of *Arcadia* or *Epsom Downs.* This passion for crowds is no where feasted so full as in London. The man must have a rare *recipe* for melancholy, who can be dull in Fleet-street. I am naturally inclined to *hypochondria,* but in London it vanishes, like all other ills. Often when I have felt a weariness or distaste at home, have I rushed out into her crowded Strand, and fed my humour, till tears have wetted my cheek for inutterable sympathies with the multitudinous moving picture, which she never fails to present at all hours, like the shifting scenes of a skilful Pantomime."

"The very deformities of London, which give distaste to others, from habit do not displease me. The endless succession of shops, where Fancy (miscalled Folly) is supplied with perpetual new gauds and toys, excite in me no puritanical aversion. I gladly behold every appetite supplied with its proper food. The obliging customer, and the obliged tradesman—things which live by bowing, and things which exist but for homage, do not affect me with disgust; from habit I perceive nothing but urbanity, where other men, more refined, discover meanness. I love the very smoke of London, because it has been the medium most familiar to my vision." [149]

The above passages have been quoted at length, because they serve to show the close union between the familiar letter and the

---

[148] Op. cit., p. 210.
[149] Ibid., vol. I, pp. 401-02.

familiar essay. It is as if we went "behind scenes" with the author and saw the raw material of his paper take form. This alchemy of the letter into the essay was effected by Lamb in several instances: "On the Ambiguities arising from Proper Names"; [150] "On the Custom of Hissing at the Theatre, with some account of a Club of Damned Authors"; [151] "The Two Races of Men"; [152] "The Last Peach"; [153] "A Dissertation upon Roast Pig"; [154] "A Death-Bed." [155] In three of these essays Lamb takes the topic from a letter and fashions his essay upon it. Thus, the germ of "The Two Races of Men" will be found in a letter to Wordsworth, April 9, 1816, where he says: "I have not bound the poems yet. I wait till People have done borrowing them. I think I shall get a chain, and chain them to my shelves more Bodleiano, and People may come and read them at chain's length. For of those who borrow, some read slow, some mean to read but don't read, and some neither read nor meant to read, but borrow to leave you an opinion of their sagacity." [156]

In a letter to Baron Field (August 31, 1817) Lamb speaks of the difficulties of writing "from one end of the globe to another," because half of the truths in his letters will become lies and some of the lies may become sad realities. [157] This idea forms the nucleus of the Elia essay, "Distant Correspondents" addressed to "My dear F." [158]

Writing to Bernard Barton (December 1, 1824), [159] Lamb refers to the fate of Henry Fauntleroy, the banker who was hanged for forgery in 1824. In "The Last Peach" he returns to the subject, and writes in a style similar to the letter. As Mr. Binkley has observed, [160] "here . . . there is a perfect identity of mood in the

---

[150] *Reflector*, No. 2.
[151] Ibid., No. 3.
[152] *London Magazine*, December, 1820.
[153] Ibid., April, 1825.
[154] Ibid., Sept., 1822.
[155] *Hone's Table Book*, vol. 1, cols. 425-26, 1827.   Reprinted in *Last Essays of Elia*, 1833.
[156] *Works*, vol. VI, p. 484.
[157] Ibid., p. 501.
[158] Ibid., vol. II, p. 104.
[159] Ibid., vol. VII, p. 662 f.
[160] Harold C. Binkley, "Essays and Letter Writing," *P.M.L.A.*, vol. 41, 1926, p. 356.

two versions, the same humorous droop of phrase, and the same wry twist of fanciful notions." Likewise the germ of the Elia essay "Blakesmoor in H-shire" is to be found in a letter written to Southey, October 31, 1799.[161]

In the examples just cited the letters provide little more than themes for the essays. In contrast to these are two other essays of Lamb's of which his letters furnish the entire material. In a letter to Wordsworth (February 1, 1806),[162] Lamb tells the amusing incident of a young man who confused William Robert Spencer (1769-1834), author of *jeux d'esprit* and verse, with the poet Edmund Spenser. We find the same incident recounted in the essay "On the Ambiguities Arising from Proper Names" (*Reflector*, No. 2, 1811).[163] A comparison of the letter with the essay reveals little change, except a more formal arrangement of the material. The following is characteristic of the type of change: *Letter:* "Then pausing, and looking sad, he ejaculated 'Poor Spencer'!" (p. 334). *Essay:* "But presently after, assuming a grave look, he compassionately muttered to himself 'poor Spencer.'" (p. 69). *Letter:* "I begged to know the reason of his ejaculation, thinking that Time had by this time softened down any calamities which the Bard might have endured—'Why, poor fellow!' said he, 'he has lost his Wife!' 'Lost his Wife?' said I, "Who are you talking of?' 'Why, Spencer,' said he. 'I've read the Monody he wrote on the occasion and *a very pretty thing it is.'*" (p. 334). *Essay:* "There was something in the tone with which he spoke these words that struck me not a little. It was more like the accent with which a man bemoans some recent calamity that has happened to a friend, than that tone of sober grief with which we lament the sorrows of a person, however excellent, and however grievous his afflictions may have been, who has been dead more than two centuries. I had the curiosity to enquire into the reasons of so uncommon an ejaculation. My young gentleman, with a more solemn tone of pathos than before, repeated 'poor Spencer,' and added 'he has lost his wife.'" (p. 69).

---

161 *Works*, vol. VI, p. 149 f.
162 Ibid., p. 332 f.
163 Ibid., vol. I, p. 69 f.

The other example of close identity between letter and essay is to be found in "A Death Bed—In a Letter to R. H. Esq. of B——." It is not, properly speaking, an essay but was included in the first edition of the *Last Essays of Elia.* It originally appeared in Hone's *Table Book* (vol. 1, cols. 425-26, 1827) signed "L," and dated February 10, 1827. The "essay" is almost identical to a letter written by Lamb to Crabb Robinson (January 20, 1827),[164] describing the death of Randal Norris, whose wife was a friend of Mrs. Field, Lamb's grandmother. The only changes made in the essay are for the purpose of disguising the identity of the family. Of course it would have been impossible to write the essay word for word like the letter if Lamb had not had a copy of the letter before him, which perhaps may be accepted as proof that he made conscious use of letters and was not simply recollecting incidents.

Midway between the instances just cited of letters furnishing the germ of ideas for the essays, and the material of the letter being transferred entire to the essay, is a third treatment of subject matter, in which the incidents related in a letter are used to form *part* of an essay. "A Dissertation upon Roast Pig," in addition to a Chinese fable, contains two incidents: the gift of a pig, and Lamb's childhood generosity to a beggar. Both incidents are to be found in a letter which Lamb wrote to Coleridge, March 9, 1822.[165] It is difficult to determine which is the more delightful, the letter or the essay. It is as if Lamb vied with himself upon a chosen theme. The delicious humor, the intimate, almost tender mood, the highly individual style are the same. Perhaps more than any other instance, this illustrates the occasional identity of the familiar letter with the essay. One example will suffice:

Letter: "Teals, wigeons, snipes, barn-door fowl, ducks, geese— your tame villatic things—Welsh mutton, collars of brawn, sturgeon, fresh or pickled, your potted char, Swiss cheeses, French pies, early grapes, muscadines, I impart as freely unto my friends as to myself. They are but self-extended; but pardon me if I stop somewhere—where the fine feeling of benevolence giveth a higher smack than the sensual rarity—there my friends (or any good

---

[164] *Works*, vol. VII, pp. 720-21.
[165] Ibid., p. 561 f.

man) may command me; but pigs are pigs, and I myself therein am nearest to myself. Nay, I should think it an affront, an under-valuing done to Nature who bestowed such a boon upon me, if in a churlish mood I parted with the precious gift." [166]

Essay: "Hares, pheasants, partridges, snipes, barn-door chicken (those "tame villatic fowl"), capons, plovers, brawn, barrels of oysters, I dispense as freely as I receive them. I love to taste them, as it were, upon the tongue of my friend. But a stop must be put somewhere. One would not, like Lear, 'give every thing.' I make my stand upon pig. Methinks it is an ingratitude to the Giver of all good flavours, to extra-domiciliate, or send out of the house, slightingly, (under pretext of friendship, or I know not what) a blessing so particularly adapted, predestined, I may say, to my individual palate—it argues an insensibility." [167]

Lamb in his early essays modeled upon those of the *Spectator* freely uses the letter form. "On the Inconveniences resulting from being Hanged" [168] is an excellent example of the correspondent's letter-to-the-paper type of essay which Steele and Addison used to such good purpose. Lamb's letter is couched in the same humorous vein as the letters of the periodical essayists; and likewise employs a fictitious signature, a take-off on names drawn from classical lore. It begins in the customary fashion of a correspond-ent seeking advice: "Sir—I am one of those unhappy persons whose misfortunes, it seems, do not entitle them to the benefit of pure pity," and ends: "Permit me to subscribe myself, Mr. Editor, your unfortunate friend, Pensilis." Lamb, in the same essay, em-ploys the device of inserting a letter within a letter, which serves to introduce the "love-lorn" note so characteristic of the eighteenth century correspondents. He begins and ends his letter in the same gay, mock-serious, bantering tone, but interpolates a para-graph in true essay fashion in which the subject of hanging is treated "as a topic." He refers to the politest authors—Shakes-peare, Swift, Pope, Prior, Gay, Fielding, Smollett—who have made use of hanging as a source of the ridiculous. He carries on a

---

[166] Op. cit., p. 561.

[167] Ibid., vol. II, p. 125.

[168] Ibid., vol. I, p. 56 f.   (Originally appeared in *The Reflector*, No. 2, 1811.)

sort of implied mental dialogue with the editor, and in one instance indicates in italics what the editor would have said to the correspondent. Here we have an excellent example of the letter passing by almost imperceptible degrees into the essay and back again without marked change in style or mood.

Another essay in letter form which reflects the style of the *Spectator* is "Edax on Appetite" [169] in which Lamb addresses "Mr. Reflector" as follows: "I am going to lay before you a case of the most iniquitous persecution that ever poor devil suffered" [170]; and then proceeds to lay bare the secret of his "appetite for *food.*" The paper is evidently a burlesque on a rather common practice of filling up the papers with stories of great eaters,—"those tales," which Lamb says, "are renewed as often as the editors of papers want to fill up a space in their unfeeling columns, of great eaters,— people that devour whole geese and legs of mutton *for wagers,* are sometimes attempted to be drawn to a parallel with my case." [171] The essay is couched in the mannered style of the eighteenth century, and the idea of it may have originated from the exaggerated stories of the hack writers of the period, which are ridiculed by Steele in the *Spectator.* "*Hospita* on the Immoderate Indulgence of the Pleasures of the Palate" [172] is a companion piece to "Edax on Appetite" which it preceded when printed in the *Reflector.* It, too, is addressed to "Mr. Reflector" and is in the form of a letter seeking advice, but its style has no likeness to that of Addison or Steele; it resembles the periodical letters only in the spirit of ridicule in which it is written.

After the publication of the *Essays of Elia,* Lamb again turned to the writing of essays in letter form. His "Letter to an Old Gentleman whose Education has been Neglected" appeared in the *London Magazine,* January, 1825. It was intended as a parody on De Quincey's "Letters to a Young Man whose Education had been Neglected" which appeared in the *London Magazine,* January to July, 1824. Lamb doubtless planned to have his letter (dated April 1, 1823) appear at the same time, but "Taylor and Hessey

---

[169] *Reflector,* No. 4. *Works,* vol. I, p. 118 f.

[170] *Works,* vol. I, p. 122.

[171] Ibid.

[172] *Reflector,* No. 4. *Works,* vol. I, p. 124 f.

would not print it." [173] This letter is of particular interest because it shows how Lamb could alter his style at will, and perfectly imitate another's manner of writing. After several pages of banter, Lamb changes his style to that of Milton in his tractate *Of Education.* He marks the transition by the following paragraph: "And now, my dear Sir, if in describing such a tutor as I have imagined for you, I use a style a little above the familiar one in which I have hitherto chosen to address you, the nature of the subject must be my apology. *Difficile est de scientiis inscienter loqui,* which is as much as to say that 'in treating of scientific matters it is difficult to avoid the use of scientific terms.' But I shall endeavour to be as plain as possible." [174] Lamb closes his letter with a quotation from Milton's tractate.

In 1825 Lamb contributed two humorous letters to *Hone's Everyday Book.* In the first one, addressed to the Editor and signed "Twenty-ninth of February" (vol. 1, May 1, 1825), Lamb writes as if he were the "day," protesting against having been omitted from Hone's *Book* which made no mention of the leap year date. In the second letter, entitled "Twelfth Day of August" (vol. 1, August 12, 1825), he again writes in the same vein under character of the day.[175] These letters are of interest because Lamb had made use of their themes in a previous essay, "Rejoicings upon the New Year's coming of Age" which had appeared in the *London Magazine,* January 1823. In this essay he more than once comments upon the forlorn condition of February twenty-ninth, and represents the Twelfth of August "a jealous old Whig gentlewoman" as disputing with the Twenty-third of April "a new fangled lady of the Tory stamp."

---

[173] See Lamb's letter to Bernard Barton, March 5, 1823. Lamb wrote Miss Huchinson (Jan., 1825) that: "De Quincey's Parody was submitted to him before printed, and had his Probatum." (*Works,* vol. I, p. 474 (notes).) In a note which prefaced the "letter" when it was printed in the *London,* Lamb says he is sending "a bantering epistle" which "was *suggested* by some Letters of your admirable Opium-Eater." It was not, he says, in the remotest degree his intention to ridicule De Quincey's letters. (*Works,* vol. I, p. 213.)

[174] *Works,* vol. I, p. 216.

[175] Its occasion was the birthday of George IV, who was born August 12, 1762, but who adopted St. George's Day, April 23, as his natal day after his accession to the throne.

Other essays, addressed to "Mr. Reflector" are "On the Danger of confounding Moral with Personal Deformity" (*Reflector* No. 2) ; "On the Custom of Hissing at the Theatres, with some account of a Club of Damned Authors" (*Reflector* No. 3) and "On Burial Societies" (*Reflector* No. 3). These papers exhibit none of the characteristics of the familiar letter, but are essays to which have been appended a salutation and a signature. "On the Custom of Hissing at the Theatres," is based on an actual incident: the failure of Lamb's farce *Mr. H——*, which Lamb recounted in a letter to Manning.[176]

Still another use Lamb made of the letter was to introduce it into the essay, as in "The Old and the New Schoolmaster" [177] (*London Magazine,* May, 1821), where he professes to quote from a letter supplied him by his cousin Bridget.[178]

Lamb's use of the letter in the essay may be summed up as follows: (1) The contents of his own letters, slightly modified, form the material of the essay, as in "The Londoner"; (2) Topics discussed in his personal letters are made the themes of his essays, such as the "Two Races of Men," "The Last Peach" and "The Dissertation upon Roast Pig"; (3) Incidents recounted in his letters are transferred to his essays without change of mood, as for example, "The Ambiguities arising from Proper Names." Also the entire essay is sometimes cast in letter form, and in some instances the letter is introduced into the essay. In these latter practices, Lamb was following the example of the eighteenth century essayists.

Hunt employs the letter-form in his periodicals in a manner similar to that of Steele in the *Tatler;* he adopts the harmless fiction of writing letters to himself as editor. Like Steele he possesses the art of imitating the style and sentiment of his would-be correspondents, but his success in this respect falls short of that achieved by Dr. Johnson. The letters in Hunt's *Tatler* and *Indi-*

---

[176] *Works,* vol. I, p. 412 (notes). This letter is not dated, therefore it has not been included among those which furnished a theme for the essays.

[177] Ibid., vol. II, p. 49 f.

[178] Lamb is said to have had a hand in "Original Letters of Sir John Falstaff" which were published in 1796; as the work of White. Mr. Lucas believes that the *Dedication* is wholly Lamb's. (See E. V. Lucas, *Life of Lamb,* vol. I, p. 116, 1905.)

cator bear closest resemblance to their eighteenth century prototypes. Like those of the earlier periodicals they frequently voice
a complaint, as in "Against Fantastical Scrupleness." [179] which
protests against the banishment of old customs, such as hanging
the mistletoe. In voicing his protest, Hunt refers to the earlier
periodicals: "This brings me to the grievance which caused me to
trouble you with so long a letter: for they will mind what you
say, because it appears in a *modern* publication; whereas if I quote
from the Spectator or Tatler, I am reminded that these are writers
whose notions are gone by, that manners have changed as well as
fashions, and that it would be as ridiculous to copy the usages of
other times, as it would be to appear at the Opera in a wig like Sir
Richard Steele's." Also like those of Steele's *Tatler,* some of the
letters purport to have been written by young women, who seek
advice in affairs of the heart, and various matters of feminine
interest. "On Jealousy in Marriage" [180] is from "a fair author,"
who contrary to the usual practice does not solicit advice, but tells
how she followed it. Hunt's sympathy with the problems of the
fair sex, in an age when standards for women were undergoing
modification is expressed in several *Indicator* letters. In *Indicator*
No. 72 under the caption "Old Maids" he writes in defense of
spinsterhood, and in the same number expresses a sympathetic
attitude toward a broader education for women.

Hunt also employs the fiction of a letter received from a reader,
when he reprints stories and other articles to take the place of
original matter, which he himself was unable to contribute. For
example he prefaces "The Japanese Widow and her Sons," [181]
taken from the *Histoire de Japan,* by P. Charlevoix, with a letter
purporting to come from "A Constant Reader," and in like manner
introduces "The Englishman in Paris," [182] a translation from the
Life of Goretry.

Another likeness to the use of the letter by the *Tatler* and *Spectator* is to be seen in Hunt's adoption of the epistolary form for

---

[179] *Indicator,* No. 66. (Reference is to original periodical and not to
Indicator in book form.)
[180] Ibid., No. 60. (See note under cit. 179.)
[181] Ibid., No. 72. (See note under cit. 179.)
[182] Ibid., No. 74. (See note under cit. 179.)

literary and dramatic criticism. He uses it in *Indicator* No. 73 to criticize the French and English drama. The critical essay on "Nautical Poetry," [183] signed by J. C. H. and probably written by John Hunt, is in the form of a letter. Literary criticism in Hunt's *Tatler* is frequently written in letter form.[184] Essays in epistolary style dealing with fashion and the lesser moralities also appear in Hunt's *Tatler,* as for example "Tests of Respectability." [185]

Hunt made still further use of the letter in his Italian travel sketches which appeared in the *Liberal* as "Letters from Abroad." In the first of the series Hunt explains that he adopted the letter form because he "found the use of one's plural privileges inconvenient in travelling. An author must reverse on these occasions the custom of his legitimate brother *we's* and travel *cognito;* otherwise his personal experiences will sometimes have a very ludicrous and inconsistent effect. He will not be able to move about with so much freedom, or give the results of his impressions with such vivacity, as if he were unhampered with a body corporate." [186] In thus using the letter to record his travel impressions, Hunt was following the example of James Howell, Lady Mary Wortley Montague, Horace Walpole, and others. In some of Hunt's "Letters from Abroad" the familiar tone is further emphasized by personal references. Letter III is addressed to "My dear N" and begins as if written to an actual correspondent: "I write you, as you request, a very long letter 'on the largest sized paper, and in the smallest hand-writing.' " [187] Letter IV, addressed to "Dear C—" also opens in a personal vein: "I hope you have not forgotten the thoughts you entertained of visiting Italy. I set your father longing to accompany you, when I saw him. N's holidays are approaching; and I should like to know what all three of you could do better than to come arm-in-arm, joking and to joke, and see who hungers and thirsts after his old friends." [188] Except for these familiar passages, the "Letters from Abroad" are essays in their

---

183 Op. cit.,
184 *Tatler,* vol. I, pp. 21, 27, 51, 73.
185 Ibid., No. 8.
186 *Liberal,* vol. 1, p. 97.
187 Ibid., vol. II, p. 47.
188 Ibid., p. 7.

general tone and style. They are addressed to the impersonal, general reader, and are intended to be read by many instead of one.

"A Walk from Dulwich to Brockham" [189] records Hunt's impressions in "a letter to a friend." The paper is written in an informal entertaining manner, and well illustrates the close connection between the travel sketch, the essay and the letter. In describing the walking trip he took with two companions, Hunt might equally well be writing to an interested friend, or sharing his pleasure, as in this instance, with the wider circle who composed his periodical audience. Descriptions of places and people, anecdotes, recollections and events of historic interest are woven into a charming whole which gives the flavor of the familiar essay in its numerous and happy digressions, and intimate style; and retains the nature of the travel sketch in the information provided, and in the personal impressions, the result of first hand observation. Not only does Hunt describe what he actually sees on his walk, but he links the present with the past, transporting us to the eighteenth century with the magic ease of a wishing carpet.

"A Letter to the Bells of a Parish Church in Italy" contributed by Hunt to the *New Monthly Magazine* in 1825, offers an interesting variation of the familiar essay in letter form. The "letter" is written in this instance not to a supposed correspondent, but to the bells themselves, whom Hunt addresses in a friendly manner.

Hunt's use of the letter form, while not as extensive as Lamb's, clearly shows his indebtedness to the eighteenth century periodical essayists in the manner in which he introduces it to voice complaints, to give advice to the fair sex, and for literary and dramatic criticism. It is not possible to draw parallels between Hunt's personal letters and his essays. There is no transference of material from one to the other as in the case of Lamb. Hunt's personal letters are in fact peculiarly wanting in the intimate charm which characterizes his familiar essays.

Hazlitt's use of the letter form in his familiar essays is very slight compared to that of Hunt and Lamb. He does not vary the form of his essays by introducing into them so-called letters, but in a few instances he begins and ends his essays in letter style.

---

[189] *Companion*, N. Y. 1845, No. 14. (Bound with the *Indicator*.)

This is however but an editorial device, and no attempt is made to give the material the tone of a familiar letter, implying an audience of one. "On the Love of Country" [190] is addressed "To the Editor of the *Round Table*," but this essay appeared originally in the *Examiner* (November 27, 1814) as one of a series called "Commonplaces," prior to the Round Table essays, and was not therefore addressed to the Round Table Editor, when first written. The germ of "My First Acquaintance with Poets" which appeared in the *Liberal* (No. 3, 1823) is to be found in a letter addressed "to the Editor of the Examiner." [191] The letter voices a complaint and is familiar in tone. When taken over into the essay, it did not reappear as a letter, but as an integral part of the essay, from which it is not to be distinguished.

The greatest effect of the letter upon Hazlitt's essays is to be found not in his use of the form, but in the manner in which he weaves the subject matter of letters—quotations from them, and references to them, into his essays. "On Manner" [192] quotes from Lord Chesterfield's *Letters to his Son* (No. cxxx), and takes its theme from Chesterfield's opinion that manner is of more importance than matter. The letters of Horace Walpole are made the subject of a paper by Hazlitt, contributed to the *Edinburgh Review*, December 1818.[193] This essay quotes freely from Walpole's *Letters*, whose author it characterizes as "an inimitable gossip —a most vivacious garrulous historian of fair-haired women, and curious blue china." [194] Hazlitt opens his essay "On Different Sorts of Fame" [195] with a quotation on the futility of posthumous fame from William Melmoth's *Fitzosborne's Letters* (1742-47). He uses the passage as a point of departure for the opposite viewpoint which he develops in his paper. He follows the same method in his essay "On the Literary Character," only instead of quoting directly from letters, in this instance the *Correspondence of Baron Grimm* (1812-14), he quotes from Jeffrey's article on the *Corre-*

190 *Works*, vol. I, p. 17 f.
191 *Examiner*, Jan. 12, 1817.
192 *Works*, vol. I, p. 41 f.
193 "Letters of Horace Walpole," Ibid., vol. X, p. 159 f.
194 Ibid., p. 167.
195 Ibid., vol. I, p. 93 f.

spondence in the *Edinburgh Review* (July, 1813), and uses his disagreement with Jeffrey's statements as the thesis of his paper. This essay originally appeared in the form of a letter in *The Morning Chronicle* (Oct. 28, 1813), entitled "Baron Grimm and the Edinburgh Reviewers."

Hazlitt also makes telling use of the letter to express his critical and political opinion, and as a weapon of invective, as for example in "A Letter to William Gifford, Esq.," [196] written to refute Gifford's criticism of the *Round Table,* and his "Free Thoughts on Public Affairs, or Advice to a Patriot, in a Letter Addressed to a Member of the Old Opposition" (1808).[197] Such material, however, lies outside the field of the familiar essay.

In general it may be said that the early nineteenth century familiar essayists further demonstrated the close union between the familiar essay and the familiar letter by: (1) introducing letters into their essays in the manner of the eighteenth century essayists; (2) employing a style in their essays characteristic of the familiar letter; (3) using material from actual letters either as part of their essays, or to furnish a theme for them.

---

[196] Op. cit., p. 365 f.
[197] Reprinted as "Advice to a Patriot," Ibid., vol. III, p. 1 f.

PART II

ROMANTIC ELEMENTS IN THE FAMILIAR ESSAY

CHAPTER IV

INTEREST IN NATURE AND THE PICTURESQUE

One of the strongest influences upon the English familiar essay in the early nineteenth century was that of the Romantic Revival. In the essays of Hunt, Hazlitt and Lamb may be traced Romantic elements which parallel those found in the early nineteenth century poets. The friendship between Lamb and the Lake poets, and Hunt's connection with Byron, Shelley and Keats have often been emphasized. Lamb's friendship with Coleridge, begun at Christ's Hospital where they were fellow-students, continued throughout life, and was a tie so strong that his grief at Coleridge's death is thought to have hastened his own. Coleridge brought Lamb and Southey together when they were both young men, and although the friendship never became an intimate one, their literary correspondence proved an intellectual stimulus to Lamb. As early as 1797 Lamb was with the Wordsworths at Nether Stowey, where he visited Coleridge, and it was after this visit that he commenced work upon *John Woodvil* and *Rosamund Gray*. The latter work, inspired by Mackenzie's *Julia de Roubigné,* is infused with romantic feeling and childlike simplicity, and has been looked upon as Lamb's contribution to the war against convention in which the *Lyrical Ballads* played such a conspicuous part.[1] Hunt's and Keats' residence together has already been noted, as well as Hunt's indebtedness to Keats for suggestions for one of his essays. It was under Hunt's roof that Keats and Shelley became acquainted. The friendship between Hunt and Shelley is one of the most beautiful in literary annals, and it is significant that both Shelley and Keats celebrated Hunt in their poetry. Hazlitt's admiration and friendship for Wordsworth and Coleridge were tempered by political differences, but he freely acknowledged their influence upon his life. It was in Hazlitt's youth that he made the acquaint-

---

[1] *The Works of Charles and Mary Lamb,* ed. by E. V. Lucas, vol. I, p. 389.

ance of Coleridge, and he tells us that he owed it to Coleridge that
his understanding "did not remain dumb and brutish," but "at length
found a language to express itself." [2] In the same impressionable
period he met Wordsworth. He read the *Lyrical Ballads* while
they were still in manuscript, and he dates his insight into poetry
from the commencement of this acquaintance with Wordsworth
and Coleridge.[3] The familiar essayists, and the romantic poets of
the early nineteenth century, therefore, were not isolated groups
each working under a common influence, but were linked by
friendship and bonds of mutual interest.

As critics no less than as familiar essayists, Hunt, Lamb and
Hazlitt contributed to the Romantic Revival. Their sane and
appreciative criticism helped to create a favorable attitude toward
the new poetry in the midst of much adverse comment on the
part of critics. Their criticism is also valuable as showing their
own attitude toward romanticism. Lamb's review of Wordsworth's *Excursion,* which appeared in the *Quarterly Review,* 1814,
is not only appreciative in high degree of Wordsworth's genius, but
is interpretive of the movement which the *Lyrical Ballads* pro-
claimed. That Lamb was in sympathy with the pronouncements
of the *Preface* to the *Ballads* is evident from his article, but it
also shows that he considered Wordsworth's theories needed both
interpretation and defense. Hazlitt in his "Lectures on the English
Poets" (1818)[4] has freely expressed his opinion of the Lake
Poets, upon whom he bestows both praise and censure, the latter
colored by political animosity. It is noteworthy that he selects
for commendation those qualities which were characteristic likewise of the nineteenth century familiar essay. He admires Wordsworth's poetry because "he furnishes it from his own mind, and
is his own subject." [5] He praises the shorter personal compositions
of Southey, in which "there is an ironical mixture of the quaint
and serious, such as his lines on a picture by Gaspar Poussin, the
fine tale of Gaulberto, his Description of a Pig, and the Holly-tree,
which is an affecting, beautiful and modest retrospect on his own

---

[2] "My First Acquaintance with Poets," *Works,* Vol. XII, p. 260.

[3] "On Reading Old Books," Ibid., vol. VII, p. 226.

[4] "Lectures on the English Poets," Ibid., vol. V, p. 143 f.

[5] Ibid., p. 156.

character." [6] He singles out for appreciation Coleridge's great imaginative and descriptive powers. "His thoughts," Hazlitt says, "did not seem to come with labour and effort; but as if borne on the gusts of genius, and as if the wings of his imagination lifted him from off his feet." [7]

Hunt selects for comment the contemplative, retrospective and melancholy aspects of Wordsworth's poetry. He considers Wordsworth, with the exception of Shakespeare, "the greatest contemplative poet" [8] that England has produced. He finds him "almost entirely a retrospective poet" [9] and remarks that "a vaporous melancholy" hangs over his most beautiful landscapes. He is not in sympathy with either Wordsworth's melancholy or his didactic tendency, and says if " 'no mirth indeed can be found in his melancholy,' . . . it is to be feared there is always 'some melancholy in his mirth.' " [10] Very self-revealing is Hunt's comment that Wordsworth "seems always girding himself up for his pilgrimage of joy, rather than enjoying it; and his announcements are in a tone too exemplary and didactic. We admire him; we venerate him; we would fain agree with him: but we feel something wanting on his own part towards the largeness and healthiness of other men's wider experience; and we resent . . . that he should insist upon squaring all which is to come in the interminable future with the visions that bound a college cap." [11] On the other hand, Hunt had the highest admiration for Coleridge as a poet, and considered him "the greatest master of his time," of pure poetry. [12]

It is interesting to compare the critical attitude of Hunt and Hazlitt toward Shelley. Hunt found Shelley's poetry "full of mountains, seas, and skies, of light, and darkness, and the seasons, and all the elements of our being, as if Nature herself had written it, with the creation and its hopes newly cast around her." But

---

[6] Op. cit., p. 164.
[7] Ibid., p. 167.
[8] The *Seer*, Vol. 1, p. 205.
[9] Ibid., p. 207.
[10] Ibid., p. 208.
[11] Ibid., pp. 208-209.
[12] *Imagination and Fancy*, Lond. 1891, p. 250.

he thought it contained "too indiscriminate a mixture of great and small, and a want of sufficient shade,—a certain chaotic brilliancy 'dark with excess of light.' " [13]   Hazlitt considered Shelley a genius, and particularly admired his shorter poems. His style, he says, "is to poetry what astrology is to natural science— a passionate dream, a straining after impossibilities, a record of fond conjectures, a confused embodying of vague abstractions,— a fever of the soul, thirsting and craving after what it cannot have, indulging its love of power and novelty at the expense of truth and nature, associating ideas by contraries, and wasting great powers by their application to unattainable objects." [14]

Keats, Hunt says, "never beheld an oak-tree without seeing the dryad." [15]   His imagery drawn from Nature particularly appealed to Hunt. "In what other English poet," he asks, . . . "are you so *certain* of never opening a page without lighting upon the loveliest imagery and the most eloquent expressions?" "His region is 'a wilderness of sweets,'—flowers of all hue, and 'weeds of glorious feature' . . . There . . . is the 'rain-scented eglantine,' and bushes of Mayflowers, with bees and myrtle, and hay,—and endless paths into forests haunted with the loveliest as well as gentlest beings; and the gods live in the distance, amid notes of majestic thunder." [16]

After Gifford's critical attack upon Keats, Hazlitt defended him in *The Spirit of the Age,* and showed his sympathy and regard for "poor Keats." He considered the fault in Keats' poetry was "a deficiency in masculine energy of style." He criticizes *Endymion* for its lack of "hardy spirit or rigid forms of antiquity." Keats, says Hazlitt, "painted his own thoughts and character and did not transport himself into the fabulous and heroic ages." [17] Lamb expresses his admiration for Keats in his review of "St. Agnes' Eve," which he contributed to the *New Times.* Of the romantic poets, he believed Keats next in genius to Wordsworth.

Hazlitt's criticism of Byron in *The Spirit of the Age* is just and

---

[13] Op. cit., pp. 268-69.
[14] "Shelley's Posthumous Poems," *Works,* Vol. X, p. 256.
[15] "Keats," *Imagination and Fancy,* p. 283.
[16] Ibid., p. 284.
[17] "On Effeminacy of Character," *Works,* vol. VI, pp. 254-55.

penetrating. *Intensity* is "the great and prominent distinction" of Byron's writing.[18] It is his power to elevate his work by the force of his own feelings that keeps them from being dull. Hazlitt also notes that Byron does not exhibit "a new view of nature, or raise insignificant objects into importance by the romantic associations with which he surrounds them; but generally . . . takes commonplace thoughts and events, and endeavours to express them in stronger and statelier language than others." [19]   The self-revelatory aspect of Byron's work is also mentioned: "he hangs the cloud, the film of his existence over all outward things—sits in the centre of his thoughts, and enjoys dark night, bright day." [20] "In reading Lord Byron's works," Hazlitt says, "he himself is never absent from our minds." [21]

In this criticism of the Romantic poets by Hunt, Lamb and Hazlitt may be seen a tendency to emphasize those elements which were prominent in the work of the essayists themselves.

It is not surprising that the work of both poets and essayists should exhibit similar characteristics of a romantic kind. Eighteenth century formalism, decorum, and lifeless abstractions no longer satisfied the new spirit of inquiry and curiosity which science, politics and industrialism were helping to create. The reaction was away from imitation and a narrow social attitude toward originality and the expression of individuality.   Men were struggling to break through the barriers of convention and an outworn social order, to first principles and eternal verities.   Romanticism is an attitude toward life; it is a way of viewing the external world, and of trying to effect a compromise between man's natural inclinations and feelings and the limitations imposed upon him by the world in which he finds himself. The adjustment was characterized by struggle and revolt.   Out of this struggle came cries straight from the heart, and hence a lyricism which finds expression in the prose as well as the poetry of the early nineteenth century.

The criticism of the age had much to say of romanticism and its differences from classicism.   "The most obvious distinction," says

---

18 "Lord Byron," *Works*, vol. IV, p. 256.
19 Ibid., p. 257.
20 Ibid., p. 255.
21 Ibid., p. 256.

Hazlitt, "between the two styles, the classical and the romantic is, that the one is conversant with objects that are grand or beautiful in themselves, or in consequence of obvious and universal associations; the other with those that are interesting only by the force of circumstances and imagination. . . . The classical idea or form of anything . . . remains always the same, and suggests nearly the same impressions; but the association of ideas belonging to the romantic character may vary infinitely, and take in the whole range of nature and accident." "The classical appeals to sense and habit; the Gothic or romantic strikes from novelty, strangeness and contrast.   Both are founded in essential and indestructible principles of human nature." [22]

Novelty, strangeness, contrast, originality, individuality, subjectivity, are characteristics of the Romantic Movement, and the chief notes or manifestations of Romanticism in the nineteenth century were briefly as follows: (1) Frank self-revelation, showing all degrees of feeling from sensibility to passion.   This out-pouring of personal experience is sometimes accompanied by sentimentality and sentimental melancholy; (2) Stressing of the dignity and worth of human nature as exemplified in the ordinary man, and sympathy for the suffering of the individual; (3) A turning to the past or the future for enjoyment, attended by impassioned recollection or a contemplative mood; (4) An interest in physical nature, especially in the picturesque, and the assertion of a sympathetic tie between man and the physical world; (5) The exaltation of the feelings or the intuitive faculties of the mind above the reasoning faculties; and the dwelling upon the imaginative pleasure to be derived from the association of ideas; (6) A delight in the concrete and particular as opposed to the abstract and universal. The passion for underlying truth, the portrayal of the universal in human nature, as opposed to the merely conventional, lies at the heart of the Romantic Movement.   It is an interpretation of the natural mind in its relation to the external world.

Before tracing the influence of the Romantic Revival upon the familiar essayists, their views of the close connection between prose and poetry should be noted.   The distinction between prose

---

[22] "Lectures on the Age of Elizabeth," *Works*, vol. V, p. 348.

and poetry was no longer considered one of form. It was recognized that a great deal of verse was not poetry, and that prose could be in the best sense poetic.

Hazlitt defines poetry as "the universal language which the heart holds with nature and itself. . . . There is no thought or feeling that can have entered into the mind of man, which he would be eager to communicate to others, or which they would listen to with delight, that is not a fit subject for poetry. It is not a branch of authorship: it is 'the stuff of which our life is made.' . . . It is strictly the language of the imagination; and the imagination is that faculty which represents objects, not as they are in themselves, but as they are moulded by other thoughts and feelings, into an infinite variety of shapes and combinations of power. . . . Poetry is the high-wrought enthusiasm of fancy and feeling." [23]

Hazlitt further observes that all is not poetry that passes for such, and that verse does not make the whole difference between poetry and prose. He considers *Pilgrim's Progress, Robinson Crusoe,* and the *Tales of Boccaccio* to be prose works which come as near to poetry as possible without being such. "If it is of the essence of poetry," he says, "to strike and fix the imagination, whether we will or no, to make the eye of childhood glisten with the starting tear, to be never thought of afterwards with indifference, John Bunyan and Daniel Defoe may be permitted to pass for poets in their way." [24]

Hazlitt, like Wordsworth, was deeply interested in the diction of prose and poetry. He recognized that prose and poetry might speak a common language, but he also believed, as did Coleridge, that there was a language peculiar to poetry—"those flowers of speech, which . . . are strewed over the plainer ground which poetry has in common with prose." [25] Hazlitt speaks of Walton's *Complete Angler* as a "prose-poem," "perhaps the best pastoral in the language," [26] and he quotes passages from Milton's *Treatise on Education,* of which he says, "The poet breaks through the ground-

---

[23] "On Poetry in General," *Works,* vol. V, pp. 1,2,4.
[24] Ibid., p. 14.
[25] "Coleridge's Literary Life," Ibid., vol. X, p. 155.
[26] "Lectures on the English Poets," Ibid., vol. V, p. 98.

work of prose, as it were, by natural fecundity and a genial, un-restrained sense of delight." [27]

The correspondence between Hazlitt's and Hunt's definitions of poetry is a close one. Hunt defines poetry as "the utterance of a passion for truth, beauty, and power, embodying and illustrating its conceptions by imagination and fancy, and modulating its language on the principle of variety in uniformity. Its means are whatever the universe contains; and its ends, pleasure and exaltation." "Poetry," he further says, "stands between nature and convention, keeping alive . . . the enjoyment of the external and spiritual world." [28]

Hunt also shows his interest in the discussion as to whether poetry should be written in verse, or should be conveyed through the medium of prose. He disagrees with those who think prose a fitting medium. "The reason why verse is necessary to the form of poetry," he says, "is that the perfection of poetical spirit demands it;—that the circle of its enthusiasm, beauty and power, is incomplete without it." [29]

When we turn to the discussion by the Romantic poets of what constitutes poetry, we find a similarity in thought between them and the essayists just quoted.

Shelley in his *Defence of Poetry* emphasizes the universality of poetry, and the inclusiveness of its province. "A poem," he says, "is the very image of life expressed in its eternal truth." It "is universal, and contains within itself the germ of a relation to what-ever motives or actions have place in the possible varieties of human nature." [30] Poetry in its general sense he defines as "the expression of the imagination." [31] Shelley also concerns himself with the difference between prose and poetry. "The distinction between poets and prose writers" he declares to be "a vulgar error." "Lord Bacon," he says, "was a poet. His language has a sweet and majestic rhythm, which satisfies the sense, no less than the almost

---

[27] "On Milton's Sonnets," *Works*, vol. VI, p. 180.

[28] *Imagination and Fancy*, p. 1.

[29] Ibid., p. 31.

[30] "A Defence of Poetry," *Prose Works*, ed. by H. B. Forman, vol. III, Lond. 1880, p. 108.

[31] Ibid., p. 100.

superhuman wisdom of his philosophy satisfied the intellect. . . . " [32] He also believed that Rousseau was "essentially a poet." [33]   But he further observes that "the language of poets has ever affected a certain uniform and harmonious recurrence of sound, without which it was not poetry, and which is scarcely less indispensable to the communication of its influence than the words themselves, without reference to their peculiar order." [34]

Coleridge in his *Biographia Literaria* (1817), defines a poem as "that species of composition, which is opposed to works of science, by proposing for its *immediate* object pleasure, not truth; and from all other species—(having this object in common with it)—it is discriminated by proposing to itself such delight from the *whole* as is compatible with a distinct gratification from each component part." [35]   Coleridge mentions as the two cardinal points of poetry: "the power of exciting the sympathy of the reader by a faithful adherence to the truth of nature, and the power of giving the interest of novelty by the modifying colours of the imagination." [36] The difference between prose and poetry, he considers, is not a metrical one, and mentions the works of Plato and Jeremy Taylor, and the *Theoria Sacra* of Burnet, as proof "that poetry of the highest kind may exist without metre, and even without the contradistinguishing objects of a poem." [37]   Coleridge, however, takes exception to Wordsworth's dictum in his Preface to the *Lyrical Ballads* (1798) "that there neither is, nor can be, any *essential* difference between the language of prose and metrical composition." He grants that many specimens may be found of a style which is common to both prose and poetry, but he believes that there is a difference between the language of the two, owing to the fact that the very act of poetic composition produces a state of excitement which "justifies and demands a correspondent difference of language." [38]

---

[32] Op. cit., p. 107.
[33] Ibid., p. 133 (note).
[34] Ibid., pp. 166-67.
[35] *Biographia Literaria*, N. Y., 1926, p. 195.
[36] Ibid., p. 190.
[37] Ibid., p. 196.
[38] Ibid., p. 238.

This concern with the diction of prose and poetry, and the essential elements of poetry, whether written as prose or in metrical form, undoubtedly had its influence upon the familiar essayists. Their prose is not only frequently rhythmical, but in its allocation of words, its phraseology, its poetic diction, and its lyricism, it often partakes of the nature of poetry. Many passages in the familiar essays of Hunt, Lamb and Hazlitt might be correctly termed prose-poetry. Such prose is a fitting medium for the expression of exaltation of feeling and other emotional moods of the essayist.

A parallel may also be drawn between the familiar essayists and the Romantic poets in the way in which they invest the common experiences and the ordinary things of life with imagination, and reveal truth and beauty. The essayists interpret life subjectively, not in a metaphysical and reasoning manner, but in an imaginative and intuitive manner, analogous to that of the poet who "lifts the veil from the hidden beauty of the world, and makes familiar objects be as if they were not familiar." [39]   Their conclusions are given in flashes and often at random, as if their imagination playing over a subject, suddenly struck from it a light, which reveals a new perception of an old truth. This strong imaginative element was new to the essay. There is nothing comparable to it in the earlier essayists. Those of the seventeenth century when they turn to familiar subjects, are still under the influence of dialectics. Their imagination hampered by reason, can take but short flights. It usually expresses itself in quaint conceits, but even these are carefully pruned. "Take part always with thy judgment against thy fancy in anything wherein they shall dissent," advises Thomas Fuller. "If thou suspectest thy conceits too luxuriant, herein account thy suspicion a legal conviction, and damn whatsoever thou doubtest of." [40]

The periodical essayists of the eighteenth century reflect the realism and classicism of their age. They have imagination in the sense of invention but seldom in the poetic sense. Their concern with life is usually not deep enough to give us a fresh revelation

---

[39] Percy Bysshe Shelley. "A Defence of Poetry," *Prose Works*, vol. III, p. 111.

[40] "Of Fancy," *Seventeenth Century Essays*, ed. by Jacob Zeitlin, p. 176.

of truth or beauty, nor do they show any real depth of emotion or intensity of feeling. Present-day criticism stresses Addison's contribution to the Romantic movement, but his appreciation of the natural and simple in poetry, especially in the old ballads, is owing to its likeness to the classical rather than to the romantic. Steele was sensitive to natural beauty, but, as the following illustrates, his poetic fancy did not wing its flight very far: "To one, used to live in a City the Charms of the Country are so exquisite, that the Mind is lost in a certain Transport which raises us above ordinary Life, and yet is not strong enough to be inconsistent with Tranquility. This State of Mind was I in, ravished with the Murmur of Waters, the Whisper of Breezes, the Singing of Birds; and whether I looked up to the Heavens, down on the Earth, or turned on the Prospects around me, still struck with new Sense of Pleasure. ... [41] There is a wide difference between such writing and Hazlitt's exclamation—"I laugh, I run, I leap, I sing for joy. From the point of yonder rolling cloud, I plunge into my past being, and revel there, as the sunburnt Indian plunges headlong into the wave that wafts him to his native shore." [42] Steele tells of his emotion and not very convincingly; Hazlitt communicates his through its intensity.

Imagination has been variously defined in different periods and in the nineteenth century it came to have new meaning and force. We have but to turn to the familiar essayists and Romantic poets for its definition in accord with the tenets of Romanticism. Hazlitt was particularly interested in the imaginative faculty, and has discussed it in many of his essays. He emphasizes the part the passions play in imaginative expression, and the excess of feeling and sensibility which accompanies imagination. "Our existence," he says, "is a tissue of passion, and our successive years only present us with fainter and fainter copies of the first proof-impressions. ... Imagination is, in this sense, sometimes truer than reality; for our passions being 'compacted of imagination,' and our desires whetted by impatience and delay, often lose some of their taste and essence with possession." [43] He defines imagination as "that

---

[41] *Spectator*, No. 118.
[42] "On Going a Journey," *Works*, vol. VI, p. 182.
[43] "On Novelty and Familiarity," Ibid., vol. VII, p. 302.

faculty which represents objects, not as they are in themselves, but as they are moulded by other thoughts and feelings, into an infinite variety of shapes and combinations of power." [44] Genius, imagination, feeling, taste, he says, have been indifferently used to express the same thing. "The more ethereal, evanescent, more refined and sublime part of art is the seeing nature through the medium of sentiment and passion, as each object is a symbol of the affections and a link in the chain of our endless being. But the unravelling this mysterious web of thought and feeling is alone in the Muse's gift, namely, in the power of that trembling sensibility which is awake to every change and every modification of its ever-varying impressions, that

'Thrills in each nerve, and lives along the line.'

This power is indifferently called genius, imagination, feeling, taste; but the manner in which it acts upon the mind can neither be defined by abstract rules, as is the case in science, nor verified by continual unvarying experiments, as is the case in mechanical performances." [45] In his essay "On Genius and Common Sense," Hazlitt makes a distinction between genius and imagination: "Genius or originality is, for the most part, *some strong quality in the mind, answering to and bringing out some new and striking quality in nature.* Imagination is, more properly the power of carrying on a given feeling into other situations, which must be done best according to the hold which the feeling itself has taken of the mind." [46]

Hunt, in defining imagination, distinguishes between it and fancy: "Imagination, purely so called, is all feeling; the feeling of the subtlest and most affecting analogies; the perception of sympathies in the natures of things, or in their popular attributes. Fancy is the sporting with their resemblances, real or supposed, and with airy and fantastical creations." [47]

Shelley in "A Defence of Poetry" distinguishes between the reason and the imagination: "Reason is the enumeration of quantities already known; imagination is the perception of the value of

---

[44] "On Poetry in General," *Works*, vol. V, p. 4.
[45] "The Indian Jugglers," Ibid., vol. VI, pp. 82-83.
[46] Ibid., vol. VI, p. 42.
[47] "What is Poetry," *Imagination and Fancy*, p. 27.

those quantities, both separately and as a whole. Reason respects the differences, and imagination the similitudes of things." [48]

Coleridge recognizes two kinds of imagination, primary and secondary. The primary imagination he defines as "the living power and prime agent of all human perception, and as a repetition in the finite mind of the external act of creation in the infinite I AM." The secondary imagination is "an echo of the former. . . . It dissolves, diffuses, dissipates, in order to recreate." [49]

From these definitions it is clear that the imagination has creative and selective power, and that it is closely associated with passion, feeling, sentiment and sensibility. The effect of passion upon the imagination is further emphasized by Hazlitt: "The light of poetry is not only a direct but a reflected light, that while it shows us the object, throws a sparkling radiance on all around it: the flame of the passions communicated to the imagination, reveals to us with a flash of lightning, the inmost recesses of thought, and penetrates our whole being. Poetry represents forms chiefly as they present other forms; feelings as they suggest form, or other feelings." [50] Wordsworth voices a similar idea when he says that poetry is "the image of man and nature . . . the spontaneous overflow of powerful feelings: it takes its origin from emotion *remembered* in tranquillity." [51] The poet, therefore, by means of his imaginative faculty, perceives analogies between things and expresses what he sees, not as it ordinarily appears, but as it appears to him, colored by the intensity of his feelings.

These definitions of poetry and of the part imagination plays in poetry, it will be noted, are not concerned with poetic *form,* but poetic *content.* They may therefore be applied to poetic prose as well as to verse. The way in which the familiar essayist views life, his musing upon its meaning and his emotional reaction to its experiences, the free outpouring of his feelings, his discovery of truth in simple things, his illumination of his subject by unexpected analogies, are comparable to the creative and imaginative processes of the poet or "maker." Like him, the essayist handles his material

---

[48] "A Defence of Poetry." *Prose Works,* vol. III, p. 100.
[49] *Biographia Literaria,* pp. 189-90.
[50] "On Poetry in General," *Works,* vol. V, p. 3.
[51] Preface to the *Lyrical Ballads.*

in a creative and artistic manner, revealing truth and beauty, and writing not for his generation alone.

In discussing the romantic elements in the work of the familiar essayists, it is necessary to distinguish between romantic subject matter, and romantic treatment of subject matter. Romantic treatment consists of the emotional, imaginative and personal qualities with which the writer infuses his work, so that even the most ordinary and commonplace subjects are invested with romantic interest. Such elements are present in much of the writing of the familiar essayists, especially that of Lamb and Hazlitt. Their subject matter is seldom romantic in itself. As has already been noted, they frequently choose to write upon the same themes as earlier essayists. It is their handling of these themes in an imaginative and subjective manner which clearly distinguishes their work from what went before. Romantic and imaginative elements are particularly to be found in their treatment of natural objects, of picturesque scenery, of city life, and in their self-revelation.

A striking feature of the Romantic Revival was a reawakened sense of the beauties of nature. In the late eighteenth century a growing appreciation of natural scenery, especially that of wild and rugged landscape, is evidenced in both literature and painting. And in the early nineteenth century a delight in the picturesque characterizes much of the poetry of Wordsworth, Byron and Shelley. Still more important, nature was felt to have a spiritual significance, and a bond was recognized between man and nature which transcended the physical and brought man into closer communion with the divine.

The various aspects of this new love of nature found in the poetry of the period are present no less in the prose. The familiar essayists not only describe the beauties of nature, but discuss nature in its relation to art and life. Hazlitt expresses his theories concerning nature and its relation to poetry and art in many of his essays, and gives added emphasis to his ideas by frequently quoting from Wordsworth, whose treatment of nature is in accord with Hazlitt's theories. Hazlitt defines nature and natural objects as "those objects which exist in the universe at large, without, or in spite of, the interference of human power and contrivance, and those interests and affections which are not amenable to the human will." [52]   In his Round Table essay "On the Love of the Country" he seeks to explain man's attachment to natural objects, and "that soothing emotion which the sight of the country hardly ever fails to infuse into the mind." "It is not," he says, "the beautiful and magnificent alone that we admire in Nature; the most insignificant and rudest objects are often found connected with the strongest emotions." Therefore he concludes that it is because natural objects "have surrounded us in almost all situations, in joy and in sorrow, in pleasure and in pain; because they have been one chief source and nourishment of our feelings, and a part of our being, that we love them as we do ourselves." [53]   Always interested in searching out underlying principles, Hazlitt attributes this attachment not only to the association of ideas but to the fact that the associations connected with any one natural object extend to the whole class.   He illustrates this idea by recalling that when he was abroad: "the trees, and grass, and wet leaves, rustling in the walks of the Thuilleries, seemed to be as much English, to be as much the same trees and grass, that I had always been used to, as the sun shining over my head was the same sun which I saw in England." [54]

This theory of Hazlitt's seeks to explain man's attachment to natural objects, but it does not altogether account for the romantic sentiment with which he invests them. But for this too Hazlitt has an explanation.   "The most opposite kinds and remote trains of feeling," he says, "gradually go to enrich the same sentiment; and in our love of Nature, there is all the force of individual attachment, combined with the most airy abstraction.   It is this circumstance which gives that refinement, expansion, and wild interest to feelings of this sort, when strongly excited, which every one must have experienced who is a true lover of Nature." [55]

The power of the most humble of nature's objects to call forth the most tender sentiments and the most exalted feeling in man, Hazlitt expresses in poetic prose that parallels in thought Wordsworth's lines beginning "To me the meanest flower that blows." "I love," he writes, "to see the trees first covered with leaves in

---

[52] "Pope, Lord Byron, and Mr. Bowles," *Works*, vol. XI, p. 498.
[53] "On the Love of the Country," Ibid., vol. I, p. 18.
[54] Ibid., p. 19.
[55] Ibid., p. 18.

the spring, the primroses peeping out from some sheltered bank, and the innocent lambs running races on the soft green turf; because, at that birth-time of Nature, I have always felt sweet hopes and happy wishes—which have not been fulfilled! The dry reeds rustling on the side of a stream,—the woods swept by the loud blast,—the dark massy foliage of autumn,—the grey trunks and naked branches of the trees in winter,—the sequestered copse and wide extended heath,—the warm sunny showers, and December snows,—have all charms for me; there is no object, however trifling or rude, that has not, in some mood or other, found the way to my heart." [56]

Hazlitt's comment on the romantic poets' treatment of nature further shows his attitude toward the subject. In his essay "On Mr. Wordsworth's Excursion," he particularly notes Wordsworth's power of associating his feelings with natural objects. "He does not," he says, "present the reader with a lively succession of images or incidents, but paints the outgoings of his own heart, the shapings of his own fancy. . . . His descriptions of natural scenery are not brought home distinctly to the naked eye by form and circumstances, but every object is seen through the medium of innumerable recollections, is clothed with the haze of imagination like a glittering vapour, is obscured with the excess of glory, has the shadowy brightness of a waking dream. The image is lost in the sentiment, as sound in the multiplication of echoes." [57]

It is this union of imagination and reality that constitutes for Hazlitt the charm of poetry. He considered Shelley was not a poet, because he gave "for representations of things, rhapsodies of words." "He does not," says Hazlitt, "lend the colours of imagination and the ornaments of style to the objects of nature, but paints gaudy, flimsy, allegorical pictures on gauze, on the cobwebs of his own brain." "To embody an abstract theory, as if it were a given part of actual nature," Hazlitt thought "an impertinence and an indecorum. The charm of poetry . . . depends on the union of fancy with reality, on its finding a tally in the human breast." [58]

Hazlitt found in Keats "a want of strength and substance." He

---

[56] Op. cit., pp. 19-20.

[57] *Works*, vol. I, p. 112.

[58] "On People of Sense," Ibid., vol. VII, p. 246.

speaks of his *Endymion* as "a very delightful description of the illusions of a youthful imagination, given up to airy dreams—we have flowers, clouds, rainbows, moonlight, all sweet sounds and smells, and Oreads and Dryads flitting by—but there is nothing tangible in it, nothing marked or palpable." [59]

In his essay "Pope, Lord Byron, and Mr. Bowles," Hazlitt takes exceptions to Byron's answers to what constitutes the poetical, and what is natural, and artificial in poetry. Hazlitt's refutation of Byron's theories leads him to define the difference between art and nature, which he sums up as follows:

"Natural objects are common and obvious, and are imbued with an habitual and universal interest, without being vulgar. Familiarity in them does not breed contempt as it does in the works of man. They form an ideal class: their repeated impression on the mind in so many different circumstances, grows up into a sentiment. The reason is, that we refer them generally and collectively to ourselves, as links and mementos of our various being; whereas, we refer the works of art respectively to those by whom they are made or to whom they belong. This distracts the mind in looking at them, and gives a petty and unpoetical character to what we feel relating to them." . . .

"Natural objects are more akin to poetry and imagination, partly because they are not our own handy-work, but start up spontaneously, like a visionary creation, of their own accord, without our knowledge or connivance. . . . They have this advantage over the works of art, that the latter either fall short of their preconceived intention, and excite our disgust and disappointment by their defects; or, if they completely answer their end, they then leave nothing to the imagination, and so excite little or no romantic interest that way." [60]

In these theories and definitions of Hazlitt's concerning nature, it will be observed that he was a true Wordsworthian. His own ideas coincided with, or perhaps were derived from, Wordsworth's treatment of natural objects. With the other Romantic poets of his generation who did not treat nature in the manner of Wordsworth, he was not in entire sympathy. Like Wordsworth, he

---

[59] "On Effeminacy of Character," *Works*, vol. VI, pp. 254-55.
[60] "Pope, Lord Byron and Mr. Bowles," Ibid., vol. XI, pp. 502-03.

looked upon nature as sentient. "There is this great difference," he says, "between nature and art, that the one *is* what the other *seems,* and gives all the pleasure it expresses, because it feels it itself." [61]

Hazlitt recognized nature as the fountain head of art, the Hyperian spring from which the artist as well as the poet drinks. "Nature is the soul of art. There is a strength in the imagination that reposes entirely on nature, which nothing else can supply." [62] In his essay "On the Ideal," he writes, "He is the greatest artist, not who leaves the materials of nature behind him, but who carries them with him into the world of invention." [63] He defines originality as "seeing nature differently from others, and yet as it is in itself." Nature does not reveal herself to every one, he believes: "It is only minds on whom she makes her fullest impression that can penetrate her shrine or unveil her *Holy of Holies.*" The man who is capable of portraying one aspect of nature is a genius. He is able to do this "by some quality of mind in which the quality of the object sinks deepest, where it finds the most cordial welcome, is perceived to its utmost extent, and where again it forces its way out from the fulness with which it has taken possession of the mind of the student." [64]

Hazlitt's love of nature, which he expresses in many of his familiar essays, shows qualities characteristic of the nineteenth century romantic poets, especially Wordsworth. Hazlitt delighted in the out-of-doors; he liked to take long walks, meditating as he went. "Give me," he writes, "the clear blue sky over my head, and the green turf beneath my feet, a winding road before me, and a three hours' march to dinner—and then to thinking! It is hard if I cannot start some game on these lone heaths. I laugh, I run, I leap, I sing for joy. From the point of yonder rolling cloud, I plunge into my past being, and revel there, as the sunburnt Indian plunges headlong into the wave that wafts him to his native shore. Then long-forgotten things, like 'sunken wrack and sumless treasuries,' burst upon my eager sight, and I begin to feel,

[61] Op. cit., p. 501. Also "The Opera," *Works*, vol. XI, p. 427.

[62] "On the Progress of Art," Ibid., vol. I, p. 162.

[63] Ibid., vol. XI, p. 223.

[64] "On Genius and Common Sense," Ibid., vol. VI, pp. 46-47.

think, and be myself again." [65]   This lyric rapture expresses man's newly awakened delight in nature, and his recognition that she is the source of his inspiration.   It also recognizes the power of natural objects to awaken a train of memories, and through the association of ideas to give added pleasure to the contemplation of nature.

Like Wordsworth, Hazlitt was conscious of an animate spirit in Nature, harmonizing all her works: "There is that constant and mutual harmony among all her works, one individual spirit pervading them throughout, that, if we have once knit ourselves in hearty fellowship to any of them, they will never afterwards appear as strangers to us, but, which ever way we turn, we shall have found a secret power to have gone before us, moulding them into such shapes as fancy loves, informing them with life and sympathy, bidding them put on their festive looks and gayest attire at our approach, and to pour all their sweets and choicest treasures at our feet." [66]   In *Tintern Abbey,* Wordsworth has expressed a somewhat similar idea of the power of nature "to lead from joy to joy"; and his belief that "Nature never did betray the heart that loved her," finds a parallel in Hazlitt's theory that for the man "who has well acquainted himself with nature's works, she wears always one face, and speaks the same well-known language, striking on the heart, amidst inquiet thoughts and the tumult of the world, like the music of one's native tongue heard in some far-off country." [67]   Hazlitt again expresses his faith in Nature as a solace and means of escape from life's "tumult" in his "Farewell to Essay Writing."   When man turns from the world which has deceived him, it is nature that keeps up "the illusion of the past."   Surrounded by her beauties, Hazlitt feels "no need of book or companion."   "The days, the hours, the thoughts of my youth," he says, "are at my side, and blend with the air that fans my cheek." [68]   Hazlitt also believed in the power of nature to nourish the imagination and purify the feelings.   In contemplating nature, "our feelings carried out of themselves, lose their grossness and

---

[65] "On Going a Journey," *Works,* vol. VI, p. 182.
[66] "On the Love of the Country," Ibid., vol. I, p. 20.
[67] Ibid.
[68] Ibid., vol. XII, pp. 321-22.

their husk, are rarefied, expanded, melt into softness and brighten into beauty, turning to ethereal mould, sky-tinctured." [69]

By way of illustration of some point he is discussing, Hazlitt sometimes decorates his essays with charming natural description, little prose poems which strike "upon the inward eye" with sudden beauty. In drawing a distinction between nature and art, he writes of the thrush "that awakes us at daybreak with its song": "It sings because it is happy: it pours the thrilling sounds from its throat, to relieve the over-flowings of its own breast—the liquid notes come from and go to the heart, dropping balm into it, as the gushing spring revives the traveller's parched and fainting lips. The stream of joy comes pure and fresh into the longing sense, free from art and affectation, the same that rises over vernal groves, mingled with the breath of morning, and the perfumes of the wild hyacinth, that waits for no audience, that wants no rehearsing, that exhausts its raptures, and still—

"Hymns to good God, and carols sweet of love." [70]

This has something of the "fine, careless rapture" that we feel when Wordsworth sings of the cuckoo and the linnet.

Hazlitt's description of natural scenery shows his ability to view a scene and compose it as an artist would, and also to reveal it in the manner of the poet "in visionary grace and grandeur." The imagination necessarily aids the eye in descriptions such as the following—Hazlitt is speaking of the Scotch Highlands and the effect of northern twilight upon this romantic country—"The hills and groves and herds of cattle were seen reposing in the grey dawn of midnight, as in a moonlight without shadow. The whole wide canopy of Heaven shed its reflex light upon them, like a pure crystal mirror. No sharp points, no petty details, no hard contrasts —every object was seen softened yet distinct, in its simple outline and natural tones, transparent with an inward light, breathing its own mild lustre." [71] He compares this landscape to "an airy piece of mosaic work" or to "one of Poussin's broad massy landscapes or Titian's lovely pastoral scenes." "Is it not so," he in-

---

[69] "Why Distant Objects Please," *Works*, vol. VI, pp. 255-56.
[70] "Pope, Lord Byron, and Mr. Bowles," Ibid., vol. XI, pp. 500-01.
[71] "Liber Amoris," Ibid., vol. II, p. 318.

quires, "that poets see nature, veiled to the sight, but revealed to the soul in visionary grace and grandeur!" [72]

A romantic and picturesque treatment of nature is particularly apparent in Hazlitt's *Notes of a Journey Through France and Italy,* which originally appeared in the *Morning Chronicle,* 1824-25, and which describes a coaching tour through the Alps when he was on his second honeymoon. In the Advertisement to the work when printed in book form, Hazlitt writes: "My object has been to describe what I saw or remarked myself; or to give the reader some notion of what he might expect to find in travelling the same road. There is little of history or antiquities or statistics; nor do I regret the want of them. . . . " The author's impressions are conveyed in a series of essays, which have continuity in that they record his observations as he moved from place to place in the course of his journey. The essay-like character of the work is evident in its many digressions; in the way in which the progress of the narrative is frequently interrupted while he indulges in theatrical or art criticism; in the intimate manner in which he shares his observations, impressions and reflections with the reader. The informal character of the sketch is suggested by the use of the word *Notes* in the title. In many respects the account has the characteristics of a journal, particularly in the minute manner in which details are recorded. It is suffused with the writer's personality, although not to a degree evident in some of his familiar essays. It differs from the travel literature of the eighteenth century, not so much by reason of its familiar elements, as by its romantic spirit shown in a love of the picturesque, in its recognition of the close union between man and nature, in its imaginative fancy, and reflection, and in the spirit of enjoyment which animates it.

The romantic elements in *A Journey Through France and Italy* are particularly evident in Hazlitt's description of Alpine scenery, and of Italian cities whose atmosphere recalls past glories. The words "picturesque," "enchanting," "romantic" are used again and again. He writes in an exuberant, joyful manner, as one whose senses are brought under a spell of enchantment by the beauty he beholds. The scenes he describes have an imaginative quality, apart from the pictorial impressions they create. His first view

---

[72] Op. cit.

of the Alps "was a magnificent sight, and in truth a new sensation. Their summits were bright with snow and with the midday sun; they did not seem to stand upon the earth, but to prop the sky. . . . The surprise," he says, "seemed to take away our breath, and to lift us from our feet. It was drinking the empyrean. . . . It was a scene dazzling, enchanting and that stamped the long-cherished dreams of the imagination upon the senses." [73] He describes his impression upon beholding Mont-Blanc as "of the most romantic and enchanting kind. The scene has an intoxicating effect; you are relieved from the toil of wishing to admire, and the imagination is delighted to follow the lead of the senses."[74] The effect of Venice standing in the sea was "magical, dazzling, perplexing."

Hazlitt distinguishes between the romantic and the picturesque; the romantic is that which appeals to our senses and our imagination; the picturesque is that which presents a scene to us, with its elements "composed" as they would be by an artist. He makes clear his idea of the picturesque in speaking of the Swiss Alps near St. Maurice. "The landscape painter," he says, "has only to go there, and make a picture of it. It is already framed by nature to his hand! I mention this the more, because that kind of *grouping* of objects which is essential to the picturesque, is not always to be found in the most sublime or even beautiful scenes. Nature (so to speak) uses a larger canvas than man, and where she is greatest and most prodigal of her wealth, often neglects that principle of concentration and contrast which is an indispensable preliminary before she can be translated with effect into the circumscribed language of art." [75] He again emphasizes the distinction between the picturesque and romantic, when he observes: "The Simplon presents more picturesque points of view; Mont Cenis makes a stronger impression on the imagination." [76]

Hazlitt confesses himself "a slave to the picturesque." [77] His

---

[73] "Notes of a Journey through France and Italy," *Works*, vol. IX, pp. 188-89.
[74] Ibid., p. 293.
[75] Ibid., p. 290.
[76] Ibid., p. 280.
[77] Ibid., p. 236.

love of the picturesque is to be noted particularly in his description
of Alpine scenery. His appreciation of the beauty of the wild and
rugged scenes through which he passed is in contrast to the prevailing feeling of terror that characterized the attitude of eighteenth
century travelers toward the grandeur and solemnity of mountainous country. This dislike of mountains, which extended to uncul-
tivated lands, is one of the reasons given for the lack of sympathy
with nature evidenced in so many eighteenth century travel records.
But a gradual change in attitude took place in the last quarter of
the century. And this seems to have been effected in part by the
works of William Gilpin, a clergyman, who published in 1782 his
*Observations on the River Wye and Several Parts of South
Wales*. This work was illustrated by the author's own drawings,
and its emphasis, both of pencil and pen, was upon the picturesque.
It was followed by other works of the same writer upon various
parts of England, including the New Forest, water-color scenes
of which adorned Gilpin's *Remarks on Forest Scenery and other
Woodland Views* (1790). These illustrated works became the
fashion and undoubtedly helped to develop a liking for the picturesque. Sir Leslie Stephen [78] attributes in part the modern taste
for mountains and natural scenery to the influence of Rousseau and
his followers. However the change in taste was effected, there is
ample proof of it in the poetry, travel literature, and landscape
painting of the early nineteenth century.

The panorama of mountain scenery which Hazlitt glowingly
paints with his pen, is presented not only as a traveler saw it, but
through the eyes of an artist, who was quick to note the details
which "compose" well for the painter. His description of the
descent of Mont Cenis conveys not only an idea of the picturesque-
ness of the country, but an impression of the sublimity and
grandeur of the scene, epic in its proportions, and of Dantesque
magnificence: "The height, the magnitude, the immovableness of
the objects, the wild contrast, the deep tones, the dance and play
of the landscape from the change of our direction and the interpo-
sition of other striking objects, the continued recurrence of the
same huge masses, like giants following us with unseen strides,

---

[78] Leslie Stephen, *The Playground of Europe*, Lond., 1910. Chapter II.

stunned the sense like a blow, and yet gave the imagination enough to contend with a force that mocked it. . . . It was not the idea of height or elevation that was obtruded upon the mind and staggered it, but we seemed to be descending into the bowels of the earth—its foundations seemed to be laid bare to the centre; and abyss after abyss, a vast, shadowy, interminable space, opened to receive us. We saw the building up and frame-work of the world —its limbs, its ponderous masses, and mighty proportions, raised stage upon stage, and we might be said to have passed into an unknown sphere, and beyond mortal limits." [79]

Of equal excellence is Hazlitt's description of Mont Blanc, in which he suggests the close union between man and nature, and an animating spirit in nature: "You stand, as it were, in the presence of the Spirit of the Universe, before the majesty of Nature. . . . The mind hovers over mysteries deeper than the abysses at our feet; its speculations soar to a height beyond the visible forms it sees around it." [80]

Hazlitt found the picturesque and romantic in cities as well as mountains. He is particularly fond of describing a scene viewed from a height. His description of Florence is sparkling, filled with an airy splendor, poetic in the truest sense. As he viewed the city from a hilltop, it was "a scene of enchantment, a city planted in a garden." . . . "Everything was on the noblest scale, yet finished in the minutest part—the perfection of nature and art, populous, splendid, full of life, yet simple, airy, embowered." [81] Of Rome he remarks, "This is not the Rome I expected to see." He misses in it the beauty of the environs of Florence, and the splendid background of Turin; "nor does it present any highly picturesque or commanding points of view like Edinburgh." [82] When Addison beheld Rome it suggested to him only classical allusions. Hazlitt notes that the air was "of an Elysian temperature, as if the winds did not dare to visit the sanctuaries of the dead too roughly. The daisy sprung beneath our feet—the fruit

---

[79] "Notes of a Journey through France and Italy," *Works*, vol. IX, pp. 194-95.
[80] Ibid., p. 292.
[81] Ibid., p. 211.
[82] Ibid., pp. 232, 233.

trees blossomed within the nodding arches." The Coliseum seemed
to "mingle with the sky . . . as if earth were a thing too gross for
it" [83]; the Pantheon had "a simplicity and grandeur like the vaulted
cope of Heaven." [84]   Ferrara, Hazlitt found enchanting, the ideal
of an Italian city. Its picturesque beauty, its faded splendors, its
"airy palaces with dark portraits gleaming through the grated
windows," its "glimmering fairy perspective" cast its spell upon
him: "You are in a dream, in the heart of a romance; you enjoy
the most perfect solitude, that of a city which was once filled with
'the busy hum of men,' and of which the tremulous fragments at
every step strike the sense and call up reflection." [85]   Tivoli he
likewise found "an enchanting—a fairy spot." "To do justice to the
scene would require the pen of Mr. Moore . . . sportive yet romantic, displaying all the fascinations of sense, and unfolding the
mysteries of sentiment." [86]   Cities that did not fulfil Hazlitt's ideal
of the picturesque and romantic failed to interest him. Basle fell
short of his expectation because it was "beyond the confines of the
picturesque."   He marvels that Rousseau, "an admirable describer
of romantic situations," should have fixed upon Vesey as the
scene of his *New Eloise,* for to Hazlitt it seems the least picturesque
part of the country bordering upon Lake Geneva.

The style in which Hazlitt clothes his romantic and picturesque
description is especially to be noted. He uses sentence structure
and words much as an artist uses line and color. His sensitive-
ness to the agreement of style with the scene pictured, is to be
seen in his criticism of Lord Byron's description of the Fall of
Terni in *Childe Harold.* He notes that the fall has "nothing of
the texture of Lord Byron's terzains, twisted, zigzag, pent up
and struggling for a vent, broken off at the end of a line, or point
of a rock, diving under ground, or out of the reader's comprehen-
sion, and pieced on to another stanza or shelving rock. Nature has

> 'Poured it out as plain
> As downright Shippen, or as old Montaigne.' " [87]

---

[83] Op. cit., p. 234.
[84] Ibid., p. 235.
[85] Ibid., p. 265.
[86] Ibid., p. 257.
[87] Ibid., p. 258.

That Hazlitt could adapt his style to whatever he is describing may be seen in the contrast between his mountain scenes and his description of the Tuilleries gardens. [88] In the former he conveys the impression of scenery wild, majestic, grand; in the latter he reproduces the ordered elegance and beauty of French landscape gardening which to him seems romantic in the very excess of its order.

Another phase of Hazlitt's romanticism is his recollection of old associations, which link themselves with the places he visited. "In travelling," he says, "we visit *names* as well as places." [89] Such recollections have for him more value than the realities before him. He finds "no trace of romance" about the inn at Moulins. The people there seem never to have heard of Sterne's *Sentimental Journey* nor of his Maria. "Is it not provoking," he exclaims, "to come to a place, that has been consecrated by 'famous poet's pen,' as a breath, a name, a fairy-scene, and find it a dull, dirty town. Let us leave the realities to shift for themselves, and think only of those bright tracts that have been reclaimed for us by the fancy, where the perfume, the sound, the vision, and the joy still linger, like the soft light of evening skies!" [90]

The *cavalier servente* of Italy recalls to him romantic associations: "One such incident, or passage in Dante or in Spenser is worth all the route between this and Paris, and all the sights in all the post-roads in Europe. Oh Sienna! if I felt charmed with thy narrow, tenantless, streets, or looked delighted through thy arched gateway over the subjected plain, it was that some recollections of Madonna Pia hung upon the beatings of my spirit, and converted a barren waste into the regions of romance!" [91]

Hazlitt from time to time thus breaks his discourse to make some remark born of reflection, which serves also to reveal his personality. He interrupts his description of the journey between Florence and Bologna to comment upon a little boy shyly clinging to his mother: "What is the map of Europe, what all the glories of it, what the possession of them, to that poor little fellow's dream,

---

[88] Op. cit., p. 159.
[89] Ibid., p. 281.
[90] Ibid., p. 178.
[91] Ibid., p. 252.

to his sidelong glance at that wide world of fancy that circles his native rocks!" [92]   Neufchatel, where the people appear to live in ease and comfort, without being either fashionable or romantic, where they enjoy the advantages of simplicity and solitude, with nothing to surprise or to disgust, seems to Hazlitt the only place he would never wish to quit: "The *golden mean* is, indeed, an exact description of the mode of life I should like to lead—of the style I should like to write; but alas! I am afraid I shall never succeed in either object of my ambition!" [93]

But Hazlitt does achieve "the golden mean" in his *Journey through France and Italy* in the nice balance he maintains between the realistic, and the picturesque and romantic.   He has left a record which is entertaining today as an account of the difficulties of European travel as late as the first half of the nineteenth century; his many comparisons between peoples of the Continent and the English are interesting as the criticism of an Englishman whose mind was not bounded by British insularity.   His pen pictures of the scenes through which he passed have a picturesque quality which likewise characterized the poetry and painting of the period.   His delight in the sensations he experienced has a romantic quality which is Elizabethan in its exuberance, but his impassioned recollection and his perception of an animate spirit in nature are characteristic of the Romantic Revival.

Hunt, like Hazlitt, has left his impressions of a trip through the Alps and of his sojourn in Italy.   He first wrote of this ill-starred journey in *"Letters from Abroad"* which appeared in the *Liberal.*   With slight change and some rearrangement these were later incorporated into his *Autobiography.* Hunt was abroad almost three years, the greater part of which he spent in Italy, and therefore had an opportunity to formulate his opinions.   But the usual vivacity, "animal spirits," and zest characteristic of his essays are wanting.   The unhappy circumstances of Hunt's life during this period undoubtedly affected his reactions to the scenes about him. It is only necessary to compare his description of the journey across the Alps with Hazlitt's account of a similar trip, and the comments of these writers upon Italian life and art, to realize how common-

[92] Op. cit., p. 263.
[93] Ibid., p. 297.

place Hunt's account is. As has been observed, this record of Hunt's journey "might have been written quite as well at Hampstead with the aid of a few books." [94] Hunt sees neither with the eye of a poet nor an artist. His description of scenery particularly betrays the lack of a "seeing eye" and his comments upon Italian art and architecture reveal his want of knowledge of these subjects. His interest in Italy is not to be found in his liking for its people, its climate, its landscape, its art or traditions, but in its literary associations which are ever-present to his mind as he travels from place to place.

The sentiment and romantic fervor frequently found in Hunt's familiar essays are likewise wanting from his account of his sojourn in Italy. He describes what he saw in a matter-of-fact manner; he seems unable to recreate Italy's romantic past, or to recall her wealth of tradition and thus invest her scenes with "the glory which was Rome's.' He does not succeed in identifying himself with his surroundings but remains the alien visitor looking about him with detachment, frequently with disappointment, and comparing Italy, to her disadvantage, with his native land. His impressions are in marked contrast to those of Hazlitt who found in Italy's art, traditions, and scenery continual interest and delight.

Hunt describes his voyage in a small brig with the matter-of-factness of Defoe. Beset by storms, threatened with shipwreck, narrowly escaping destruction by a larger vessel, the lives of his family in almost constant danger, he had to his hand material sufficiently dramatic, but he tells the story of the voyage as if he were writing a log. Only once does he convey a sense of the dramatic, when he describes how he himself saved the vessel from collision by handing up lanterns. [95] His descriptions of the sea are neither happy nor well-chosen. Becalmed in the Bay of Biscay, he remarks that "a calm is a very unresting and unpleasant thing, the ship taking a great gawky motion from side to side, as if playing the buffoon." [96] The foam thrown up by the ship at night "seems full of stars," and you devour it "as you would so much ethereal

---

[94] Monkhouse, Cosmo. *Life of Leigh Hunt*, Lond., 1893, p. 164,
[95] *Autobiography of Leigh Hunt*, p. 264.
[96] Ibid., p. 268.

syllabub." [97]   "Waves," he thinks, "might be classed, as clouds have been; and more determination given to pictures of them. We ought to have waves and wavelets, billows, fluctuosities, &c., a marble sea, a sea weltering." [98]   As the ship labors in the trough of the waves, the water on either side looks like "a hill of yeast." [99] Such description conveys but little distinct impression to the reader; it has a bookish tone divorced from real sensations and impressions. The reason is probably to be found in Hunt's distress of mind during this period. "The sea is a grand sight," he says, "but it becomes tiresome and melancholy—a great monotonous idea; at least one thinks so, when not happy." [100]

Hunt's description of the mountainous country through which he passed on his Italian tour is also curiously lacking in imagination. Hazlitt makes us feel the grandeur, the primeval Force at work in the mountains "lifting earth to heaven."   Hunt describes the Alps, the first mountains he had seen, as having "a fine sulky look, up aloft in the sky,—cold, lofty, and distant." [101]   He says he had imagined that mountains would impress him but little, but upon beholding them, he seemed "to see a piece of one's book-wonders realized,—something very earthly, yet standing between earth and heaven, like a piece of the antediluvian world looking out of the coldness of ages." [102]   He writes of the Apennines through which he passed on his way to Genoa as "undulating, barren and coarse; without any grandeur but what arises from an excess of that appearance. They lie in a succession of great doughy billows, like so much enormous pudding, or petrified mud." [103]   Of the mountainous country between Florence and Bologna, he observes, . . . "We had proper sloping Apennines, valley and mountain, with fine sweeping meadows of green, interspersed with wood." [104] When ascending the Alps, and while yet in the darkness before

---

[97] Op. cit., p. 269.
[98] Ibid., p. 270.
[99] Ibid., p. 271.
[100] Ibid., p. 261.
[101] Ibid., p. 275.
[102] Ibid.
[103] Ibid., p. 310.
[104] Ibid., p. 357.

dawn, he "beheld the top of one of the mountains basking in the sunshine." He does not attempt to describe the glory which he saw, but says "we took it with delighted reverence into our souls." [105] His first sight of Mont Blanc, however, awakens his imagination and fancy. He compares it to "a turret in the sky, amber-coloured, golden, belonging to the wall of some ethereal world." [106] But his description suffers by comparison with that of Hazlitt who says of Mont-Blanc: "It was an image of immensity and eternity. Earth had heaved it from its bosom; the 'vast cerulean' had touched it with its breath. It was a meeting of earth and sky. . . . There is an end here of variety and littleness, and all transitory jarring interests. . . . The mind hovers over mysteries deeper than the abysses at our feet." [107]

In commenting upon Italian cities, Hunt occasionally rises above the commonplace, as when he says: "Antiquity refuses to look ancient in Italy. It insists upon retaining its youthfulness of aspect. The consequence at first is a mixed feeling of admiration and disappointment; for we miss the venerable. The houses seem as if they ought to have sympathized more with humanity, and were as cold and as hard-hearted as their materials. But you discover that Italy is the land, not of the venerable, but the beautiful; and cease to look for old age in the chosen country of the Apollo and the Venus." [108]

If Hunt had no eye for the picturesque in mountains and cities, he observed it in people. A boat passes, and instantly reminds him of Titian, "yet it contained nothing but an old boatman in a red cap, and some women with him in other colours, one of them in a bright yellow petticoat." [109] He describes a religious procession in Pisa, at whose head was "a little live Virgin, about four years old, walking in much state, with a silver-looking crown on her head and a sceptre in her hand." [110] The manner in which Italian women carry themselves recalls to him Dante's simile of his mis-

---

[105] Op. cit., p. 363.
[106] Ibid., p. 364.
[107] "Notes of a Journey through France and Italy," *Works.* vol. IX, pp. 291, 292.
[108] *Autobiography*, p. 297.
[109] Ibid., p. 324.
[110] Ibid., p. 319.

tress, walking like a peacock, or a crane, *"straight above herself."* [111]

Hunt himself gives us the clue to his failure to write more inspiringly of Italy. "To me," he says, "Italy had a certain hard taste in the mouth. Its mountains were too bare, its outlines too sharp, its lanes too stony, its voices too loud, its long summer too dusty. I longed to bathe myself in the grassy balm of my native fields. But I was ill, unhappy . . . and critics, in such condition . . . should give us a list of the infirmities under which they sit down to estimate what they differ with." [112]

In a manner similar to Hazlitt, Hunt decorates his essays with little prose poems of nature. Sometimes they seem to have been suggested by the lines of a poem. In "Spring," one of the *Wishing-Cap Papers,* he opens his essay with a quotation from Gray: "Ah, happy hills! ah, pleasing shade!" and follows it by his own apostrophe to spring: "Hail, beautiful season! hail, return of the green leaves! hail, violets, daisies, and buttercups! hail, blue sky; and ye, white little silver clouds, 'gay creatures of the elements,' the posterity of your turbid sires of winter time!" [113] "Spring and Daisies," one of Hunt's essays in the *Indicator,* to which reference has already been made, contains a passage which may have been suggested by Keats' *Endymion:* "Spring, while we are waiting, is complete. . . . There are clear, crystal mornings; noons of blue sky and white cloud; nights, in which the growing moon seems to lie looking at the stars, like a young shepherdess at her flock. A few days ago she lay gazing in this manner at the solitary evening star, like Diana, on the slope of a valley, looking up at Endymion. His young eye seemed to sparkle out upon the world; while she, bending inwards, her hands behind her head, watched him with an enamored dumbness." [114] Hunt's faults of taste, so apparent in his poetry, are likewise evident in his prose-poetry. In the passages just quoted, "turbid sires of winter time," and "enamored dumbness" are illustrative of his lack of critical acumen.

Hunt again borrows the imagery of poetry in his description of

---

[111] Op. cit., p. 306.
[112] Ibid., p. 335.
[113] *Wishing-Cap Papers,* p. 4.
[114] *Indicator,* pt. 1, N. Y., 1845, p. 189.

sun-rise, in his essay "A Now—Descriptive of a Hot Day." "Now the rosy—(and lazy)—fingered Aurora, issuing from her saffron house, calls up the moist vapors to surround her, and goes veiled with them as long as she can; till Phoebus, coming forth in his power, looks everything out of the sky, and holds sharp uninterrupted empire from his throne of beams." [115]

" . . . Poetry without the fit sculpture of verse," Hunt says, "is no more to be called poetry, than beauty conceived is beauty accomplished. . . . But I have the wish to be a poet, and thoughts will arise within me as painful not to express as a lover's. I therefore write memorandums for verse;—thoughts that might perhaps be worthy of putting into that shape, if they could be properly developed;—hints and shadows of something poetical, that have the same relationship to actual poetry as the little unborn spirits that perish by the waters of Lethe have to the souls that visit us, and become immortal." [116] Hunt calls his "memorandums for verse" —"Dreams on the Borders of the Land of Poetry." Two of these are nature descriptions: "Spring and Summer," and "Rain and Sunshine in May," and are less poetic in expression than some of his other writing. He speaks of the rains as "well-tempered" and describes the birds which "come by fives and tens in the meadows," as "agile, . . . springing away with a song." That Hunt's imagery, however much he may have been striving for poetic effect, is not always poetic, may be seen from the following: "I speak of a season when the returning threats of cold, and the resisting warmth of summer-time, make robust mirth in the air; when the winds imitate on a sudden the vehemence of winter; and silver-white clouds are abrupt in their coming-down; and shadows in the grass chase one another, panting, over the fields, like a pursuit of spirits. With undulating necks they pant forward, like hounds or the leopard." [117]

Clouds "abrupt in their coming down" and shadows "panting," belie Hunt's power of observation. He can, however, in a few words, flash upon the mind a picture which creates its own atmos-

---

[115] Op. cit., pt. 2, p. 17.

[116] "Dreams on the Borders of the Land of Poetry," Leigh Hunt, *Essays (Selected)*, N. Y., 1929, pp. 212, 213 (Everyman edition).

[117] "Rain and Sunshine in May," Ibid., p. 215.

phere, as when he describes his walk home by night through the London suburbs: "How still the trees! How deliciously asleep the country! How beautifully grim and nocturnal this wooded avenue of ascent, against the cold, white sky!" [118] Or when he writes of the oncoming of spring, so that the air seems full of fragrance: "Honey-suckles . . . are detected in blossom: the hazel follows; the snowdrop hangs its white perfection, exquisite with green; we fancy the trees are already thicker; voices of winter birds are taken for new ones; and in February new ones come—the thrush, the chaffinch, and the wood-lark. Then rooks begin to pair; and the wagtail dances in the lane." [119] Such description reminds one of Gilbert White's *Natural Antiquities of Selborne*, a book of which Hunt was very fond.

When he writes of nature and the seasons, his thoughts are often intertwined with personal recollection. The Italian spring suggests the coming of spring in England, and he is seized with longing to see the fields of his homeland, "rich with grass and powdered with flowers." "I am," he says, "in a world of poetry and romance, of vines and olives, and myrtles, . . . of blue mountains and never-ending orchards. . . . What signifies? I think of an English field in a sylvan country, a cottage and oaks in the corner, a path and a stile, and a turf full of daisies." [120] Nature also frequently suggests to Hunt some literary allusion, the recollection of which gives added charm to the scene before him. Writing from Maiano, he says: . . . "The valley which I look upon from my window sparkles in the *Decameron* with a perpetual green. Nature inspires great authors, and they repay her by rescuing her very self from oblivion, and keeping her transitory pictures fresh in our hearts. *They,* thank God, as well as the fields, *are* Nature; and so is every great and kindly aspiration we possess." [121] He had intended, he says, to sprinkle his essay "with some flowers out of the Italian poets," but their observations upon nature "are not true." He prefers "the cockney satisfactions of Chaucer,

---

[118] "Walks Home by Night," *The Companion*, N. Y., 1845, p. 187. (Bound with the *Indicator*.)
[119] "Fine Days in January and February," *Ibid*, pp. 179-80.
[120] "Spring," *Wishing-Cap Papers*, p. 79.
[121] Ibid.

Spenser, and Milton, who talk of 'merry London,' of lying whole hours looking at the daisies, and of walking out on Sunday mornings to enjoy the daisies and green fields." [122]   Perhaps it was nostalgia that caused Hunt to recall so often the beauties of his native land while he was in Italy.   The *Wishing-Cap Papers* contain many references to the English country-side, which he contrasts with that of Italy, to the latter's disadvantage.   In his essay "Love and the Country," written while in Tuscany, he imagines himself in an English meadow lying among the hay, building castles in the air.   "I love to see trees," he says, "that look as if they were good for nothing but to walk under, and to furnish us with a sentiment. . . . I know they do not exist for nothing; and I take them for what they are,—memorandums of the abundance and poetry of Nature." [123]

Hunt, like the Romantic poets, takes the weather and the elements for his theme, and writes of "A Rainy Day," "Mists and Fogs," "Bad Weather," "East Wind," etc.   These papers seldom possess imaginative power, such as we find for instance in Shelley when he writes of the elements.   They are a blend of realistic detail and fancy.   "A Rainy Day" may have been suggested to Hunt by some verses of Swift's, which originally appeared in the *Tatler*.   Part of Swift's poem is quoted by Hunt in his essay, together with the introduction given it by "hearty, unenvying Steele."   In its realistic detail, Hunt's picture of a rainy day in the city may be compared to that of Swift.   Hunt describes the "poor girls with bandboxes" who "trip patiently along, with their wet curls over their eyes, and a weight of skirt," [124] and Swift writes:

> "The tucked-up seamstress walks with hasty strides,
>   While streams run down her oiled umbrella's sides."

Hunt introduces a philosophical or moralizing note into his essay by discussing the way to make the best of a bad day.   *"Think of something superior to it,"* he says, "make it yield entertaining and useful reflection, as the rain itself brings out the flowers." [125]

---

[122] Op. cit.
[123] Ibid., p. 106.
[124] *The Seer*, vol. I, p. 158.
[125] Ibid., pp. 160-61.

"Mists and Fogs," which originally appeared in the *Indicator* is typical of Hunt's other essays on the elements. Fogs and mists are "clouds unrisen." "The city of London . . . is literally a city in the clouds. Its inhabitants walk through the same airy heaps which at other times float over their heads in the sky, or minister with glorious faces to the setting sun." [126] The essay is largely devoted to literary allusions and quotations from poets who have "done justice," as he expresses it, "to these our melancholy visitors." [127] Homer, Ovid, Apollonius Rhodius, Dante, Spenser, Milton are all drawn upon for illustration.

In his essay "Bad Weather," Hunt creates for the reader the illusion of a cozy, warm interior, in sharp contrast to the winter storm without. After describing the distress caused by such a storm, he draws a picture of the warmth and comfort indoors: "How pleasant is this rug! How bright and generous the fire! How charming the fair makers of the tea!" [128] He devotes more than half of his paper to moralizing. "It is not by grumbling against the elements that evil is to be done away with; but by keeping one's-self in good heart with one's fellow-creatures, and remembering that they are all capable of partaking our pleasures." [129] In the "East Wind" he expresses his oft-repeated belief in the triumph of good over evil. Evil, he thinks, "is in its nature fugitive; and . . . it is the nature of good, when good returns, to outlast it beyond all calculation." [130]

The spirit of reform in these nature essays of Hunt's is another reflection of the Romantic movement. He shared with the poets, notably Shelley, the desire to help men to a better way of life, and in giving voice to this in his essays, he was following the example of the earlier periodical essayists, and was at the same time in the current of contemporary thought.

Hunt had a definite gospel of beauty, which he has made the theme of several of his essays. He desired to bring beauty into the life of everyone, even the poorest, and to make men mindful of beauty in the simplest things. In this he anticipated Ruskin

---

[126] *Indicator*, pt. I, p. 55.
[127] Ibid., p. 56.
[128] *The Companion*, p. 175.
[129] Ibid., p. 175.
[130] *The Seer*, vol. I, p. 166.

and William Morris. He believed that the pleasure to be derived from the world about us is to be found not only in things themselves, but in what they suggest. Thus the more a man knows and the more sensitive he is to beauty, the more pleasurable is his existence. In his essay "On a Pebble," he emphasizes the way in which one thing suggests another, and the consequent enriching of the enjoyment of life. He illustrates the pleasures to be derived from the association of ideas by quoting Wordsworth's lines beginning "A violet by a mossy stone," suggested to Hunt by "sight of a common stone," which also reminds him of the opening lines of Keats' *Hyperion* which contain the phrase "quiet as a stone." [131] In his essay, "Pleasure" he insists that even the poor and struggling man, "when he wants recreation for his thoughts, can make them flow from all the objects, or the ideas of those objects. . . . The commonest goods and chattels are pregnant to him as fairy tales, or things in a pantomime. His hat, like Fortunatus's wishing-cap, carries him into the American solitudes among the beavers, where he sits in thought, looking at them . . . and hearing the majestic whispers in the trees. . . . His coat shall carry him, in ten minutes, through all the scenes of pastoral life and mechanical,—the quiet fields, the sheep-shearing, the feasting, the love-making, the downs of Dorsetshire." [132] Hunt's emphasis is always upon the pleasure to be derived from natural objects, whether actually seen or brought to mind through recollection or through the imaginative pictures of the poet.

He not only urges his fellow-men to draw pleasure from nature, but gives them a great deal of practical advice as to the need of color in everyday living. The English in their "foggy, and too often not very brilliant" country are not fond enough of color, he believes, "not fond enough of a beauty of which Nature herself is evidently very fond, and with which, like all the rest of her beauties, it is the business of civilized man to adorn and improve his own well-being." [133] The Englishman's failure to appreciate color, Hunt attributes to "Puritanism and wars and debts, and the Dutch succession, and false ideas of utility" which "have all

[131] Op. cit., pp. 23-24.
[132] Ibid., p. 15.
[133] "Color," Ibid., p. 34.

conspired to take gladness out of our eyesight, as well as jollity out of our pockets." [134]   He finds a moral as well as material beauty in color,—"an inherent gladness,—an intention on the part of Nature to share with us a pleasure felt by herself—Colors are the smiles of Nature." [135]   Like Hazlitt, Hunt at times parallels Wordsworth in thought, and further accentuates the likeness of ideas by quoting from his poetry.   Wordsworth's lines beginning "My heart leaps up" furnish the theme for the following comment: "The rainbow reads its beauteous lecture in the clouds, showing the sweet division of the hues; and the mechanical 'philosopher,' as he calls himself, smiles with an air of superiority, and thinks he knows all about it, because the division is made.   The little child, like the real philosopher, *knows more;* for his 'heart leaps up,' and he acknowledges a glad mystery.   He feels the immensity of what he does *not* know." [136]   Hunt reveals a transcendental belief in the intuitive faculty of the mind when he says: "Beyond the dry line of knowledge lies beauty, and all which is beautiful in hope, and exalting in imagination." [137]

He further sets forth his gospel of beauty under such an apparently commonplace title as "Windows," [138] the theme of two of his essays.   After making a plea for more beautiful windows in the home, he falls into a contemplative mood.   The raindrops on the window pane suggest to him "a world of beauty and mystery and aboriginal idea, bringing . . . a thousand images of proportion and reflection, and the elements, and light and color, and roundness and delicacy and fluency, and beneficence, and the refreshed flowers, and the growing corn, and dewdrops on the bushes, and the tears that fall from gentle eyes, and the ocean, and the rainbow, and the origin of all things." [139]   Both of these essays are a mixture of matter-of-fact commonplaces, and imaginative perception.   Hunt seems to be illustrating his own theory that "matter of fact, and spirit of fact, must both be appreciated,

---

[134] Op. cit., p. 35.
[135] Ibid., p. 36.
[136] Ibid.
[137] Ibid.
[138] "Windows," and "Windows Considered from the Inside," Ibid., pp. 38 ff. and 48 ff.
[139] "Windows Considered from the Inside," Ibid., pp. 51-52.

in order to do justice to the riches of Nature"; by which he would distinguish between the senses and the imagination. Not to perceive both the matter of fact, and spirit of fact, is, Hunt believes, "to be a poor unattended creature, who walks about in the world, conscious of nothing but himself." [140]

Closely related to the romantic treatment of nature is the romantic interest with which places are invested. This is to be seen particularly in the familiar essayists' treatment of London life; in their return to the past, which they invest with imaginative fancy, and in the impassioned recollection of events, in their childhood and youth, connected with well-loved places and scenes. Hunt wrote at greater length of London life than either Lamb or Hazlitt. Therefore his papers will be considered first.

In his liking for the city where he spent most of his life, Hunt was a true Cockney. He shares with Lamb the love of London's sights and sounds, her shops and odd characters. Added to his liking for London, was his interest in people, especially those figures of London's past, which he calls forth in imagination to people her houses and streets. A familiar, gossipy style, an excellent memory for anecdotes, an interest in the history of ancestral houses and their owners, combine in Hunt to create a type of sketch of London life which if not entirely new, was lent a liveliness and grace which it had hitherto lacked. In these sketches, he skillfully weaves history, biography, antiquarian lore, anecdote and incident into a pleasing and entertaining narrative. The whole is given color and additional interest by the author's reflections and comments, which lend a familiar character to his sketches. The numerous digressions, the easy conversational style, the author's evident pleasure in his subject, which he invests with his own personality, entitle these sketches to be included in a study of the familiar essay.

Hunt's essay, "Pleasant Memories connected with Various Parts of the Metropolis" which appeared in the *Indicator,* is a forerunner of his more extended sketches—*The Town* (1848), *The Old Court Suburb* (1855) and *A Saunter through the West End of London* (1861). Early in this essay in the *Indicator,* Hunt remarks that "one of the best secrets of enjoyment is the art of cultivating

---

[140] Op. cit., p. 56.

pleasant associations," and it might be said that the art of this type of essay is the association of famous Londoners with various places in the metropolis, "pleasant associations," indeed, under Hunt's skillful guidance. In peopling London with great literary figures from Chaucer to Richardson, Hunt writes in the pleasant, entertaining manner of one who would share his own enjoyable associations with the reader. The sketch is comparatively brief and in its central idea only, is it suggestive of the travel sketches which Hunt later developed, described by Mr. Monkhouse as "gossip historical and topographical." [141]

Two papers contributed by Hunt to the *Indicator* take for their theme the shops of London.[142] "Though we are such lovers of country," says Hunt, "we can admire London in some points of view; and among others, from the entertainment to be derived from its shops." [143] He tests his liking for shops by the manner in which he can associate their contents with a pleasant train of ideas. He thinks a glass-shop a beautiful place, for it reminds him of the splendors of a fairy palace; a tavern and coffee-house "is a pleasant sight from its sociability; not to mention the illustrious club memories of the times of Shakespeare and the Tatlers"; [144] but of all shops a print-seller's pleases him most, for there he can see fine engravings, "translations from Titian and Raphael."

In "A Nearer View of Some of the Shops" Hunt describes a toy shop which recalls to him memories of his boyhood: "We still seem to have a lively sense of the smell of that gorgeous red paint, which was on the handle of our first wooden sword! The pewter guard also—how beautifully fretted and like silver did it look! How did we hang it round our shoulder by the proud belt of an old ribbon;—then feel it well suspended; then draw it out of the sheath, eager to cut down four savage men for ill using ditto of damsels!" [145] The sculptor's shop with its plaster casts awakens memories of the holiday spent in his boyhood in the gallery of the

---

[141] W. C. Monkhouse, *Life of Leigh Hunt*, p. 175.

[142] "On the Sight of Shops," *Indicator*, pt. I, p. 222 f., and "A Nearer View of Some of the Shops," *Indicator*, pt. 1, p. 230 f.

[143] "On the Sight of Shops," Ibid., p. 222.

[144] "A Nearer View of Some of the Shops," Ibid., p. 226.

[145] Ibid., p. 230.

painter, Benjamin West. It was to West's house with its art gallery that Hunt says he owes the greatest part of his love "for what is Italian and belongs to the fine arts." [146] Hunt's description of the fruitier's window in this essay, in its feeling for color and form, may be likened, in lesser degree, to Keats' power to summon forth sensuous images. In these essays there is a blend of realistic and imaginative elements that is truly delightful, because of the manner in which Hunt interrupts his narrative of things seen to indulge in fanciful speculation or to recall memories of his youth.

Under the caption "Wishing-Cap Papers," [147] Hunt contributed several essays on London to the *Examiner* in the years 1824-25. He wrote these articles while at Maiano, and they may have helped to lessen the nostalgia which he felt for London. "The title," Hunt tells us in his *Autobiography,* "was very genuine. When I put on my cap, and pitched myself in imagination into the thick of Covent Garden, the pleasure I received was so vivid,—I turned the corner of a street so much in the ordinary course of things, and was so tangibly present to the pavement, the shop-windows, and the people, and a thousand agreeable recollections which looked me naturally in the face,—that sometimes when I walk there now, the impression seems hardly more real. I used to feel as if I actually pitched my soul there, and that spiritual eyes might have seen it shot over from Tuscany, into York Street, like a rocket." [148] The persons and places mentioned in these London sketches were afterwards more fully described in *The Town,* but the "Wishing-Cap Papers" have more of the personal element, and more gusto than the later sketches.

Hunt begins "A Walk in Covent Garden" with traversing Maiden Lane, which he likes for three reasons: because he has walked there a thousand times; for its book-stalls and picture-shops; and for the visions it calls forth of Voltaire, Congreve and other wits. He peoples Covent Garden with familiar eighteenth century figures: Addison, Steele, Dryden, Garth, Colonel Brett, Mrs. Bracegirdle, etc. The character of all this neighborhood he considers "essentially gay and social, scented with snuff-boxes, and

---

[146] Op. cit., p. 237.
[147] Reprinted in book form, 1873.
[148] *Autobiography,* p. 334.

rustling with hoop petticoats." [149]   In true wishing-cap fashion he
passes from the eighteenth century into the nineteenth with a
recollection of Charles Lamb and his Thursday evening parties in
Russell Street.   "What would I not give for another Thursday
evening?   It was humanity's triumph; for whist-players and no
whist-players there for the first time met together." [150]

In "Piccadilly and the West End" Hunt again indulges in personal recollection in recalling evenings spent with the Novellos in
Oxford Street, where Charles Lamb came to "wonder at our
quaint spirits."   In this paper as in the former one, Hunt follows
the plan of peopling the squares and streets with illustrious Londoners who lived there in the eighteenth century.   He continually
breaks his narrative for the purpose of personal comment, or self-
revelation.   The informal tone of his description may be seen
from the following : "The West End may be supposed to commence
at Leicester Square.   It is but a mongrel square, a mixture of
house and shop ; but it is green in the middle, and contains a statue
of some prince.   There are people who object to these royal statues,
thinking it a pity that they are not rather those of some great
philosophers, poets, or other public benefactors.   But when they
reflect that the faces are too far off to be seen, and that few
persons know who they are, the objection perhaps will vanish." [151]

"A Walk in the City" takes the reader over "the most classical
ground in the metropolis," to the haunts of Chaucer, Shakespeare,
Spenser, Milton, Pope and Gray.   Hunt makes no attempt to
follow his theme in any systematic fashion.   His Wishing Cap
makes it possible for him, not only as he claims, to see the whole
neighborhood and what is going on in every house, but to slip
easily back and forth from century to century, with a rapidity as
amazing as it is sudden.   His preference is for crowded city streets,
or old alleys, "from Pudding Lane to Pie Corner."   He will have
none of a suburban street, which is "neither town nor country—
neither City nor West End."   "I must have," he says, "either antiquity to remind me of the past generations, or something busy and
going on to warm my heart with the present." [152]   He again takes

---

[149] "A Walk in Covent Garden," *Wishing-Cap Papers*, p. 25.
[150] Ibid., p. 27.
[151] "Piccadilly and the West End," Ibid., p. 34.
[152] "A Walk in the City," Ibid., p. 47.

the reader into his confidence when he confesses: " 'For my own private eating,' I would rather have been a citizen of the age of Elizabeth, my cheeks glowing not only with beef and pudding, but with fresh air and a hundred merry games; but, nevertheless, my content to be a sick author in the nineteenth century 'hath a preferment in it.' " [153] Austin Friars recalls to Hunt his boyhood visits to the Thornton family. "To this house with its music and its kindness," he says, "I attribute much of the coloring of my afterlife." [154]

In "Whitehall," another Wishing-Cap paper, Hunt says that what he relates has no pretensions to the notice of the antiquary: "My antiquities are all out of Pennant, with the exception of what I glean here and there from the wits and poets. The only value in my picture (if any) is in the coloring, and in the figures occasionally introduced." [155] This essay contains less digression and self- revelation than the papers just mentioned. Whitehall is pictured in the time of Queen Elizabeth, Henry VIII, and the two Charles. The banqueting-house, built by Inigo Jones, particularly interested Hunt, who says that its beautiful proportions affect him like a piece of music.[156]

The Wishing-Cap paper, "St. James Park" is interesting for its literary allusions, for the verses quoted from Waller, describing the Park in the reign of Charles II, and for the manner in which Pennant is drawn upon for anecdote and comment. To their many literary references, and to the natural and apt manner in which these allusions are introduced, Hunt's travel sketches owe part of their charm. He recalls, for example, the meeting of Bickerstaff with his friend, the upholsterer, in St. James Park, and recollects that the hero in Fielding's *Amelia* used to walk in the Mall. Painting and sculpture interested Hunt, and he frequently comments upon the works of art which adorn the buildings he describes. Music also claimed his attention; he notes that the band on parade play the best pieces of Mozart and Haydn, and that he "took home

---

[153] Op. cit., p. 49.
[154] Ibid., pp. 50-51.
[155] "Whitehall," Ibid., p. 52.
[156] Ibid., p. 57.

to school" the air of *non più andrai* long before he knew the name of Mozart.

In 1828 Hunt contributed to his *Companion,* "A Walk from Dulwich to Brockham," written in his most familiar vein.   The many digressions and lively comments he makes as he proceeds upon his journey indicate what a delightful walking companion he must have been.   He records a most interesting conversation he had at Streatham with an old man who had known Dr. Johnson, and who described his manner and his walk. "The traveller," comments Hunt, "may be in some measure regarded as a representative of wandering humanity.   He claims relationship with all whom he finds attached to a place in idea." [157]   This friendly "relationship" of Hunt to all that interests him in people and places is one of the secrets of the charm of his travel essays.   The warm, human, personal element is seldom, if ever, wanting.   His love of nature, and imaginative fancy find expression in this essay in the description of a bed of poppies: "It looked like a bed for Proserpina—a glow of melancholy beauty, containing a joy perhaps beyond joy. Poppies with their dark ruby cups and crowned heads, the more than wine color of their sleepy silk, and the funeral look of their anthers, seem to have a meaning about them beyond other flowers. They look as if they held a mystery at their hearts, like sleeping kings of Lethe." [158]

In "A Journey by Coach" originally contributed to *Leigh Hunt's London Journal,*[159] he describes a coaching trip from the White Horse in Piccadilly to Stratford-upon-Avon.   "A journey by coach," he says, "cannot be expected to furnish as much as one on foot and at leisure, but we have seen some interesting places, and had recollections awaked up from our books, and we here propose to carry something like one of our London supplements into the country." [160]   In the first paper of the series, he describes the inside of the coach, for, he says, he has never seen a description of the *inside.*   He humorously sketches the coachman, who "gathers

---

[157] *The Companion,* p. 242.
[158]Ibid.
[159] *Leigh Hunt's London Journal,* vol. II, Nos. 85, 86, 87, 89 (Nov. 14, 21, 28; Dec. 12, 1835).
[160] Ibid., No. 85.

the reins in his hands with a sort of half-gentility—a certain reticence and composure of bearing; and gives answers in the style of a man who is not to be too much troubled." [161]   Hunt's own pleasure in the journey is communicated to the reader with a gusto and holiday spirit with which all journeys should begin. "To be borne along," says Hunt, with no trouble, and yet without compulsion or mere passiveness, and with a sense of the power of commanding what you enjoy, is surely a pleasurable state of being both for body and mind." [162]

In the second paper of the "Journey" Hunt jokingly continues the fiction of a coaching tour: "The leisure and riches of your paper-traveller are immense.   He cares not at how many places he puts up, provided they are agreeable.   Noblemen's mansions fly open to him, and the portals of old time.   For him, all the steam-carriages in England shall stop at a moment's notice; and even the headlong equipages of royalty wait, till he has taken notice of the princes inside." [163]   This paper contains an appreciation of Mrs. Inchbald, whose work *Nature and Art* Hunt acknowledges, definitely influenced his opinions.

The third essay of the series is less full of personal digression, being confined largely to comment upon famous houses and places seen along the way.   Holland House, Hammersmith, Turnham Green, Sion House and Osterley Park are brought to the reader's attention by means of historic incident, legends, anecdotes, and literary allusions.

The fourth and last paper of the series opens with sympathetic reflections upon coach-horses, followed by comments upon Hounslow Heath and the neighboring district.   Hunt's interest in this part of the journey is owing to the Heath having been the scene of robberies and stage holdups in the eighteenth century, and to its association with famous writers from Chaucer to Cowley.   He planned to continue his "Journey" but it was brought abruptly to a close by the cessation of his *Journal*.

The idea for Hunt's more extended sketches of London, *The*

---

[161] Op. cit.
[162] Ibid.
[163] *Leigh Hunt's London Journal*, vol. II, No. 86.

Town, The Old Court Suburb, and *A Saunter Through the West End of London,* those agreeable "melanges of history, literature and topography," was not original with him. His interest in such sketches is shown in a letter to his friend, John Watson Dalby, written in 1834, in which he mentions not only Dalby's own contributions to this field, but those of other writers. In speaking of Dalby's work Hunt furnishes a very good description of this kind of travel writing. "I hope," he writes Dalby, "you will ramble and peregrinate on paper till your readers tell you to stop; which they will be in no hurry to do, if they are of my mind; for an enjoyment of localities, after that fashion, combines the novelty of the particular portrait with the expression of feelings common and delightful to all, . . . and I know very few kinds of writing indeed that are more desirable, especially with that mixture of verse and prose which you have adopted." [164]   Hunt mentions earlier writings of this type, among them the *Iter Boreale* of Bishop Corbett, Gay's *Epistles,* and Prior's *Down Hall.* "But," he continues, *"new* journeys are the thing; nor is it necessary to go far. The great point is to enjoy, and to feel oneself in the arms of nature and one's 'inn,' and to give way to the impulses." [165]

In 1835 Hunt contributed to the Supplement of *Leigh Hunt's London Journal* a series of papers, under the title of "The Streets of London" which later appeared in book form as *The Town.* The "Advertisement" to *The Town* calls it "an account of London, partly topographical and historical, but chiefly recalling the memories of remarkable characters and events associated with its streets between St. Paul's and St. James'." In his Introduction, Hunt makes it clear that he intends to write of the past as well as the present. "The past," he says, "is the heirloom of the world," and nowhere he believes is it more traceable than in London, where it is visibly present in old buildings, and in the names of streets. Hunt begins his account of London with the ancient Britons and brings it down to his own day. *The Town* is an agreeable mixture of antiquarianism, history, biography, anecdotes, reminiscences, theatrical criticism, and personal comment interspersed with

---

[164] *Correspondence of Leigh Hunt,* vol. I, p. 286.
[165] Ibid., p. 287.

quotations from verse and prose. Hunt's thoroughness in informing himself concerning the region he is describing may be seen
from his numerous citations of authorities. *The Town* is a kind
of glorified guide book, giving colorful pictures of "all that rich
aggregate" of London's past.

Aside from its historical and topographical features, *The Town*
gains additional interest from Hunt's personal reflections, which
frequently interrupt the narrative. It is these comments that
largely determine the essay-like nature of the work. "Merry
London," for example, causes him to think of the days of Chaucer
and healthy living, which in turn leads him to reflect: "Of all
pleasures, those are the cheapest which are bought of nature—such
as air and exercise, and manly sports; and though we allow that
the poor, in order to relish them, must be free from the melan-
cholier states of poverty, it is desirable *meanwhile* that the dispensers of knowledge should assist in hastening more cheerful
times by preparing for them, and that all classes should be told
how much the cultivation of their bodily health increases the ability, both of rich and poor, to get out of their troubles." [166] The
trees in London's streets become the theme of an essay-in-little on
the effect of nature upon the individual. Trees and flowers "re-
fresh the common-places of life, shed a harmony through the busy
discord, and appeal to those first sources of emotion, which are
associated with all that is young and innocent." [167] The book-
sellers of St. Paul's remind Hunt of Newberry, the famous seller
of juvenile books, and bring to mind recollections of his childhood
reading of "certain little penny books, radiant with gold and rich
with bad pictures." [168] The reader delays his tour of St. Paul's
while Hunt talks about reading for children.

The Old Court Suburb originally ran in Dickens' *Household
Words* in serial form from August, 1853, to February, 1854. Hunt
was sixty-nine years old when he began to write these sketches,
and they have a mellow and genial flavor, characteristic of his
later years. In writing of Kensington, Hunt was on familiar
ground, for he made his home there from 1840 until about the

---

[166] *The Town; its Memorable Characters and Events*, Lond., 1889, p. 20.
[167] Ibid., p. 22.
[168] Ibid., p. 53.

middle of 1853. From his *Correspondence* we get some idea of how much work these papers entailed. The many references had to be carefully checked, and frequently the material needed was not available. The easy style and many digressions of Hunt's travel sketches tend to make his performance seem an easy one, but a wealth of labor went into the making of this pleasant "gossip." Whenever possible, he tried to visit the great houses of which he writes, but ill-health prevented him from visiting Kensington Palace, which he describes without ever having seen its interior. Although Hunt occasionally leaned heavily upon the works of others for his factual material, he lends a freshness and individuality to his work by reason of his personality and his genius for "the right association in the right place."

Hunt early conveys to the reader the friendly and informal manner in which he intends to present his information about the "Old Court Suburb." "We shall suppose that the reader is our companion; that we are giving him what information we possess in return for the pleasure of his society; and that we say neither more nor less on any one of the objects, than might naturally be said between friends actually walking together, and equally alive to the only real interest of the subject, that is to say, of human interest." [169] It is the "human" interest which Hunt succeeds in creating that adds so much to the pleasure in reading this work. He centers the story of Kensington about its great houses: Gore, Colby, Kensington, Scarsdale, Shaftesbury, Holland, and Kensington Palace. Six chapters are devoted to Holland House, and an equal number to Kensington Palace and its gardens. The great families who have lived in these houses, their furnishings, their art treasures and their gardens chiefly occupy his attention. He does not adorn his narrative with as numerous poetic quotations as in *The Town,* but he is no less digressive. Essays-in-little are frequently introduced on any subject which happens to associate itself in his mind with the material about which he is writing. In the midst of describing Gore House, he devotes several pages to "the cultivation of the Beautiful"; the parish church and churchyard in High Street leads to a somewhat extended reflection on

---

[169] *The Old Court Suburb, or Memorials of Kensington, Regal, Critical and Anecdotal,* Phila., n.d., vol. 1, pp. 4-5.

churchyards in thoroughfares, and the custom of placing flowers on graves.

The Old Court Suburb contains many thumb nail sketches of well-known people of Kensington. Some of the most interesting of these "lives" are of people whose graves are in the High Street Churchyard. Hunt begins each sketch in the same manner, by naming the person, the year in which he died, and his age. The result is a kind of prose *Spoon-River Anthology,* without its irony. In this work Hunt expresses his optimistic faith in a new and better society, his belief in the beautiful, and his credo of cheerfulness and healthful living. He ends his sketch with a quotation from Evelyn's "Garden" essay, an appropriate ending to a work which devotes so much attention to gardens.

A Saunter Through the West End contributed by Hunt to the *Atlas* newspaper as a serial in 1847, was published in book form in 1861. It shows the same characteristics as *The Town* and *The Old Court Suburb,* and is written in the informal, conversational manner which gives to his familiar essays such genial warmth and charm. In the opening pages of *A Saunter Through the West End* he states his plan is "to go with the reader through the streets of the West End, as if the writer and he were actually so doing; that is to say as if they were lovers of local associations walking along the pavement at their leisure, and noticing any topic of interest which presented itself new or old." [170] Hunt keeps up such a lively comment on people and places that the reader's interest never flags. A large portion of the book is devoted to brief sketches and anecdotes of literary people, and of singers, dancers, and actors who in by-gone days graced the stages of the Opera House and the Haymarket Theatre. Among the writers commented upon are Madame d'Arblay, Evelyn, Dr. Arbuthnot, Mrs. Inchbald, Lady Mary Wortley Montague, Horace Walpole and Addison. The author's liking for the eighteenth century is strongly reflected in this work in the zest he shows in reconstructing the period of Queen Anne and her successors.

Hunt also includes contemporary London in his picture, and particularly interesting are his reminiscences of Hazlitt and Lamb. He recalls that "Hazlitt was as fond of tea as Dr. Johnson; and

---

[170] *A Saunter through the West End,* Lond., 1861, p. 2.

if he did not say as many bon mots over it, he delivered better criticisms, and has equal rights to have his tea recorded." [171] We see Lamb strolling up Wardour Street on a summer's day, choosing from a book stall one of his favorite authors, "the only flowers he much cared for." "He had," says Hunt, "no predilection for modern editions of his favourite writers, furnished with notes, and costing large sums of money. . . . His bookshelves accordingly had no outward attractions. They resembled an old fruitier's who makes no show. Dust and dry leaves hung about them. But within were melting peaches, and fruit for the gods." [172] On the contrary, Hazlitt "had scarcely a book in his house." [173]

Hunt's reforming spirit causes him to interrupt his *Saunter* from time to time, in order to comment on some matter which he believes indicates progress. His social outlook is always cheerful and optimistic. "At all events," he says, "advance society must; and in what better spirit can it advance, than in that of recognizing all true things for what they are, the ornamental as well as the useful, and doing its best to confirm and partake them?" [174] In another place he alludes to his belief in the coming recognition of the brotherhood of man. "A new note," he believes, "has been struck in the ears of the world, to which the wisest both among rich and poor are lending their attention; and St. James and St. Giles will yet come to know the relationship which all human beings bear to one another." [175] Hunt, like Addison and Steele, is trying to reform the "town," but his sympathies are wider in their range, and his social vision is a broader one, reflecting as it does, the ideals of the nineteenth century.

In these more extended travel sketches of Hunt's the same characteristics are discernible: lively comment upon people and things, which serves to recreate the past, as well as to present vividly the London of his own day; a genius for seizing upon significant details which lend color and interest to the narrative; a painstaking care in the accurate presentation of facts; an informal, conversa-

---

[171] Op. cit., p. 50.
[172] Ibid., p. 84.
[173] Ibid., p. 86.
[174] Ibid., p. 100.
[175] Ibid., pp. 48-49.

tional style admirably adapted to the subject matter; numerous digressions which reveal the personality and opinion of the writer; and frequent quotations from the work of other authors.   In these sketches, Hunt does not, like Lamb, deserve to be called the prose-poet of London, but he leaves a memorial of his affection for the "town" which time will not dull.   His attitude toward society, his healthy optimism, and his pleasure in natural beauty may be definitely referred to the nineteenth century.

Before turning to Lamb's essays which have to do with London life, it is worth while to review his attitude toward nature, for his essays contain no such romantic appreciation of natural beauty as characterizes the writing of Hunt and Hazlitt.   If we were to take too seriously some of Lamb's comments on natural scenery, we might conclude he was a true Cockney, wedded to his native London with no predilection for the beauties of nature.   He writes to his friend Manning (Nov. 28, 1800): "I must confess that I am not romance-bit about Nature."   And in a letter to Wordsworth, about the same time, he says, "I don't much care if I never see a mountain in my life.   I have passed all my days in London, until I have found as many and intense local attachments as any of your mountaineers can have done with dead Nature. . . . I have no passion (or have had none since I was in love, and then it was the spurious engendering of poetry and books) for groves and valleys. . . . Your sun, and moon, and skies, and hills, and lakes, affect me no more, or scarcely come to me in more venerable characters, than as a gilded room with tapestry and tapers, where I might live with handsome visible objects." [176]   It is only necessary to recall Lamb's love of exaggeration, and his sense of humor, in order to imagine his wry smile as he wrote to Wordsworth about "dead Nature."   In contrast to this, we have his declaration: "I am in love with this green earth; the face of town and country; the unspeakable rural solitudes, and the sweet security of streets." [177]   In August, 1802, Lamb visited Coleridge at Keswick, climbed to the top of Skiddaw, and waded up the bed of Lodore. "I have satisfied myself," he says, "that there is such a thing as

---

[176] Letter to Wordsworth, Jan. 30, 1801, *Life, Letters and Writings of Charles Lamb*, ed. by Percy Fitzgerald, vol. II, pp. 69-71.
[177] "New Year's Eve," *Works*, vol. II, p. 29.

that which tourists call *romantic,* which I very much suspected
before." [178]

In his review of Wordsworth's *Excursion,* Lamb attributes the
prevailing charm of the poem to the fact "that the dialogue
throughout is carried on in the very heart of the most romantic
scenery which the poet's native hills could supply." "We breathe
in the fresh air," he says, "as we do while reading Walton's Complete Angler." Moreover Lamb recognized the deeper implica-
tion in Wordsworth's love of nature: "To a mind constituted like
that of Mr. Wordsworth, the stream, the torrent, and the stirring
leaf—seem not merely to suggest associations of deity, but to be a
kind of speaking communication with it." [179] But notwithstanding
Lamb's appreciation of the romantic in nature, it did not attract
him as a theme for his own essays. Nowhere does he write in
praise of natural beauty in lyrical outbursts, such as we find in
Hazlitt. It is the city, with its myriad and teeming life, its odd
characters, its shops and its sights and sounds which is Lamb's
land of romance. To it, he transfers the romantic charm usually
associated with descriptions of nature, and in consequence he has
been aptly termed the prose poet of London. Lamb was charmed
by the manifestations of city life, as the romantic poet is by the
natural beauties he sees about him. In several of his letters to
Wordsworth, already referred to, Lamb expresses his love of the
city, and makes it the theme of his essay, *The Londoner.*

Like Hazlitt, Lamb was a keen observer; he was able to repro-
duce his impressions with great fidelity, and to recreate the atmosphere of a place. His preference is for those places and things
which have the charm of antiquity, and for those oddities in people which before him, Hogarth, and after him Dickens, so well
delineated. Lamb is especially happy in his description of old
buildings. Paradoxically, he knew how to make the ancient come
to life and burgeon under his pen. He is the poet of bricks and
stones and mortar, as Wordsworth is the poet of nature. Each
after his own fashion animates what he describes. As we are
made to feel a soul invests natural objects, so old buildings too

---

[178] E. V. Lucas, *Life of Charles Lamb,* vol. I, p. 279.
[179] "Review of 'The Excursion'," *Works,* vol. I, p. 162.

have an individuality, a personality, which is the sum and substance of the life which has inhabited them.

The romantic impulse has been defined "as an attitude of mind, a spirit given, a passion for modification, ornamentation, and recreation of material in terms of a self-originated ideal, and not a mood dictated by experience and faithfulness to material." [180] In this sense Lamb is highly romantic. He takes ordinary material and invests it with imaginative charm. His is not "a return to the past" in the sense of medievalism, but a return to the past in the flavor and spirit with which he invests objects, so that they seem to be the reincarnation of the past. We might well exclaim with him: "Antiquity! thou wondrous charm, what art thou? that, being nothing, art everything! The mighty future is nothing, being every thing. The past is every thing, being nothing!" [181] The romantic glamor of antiquity hangs over the South-Sea House which Lamb describes as "melancholy-looking" with "a desolation something like Balclutha's." [182] Its soul has long since fled. It is "a magnificent relic!" "Time . . . has not freshened it. No wind has resuscitated the face of the sleeping waters. . . . Silence and destitution are upon thy walls, proud house, for a memorial!" [183] The effect is heightened by Lamb's describing his own sensations: "To such as me, old house! there is a charm in thy quiet:—a cessation—a coolness from business—an indolence almost cloistral—which is delightful! With what reverence have I paced thy great bare rooms and courts at eventide!" [184] The atmosphere of antiquity is again created in his description of the Inner Temple where he was born and passed the first seven years of his life. He calls it "the most elegant place in the Metropolis," and pictures its "magnificent ample squares" and classic green recesses, its collegiate aspect, its terrace, its fountains and its sun-dials. Its sundials are the subject of a prose-poem by Lamb which weaves the

---

[180] W. D. MacClintock. *Some Paradoxes of the English Romantic Movement of the Eighteenth Century.* Univ. of Chicago Decennial Publications, First Series, vol. VII, Chicago, 1903, p. 346.

[181] "Oxford in the Vacation," *Works,* vol. II, p. 9.

[182] "The South-Sea House," Ibid., p. 1.

[183] Ibid., p. 2.

[184] Ibid.

spell of the past: "What an antique air had the now almost effaced
sun-dials, with their moral inscriptions, seeming coevals with that
Time which they measured, and to take their revelations of its flight
immediately from heaven, holding correspondence with the fountain of light! How would the dark line steal imperceptibly on,
watched by the eye of childhood, eager to detect its movement,
never catched, nice as an evanescent cloud, or the first arrests of
sleep! . . . It was the primitive clock, the horologe of the first
world. Adam could scarce have missed it in Paradise. It was the
measure appropriate for sweet plants and flowers to spring by, for
the birds to apportion their silver warblings by, for flocks to pasture
and be led to fold by. The shepherd 'carved it out quaintly in the
sun'; and, turning philosopher by the very occupation, provided it
with mottos more touching than tombstones." [185]

Lamb, like Addison, writes upon the tombs in Westminster
Abbey.[186] The essay shows his heartfelt appreciation of the genius
of place and his love for the past. "Is the being shown over a
place the same as silently for ourselves detecting the genius of
it?" And again he questions: "Did you ever see or hear of a mob
in the Abbey while it was free to all? Do the rabble come there,
or trouble their heads about such speculations? . . . They have,
alas! no passion for antiquities. . . . If they had, they would be
no longer the rabble." [187]

Lamb, in his sketches of figures common to London street life,
employs a theme which had occupied the pens of Steele,[188] Swift
and Goldsmith. Swift in the *Tatler* (No. 9, April 30, 1709) draws
in verse a realistic picture of London in the early morning, his
object being, he says, to make "the incidents just as they really
appear." Goldsmith in his "Adventures of a Strolling Player"
writes of the beggar and praises the freedom of his life. "We
beggars," he says, "are the very fondlings of Nature. . . . The
whole creation is filled with good things for the beggar. . . . Joy,
joy, my blood! though our estates lie nowhere, we have fortunes
wherever we go. If an inundation sweeps away half the grounds

---

[185] "Old Benchers of the Inner Temple," *Works*, vol. II, p. 83.
[186] "The Tombs in the Abbey," Ibid., p. 207 ff.
[187] Ibid., p. 208.
[188] *Spectator*, No. 430, July 14, 1712.

of Cornwall, I am content—I have no lands there; if the stocks sink, that gives me no uneasiness—I am no Jew." [189] Lamb in his "Decay of Beggars in the Metropolis" voices the same idea with regard to the beggar's freedom: "The ups and downs of the world concern him no longer. He alone continueth in one stay. The price of stock or land affecteth him not. The fluctuations of agricultural or commercial prosperity touch him not, or at worst but change his customers. He is not expected to become bail or surety for any one. No man troubleth him with questioning his religion or politics. He is the only free man in the universe." [190] Lamb deplores the removal of beggars from the London streets. They can no more be spared than the cries of London. No street corner is complete without them. "They are as indispensable as the Ballad Singer; and in their picturesque attire as ornamental as the Signs of old London. They were the standing morals, emblems, mementos, dial-mottos, the spital sermons, the books for children, the salutary checks and pauses to the high and rushing tide of greasy citizenry." [191] We have said Lamb was not a moralizer, but he makes a near approach to moralizing in this paper. His sympathy wrought to high degree, expresses itself in a kind of moral indignation against those who withhold their pennies from street beggars, lest they be imposters.

The young chimney-sweepers of London also call forth Lamb's sympathy: "Those tender novices, blooming through their first nigritude, the maternal washings not quite effaced from the cheek —such as come forth with the dawn." [192] Lamb always writes understandingly of children, but in "The Praise of Chimney-Sweepers" he displays toward these "innocent blacknesses" the depth of his kindly yearning. He enlivens his essay with the incident of a young sweeper found asleep in one of the state beds of Arundel Castle, and describes the "solemn supper" held each year in Smithfield, on St. Bartholomew's Day, when his friend, Jem White, entertained the chimney-sweepers, not yet grown to man's estate. Lamb's keen sense of humor is revealed in his

---

[189] Oliver Goldsmith. *Miscellaneous Works*, p. 302.
[190] "Decay of Beggars in the Metropolis," *Works*, vol. II, p. 116.
[191] Ibid.
[192] "The Praise of Chimney-Sweepers," Ibid., p. 108.

account of a fall he had while "pacing along Cheapside" and the mirth of a young chimney-sweeper at his discomfort. He likens him to Hogarth's urchin in the March to Finchley, and Lamb's own word painting is worthy of comparison with the work of that great artist of humble life.

The periodical essayists wrote of coffee-houses as a London institution, and Lamb writes of the dispensers of sassafras tea, thereby calling attention to another London custom. This savory drink is dispensed at way-side tea stations in the early dawn to hard-handed artisans, about to begin their daily labors, who are jostled by the rake reeling home from his midnight cups, cursing the steaming tea's "ungenial fume." Lamb also pictures the gardener transporting his cabbages at break of day from Hammersmith to Covent Garden. These vignettes of city life are comparable to those of Swift already referred to. Both writers have chosen to write of London and her humble folk, in the early hours of the morning when the city begins to stir with the life of a new day. Swift, however, does not invest his writing with sympathy, which is a predominant element in Lamb's essay. It is the union of realistic description, characteristic of the eighteenth century, with the sympathetic treatment of humble life, which was a feature of the Romantic Revival, that lends such charm to these essays of Lamb. In their human interest and in the feeling they evoke, Lamb's London street figures may be compared to Wordsworth's country folk. The method used by the essayist is similar to that of the poet. The universal qualities in human nature are illustrated by means of humble people, whose situation in life not only calls forth sympathy, but arouses interest through the realistic fidelity of the character portrayal.

Hazlitt also writes of London life. In his essay, "Londoners and Country People," he defines a cockney as "a person who has never lived out of London, and who has got all his ideas from it." [193] "A real Cockney," Hazlitt says, "is the poorest creature in the world, the most literal, the most mechanical, and yet he too lives in a world of romance—a fairy land of his own. He is a citizen of London; and this abstraction leads his imagination the

---

[193] *Works*, vol. VII, p. 66.

finest dance in the world." [194]   Every man, no matter how humble his occupation, according to Hazlitt's idea, extracts a kind of glory from the nature of his work.   The shopman enjoys the "liberty and gaudy, fluttering pride" of the well-dressed people who pass by; the tailor's stigma "is lost in the elegance of the patterns he provides, and of the persons he adorns." [195]   "Even the eye of childhood," Hazlitt believes, finds something for its delight in London, and "is dazzled . . . with the polished splendour of the jewellers' shops, the neatness of the turnery ware, the festoons of artificial flowers, the confectionery, the chemists' shops, the lamps, the horses, the carriages, the sedan-chairs." [196]   This comment recalls Hunt's entertaining essays on London shops, particularly his description of the toy shops.

Hazlitt describes the London tea-gardens, with their holiday crowd, and the Londoner, who, confined by his occupation, is shut away from knowledge of the world, and therefore retains his simplicity into manhood.   He does not agree with the picture of men in cities Wordsworth presents, in his preface to the *Excursion*. The Londoner, Hazlitt says, "lives in the eye of the world, and the world is his."   He has greater opportunity to observe life in its "larger masses and varied movements." [197]   He feels himself a part of the public, to which he is joined by bonds of fellowship, and a community of ideas.

From this brief examination of the treatment of nature by the familiar essayists, it is evident that in the amount and romantic coloring of its description, the nineteenth century essay marks a departure from the essays which had gone before.   The varied treatment of nature is an important feature of the essays of Hunt, Lamb and Hazlitt.   There are short incidental descriptions of nature, sometimes only a sentence or two in length, and more formal and extended descriptions.   Both are often poetic in feeling and expression.   Stress is laid upon the picturesque in scenery, in towns, and in people.   London and other places are invested with romantic interest, and all three writers indulge in recollections of

---

[194] Op. cit., p. 68.
[195] Ibid., pp. 68, 69.
[196] Ibid., p. 69.
[197] Ibid., p. 77.

places and scenes connected with their early life. Their treatment of nature parallels that of the Romantic poets. This likeness is further emphasized by Hazlitt's discussion of nature in its relation to art and life. His theory of man's attachment to natural objects, and the romantic sentiment with which he invests them, reflect Wordsworth's attitude as expressed in his poetry. Moreover the treatment of nature and of the romantic by Hazlitt, Hunt and Lamb is highly individualized. In Hazlitt the emphasis is upon beauty in scenery; in Hunt upon the beauty of natural objects, especially the commonplace; and in Lamb upon the romantic aspects of city life. These things give the essay a new variety, interest and beauty, and very definitely link it with the Romantic poetry of the age.

CHAPTER V

SELF-REVELATION

One of the characteristics of the Romantic Revival is the frank outpouring of personal experience and the self-revelation of the individual through the expression of his emotions and feelings. Self-revelation suffused with romantic sentiment and accompanied by impassioned recollection had in the eighteenth century made its appearance in the *Confessions* of Rousseau. The flood of romantic sentiment thus started, soon overflowed into England, where, in the later part of the century, it found an outlet in the novel, and in the "sentimental pantisocracy" of the Lake Poets. In the early nineteenth century self-revelation received a fresh impetus in the work of the English familiar essayists.

Hazlitt may be considered a link between the romantic self-revelation of Rousseau and that of the nineteenth century. A literary as well as a political disciple of Rousseau, Hazlitt early came under the influence of the *Confessions* and *La Nouvelle Heloise*. The period in which he read these works, from his eighteenth to his twentieth year, he speaks of as "the happiest of our life." In his essay, "On Novelty and Familiarity," he recalls the intense pleasure he had in reading Rousseau. Sitting on a sunny bank in a field he read the letter in the *New Eloise* in which St. Preux describes the Pays de Vaud, and never felt his "glassy essence" so much as then. The style, he says, gave him the same sensation "as the drops of morning dew before they are scorched by the sun." [198]

In the *Round Table,* in 1814, Hazlitt speaks of the *Confessions* as the most valuable of all Rousseau's writings; in 1823 he wrote his *Liber Amoris,* which in spirit and manner shows the influence of Rousseau, and in 1825 appeared his "Character of Rousseau," one of the best criticisms of Rousseau yet penned. Edmund Gosse

[198] "On Novelty and Familiarity," *Works*, vol. VII, p. 304.

in his study, "Rousseau in England in the Nineteenth Century" [199] calls attention to Hazlitt's criticism of Rousseau and to the influence exerted by the Genevese upon the Lake Poets, and Byron and Shelley. But Gosse does not mention one of the most important aspects of Rousseau's influence, the romantic impulse he gave to self-revelation in the work of the early nineteenth century familiar essayists. Self-revelation is one of the distinguishing marks of the familiar essay in the seventeenth century, and it is to be found in some degree in the eighteenth century periodical essay, but it is not accompanied by impassioned recollection or other romantic sentiment. Hunt, Lamb, and Hazlitt give to much of their self-revelation a romantic coloring which it had hitherto lacked. It is the romantic aspects of this self-revelation, and the contrasting realistic elements, which deserve consideration.

Hazlitt tells the story of his inner life by means of recalling some particular sensation or emotion. The mind, he says, is like a mechanical instrument that plays a great variety of tunes, but must play them in succession. One idea, in recalling another, excludes all others. "We cannot as it were unfold the whole web of our existence; we must pick out the single threads." [200] This provides the key to Hazlitt's self-revelation. He weaves into the tapestry of his essays, threads from his own experience, telling the story of poignant moments in his life which enable us to know the man. Talfourd speaks of Hazlitt's "intense consciousness of his own individual being," and his essays confirm this opinion. Whatever the theme, Hazlitt's interest sooner or later becomes concentrated on himself. His preoccupation with an inner world made up of his sensations and emotions leads to extended self-analysis, the purpose of which is to account for various states of mind. He carries his probing a step further than Rousseau, who is interested in his sensations as such, and not in the psychology of them. The following examples will serve to illustrate Hazlitt's method. In "Why Distant Objects Please" he analyzes the vividness of his impressions; those connected with sound, smell, and taste, he says are remembered longer than visible objects, and serve better as links in the chain of association. The reason, he believes, is that im-

[199] *Aspects and Impressions*, New York, 1922, p. 169 ff.
[200] "On Going a Journey," *Works*, vol. VI, p. 187.

pressions received by the eye are more frequent than those received
in other ways: "Where there is nothing interposed between any
two impressions, whatever the distance of time that parts them,
they naturally seem to touch; and the renewed impression recalls
the former one in full force, without distraction or competitor." [201]

When he comments upon the fact that there is a sensation in
traveling into foreign parts that is to be had no otherwise, he
analyzes the reason for this "animated but momentary hallucina-
tion," and arrives at the conclusion that to exchange our actual
for our ideal identity demands an effort, and in order "to feel the
pulse of our old transports revive very keenly, we must 'jump'
all our present comforts and connexions." [202]   This also leads
him to consider the limitation of the mind in its ability to recall
but one place at a time: "The canvas of the fancy is but of a
certain extent, and if we paint one set of objects upon it, they
immediately efface every other.   We cannot enlarge our conceptions, we only shift our point of view." [203]

Hazlitt's pleasure in recalling his sensations is the result of his
love of contemplation and his desire to relive the past.   Like
Rousseau, he enjoyed living in a world of contemplation where
he might indulge his dreams.   The impassioned fervor of his
recollections is also like Rousseau's, in that they reveal a sensitive
nature, and a remarkable memory for impressions even after a
lapse of years.   Like Rousseau, he enjoyed gathering up "the past
moments of his being."   Contemplation, emotion, sensation constituted Hazlitt's real world.   Although like Carlyle he admired
the man who sees what is to be done and does it, it was not the
world of action which personally appealed to him, but the world
of contemplation.   He confesses that what he likes best is to lie
whole mornings on his back on Salisbury Plain, "neither knowing
or caring how time passes, and thus 'with light-winged toys of
feathered Idleness' to melt down hours to moments." [104]   Somewhat of this idle humor, he says he inherited from his father.   In
his essay, "On Living to One's Self," he fondly reviews those

---

[201] "Why Distant Objects Please," *Works*, vol. VI, pp. 258-59.
[202] "On Going a Journey," Ibid., p. 189.
[203] Ibid., p. 187.
[204] "On a Sun-Dial," Ibid., vol. XII, p. 58.

years of his life when he did nothing but think. Such a dreaming existence is best he believes. "He who quits it to go in search of realities, generally barters repose for repeated disappointments and vain regrets." [205]   In the same essay Hazlitt writes at length of the contemplative life, which "is such as a pure spirit might be supposed to lead, and such an interest as it might take in the affairs of men, calm, contemplative, passive, distant, touched with pity for their sorrows, smiling at their follies without bitterness, sharing their affections, but not troubled by their passions, not seeking their notice, nor once dreamt of by them." [206]

Closely connected with Hazlitt's love of contemplation is his love of the past. It is of the nature of the dreamer to live in the past; of the man of action to anticipate the future. Hazlitt believed that "we are heirs of the past; we count upon the future as our own natural reversion." [207]   He conceives the past as a real and substantial part of our being.[208]   It is the past that gives him "most delight and most assurance of reality." "I confess," he says, "nothing at present interests me but what has been—the recollections of the impressions of my early life, or events long past, of which only the dim traces remain in a smouldering ruin or half-obsolete custom. . . . I cannot solve the mystery of the past, nor exhaust my pleasure in it. The years, the generations to come, are nothing to me. . . . The only wish I can form, or that ever prompts the passing sigh, would be to live some of my years over again—they would be those in which I enjoyed and suffered most!" [209]

The past is also inexpressibly dear to Hazlitt for the memories it revives of "the glowing image of some bright reality," "the thoughts of which," he says, "can never from my heart." [210]   The recollection of this "glowing image" runs like a leit-motif through his work. In the intensity of feeling called forth, it is like Rousseau's recollection of Madame Warens. It is Rousseau's

---

[205] "On Living to One's Self," *Works*, vol. VI, p. 92.
[206] Ibid., p. 91.
[207] "On the Feeling of Immortality in Youth," Ibid., vol. XII, p. 156.
[208] "On the Past and Future," Ibid., vol. VI, p. 22.
[209] "On a Sun-Dial," Ibid., vol. XII, pp. 55-56.
[210] "On the Past and Future," Ibid., vol. VI, p. 23.

ability to live in his own past that constitutes for Hazlitt the greatest charm of the *Confessions.* "He seems," says Hazlitt, "to gather up the past moments of his being like drops of honey-dew to distil a precious liquor from them; his alternate pleasures and pains are the bead-roll that he tells over, and piously worships; he makes a rosary of the flowers of hope and fancy that strewed his earliest years." [211] Hazlitt with equal truth might have been writing of himself. As he looked back upon his life it seemed as if he had slept it out "in a dream or shadow on the side of the hill of knowledge" where he fed "on books, on thoughts, on pictures, and only heard in half-murmurs the trampling of busy feet, or the noises of the throng below." [212] Too late, he regrets, he awoke from "the dim, twilight existence," and felt a wish to descend to the world of realities.

However bitter or disillusioning Hazlitt's experiences, he retained a childlike simplicity of spirit, revealed when he recalls the pleasures of his childhood and early youth. There is a glamor about the recollections of his childhood which reminds one of Wordsworth's "trailing clouds of glory." He remembers, for instance, the time he visited the Montpelier Tea-gardens at Walworth with his father. As he recalls this scene, he describes his emotions: "A new sense comes upon me, as in a dream; a richer perfume, brighter colours start out; my eyes dazzle; my heart heaves with its new load of bliss, and I am a child again. My sensations are all glossy, spruce, voluptuous, and fine: they wear a candied coat, and are in holiday trim. . . . All that I have observed since, of flowers and plants, and grass-plots, and of suburb delights, seems, to me, borrowed from 'that first garden of my innocence'—to be slips and scions stolen from that bed of memory." [213] In the same essay he says that "both ends of our existence touch upon Heaven," and that as we look back upon "the unsightly masses" of past experience, "the golden cloud soon rests upon their heads, and the purple light of fancy clothes their barren sides!" [214] This

---

[211] Op. cit., p. 24.

[212] "On the Fear of Death," Ibid., p. 326.

[213] "Why Distant Objects Please," Ibid., p. 257.

[214] Ibid., p. 256.

closely parallels in thought Wordsworth's "recollections of early childhood" in his *Intimations of Immortality*.[215]

Hazlitt sees a kite in the air and it seems to pull at his heart; it becomes a "thing of life" as he remembers the flutter and palpitation with which he watched his own kite when a child: "My little cargo of hopes and fears ascended with it; and as it made a part of my own consciousness then, it does so still, and appears 'like some gay creature of the element,' my playmate when life was young, and twin-born with my earliest recollections." [216] The mood of joyful recollection expressed here, the delight in recalling childhood pleasures, is essentially the same as Wordsworth's in "My Heart Leaps Up," and "To a Butterfly." [217]

The letter-bell passes and it not only fills the street with its clatter but "rings clear through the length of many half-forgotten years." It reminds Hazlitt of his first coming up to town, of the confusion of those early days, of the recollection it brought of a letter to be written, and of the picture it caused to flash upon his mind of a country scene near his home.[218] He recalls again this scene in "My First Acquaintance with Poets," where it is associated in his mind with the first time he heard Coleridge preach. A sound was in his ear "as of a Siren's song." He was "stunned, startled with it, as from deep sleep." "I was at that time," he says, "dumb, inarticulate, helpless, like a worm by the way-side, crushed, bleeding, lifeless; but now, bursting from the deadly bands that "bound them,

'With Styx nine times round them,'

my ideas float on winged words, and as they expand their plumes, catch the golden light of other years." [219] It was as if Hazlitt had heard the music of the spheres. It seemed to him that "Poetry

---

[215] "Ode on Intimations of Immortality," *Poems*, ed. by Matthew Arnold, Lond., 1903, p. 201 ff.

[216] "Why Distant Objects Please," *Works*, vol. VI, p. 258.

[217] Two of Wordsworth's poems have this title. The one referred to here begins; "Stay near me—do not take thy flight." *Poems*, p. 115.

[218] "The Letter-Bell," *Works*, vol. XII, p. 235 f.

[219] "My First Acquaintance with Poets," Ibid., p. 260.

and Philosophy had met together" and that "Truth and Genius had embraced, under the eye and with the sanction of Religion." [220]

Such impassioned recollection, associated with familiar scenes is also characteristic of the early nineteenth century romantic poets, particularly Wordsworth. The similarity between Rousseau and Wordsworth in the expression of sentiment has been noted by Hazlitt: [221] "We see no difference between them, than that the one wrote in prose and the other in poetry; and that prose is perhaps better adapted to express those local and personal feelings, which are inveterate habits in the mind, than poetry, which embodies its imaginary creations." Hazlitt prefers Rousseau's exclamation *"Ah, voila de la pervenche!"* because it "comes more home to the mind" than Wordsworth's discovery of the linnet's nest "with five blue eggs," or his address to the cuckoo. Also Hazlitt "will confidently match the citizen of Geneva's adventures on the Lake of Bienne against the Cumberland Poet's floating dreams on the Lake of Grasmere." [222] After noting the similarity between Rousseau and Wordsworth in their power to create interest out of their own feelings, in their weaving numberless recollections into one sentiment, and in their winding their own being around whatever object occurs to them, Hazlitt points out an important difference. "Rousseau . . . interests you in certain objects by interesting you in himself: Mr. Wordsworth would persuade you that the most insignificant objects are interesting in themselves, because he is interested in them. . . . This is not imagination, but want of sense." [223] Hazlitt followed Rousseau's method rather than Wordsworth's, and interests you in himself.

Hazlitt, however, in his figurative use of language resembles the poet rather than the prose writer. He speaks of sleeping out his life "in a dream or shadow on the side of the hill of knowledge," of his sensations wearing "a candied coat"; of the first "garden of his innocence." As he looks back upon the "unsightly masses" of past experience, "the golden light of fancy rests upon their heads, and the purple cloud soon clothes their barren sides." Of the

---

[220] Op. cit., p. 261.
[221] "On the Character of Rousseau," *Works*, vol. I, p. 92.
[222] Ibid., p. 92.
[223] Ibid.

fair creature whose image is engraven in Hazlitt's inmost soul, he exclaims, "Wherever she treads, pale primroses, like her face, vernal hyacinths, like her brow, spring up beneath her feet, and music hangs on every bough." [224]

But not all of Hazlitt's self-realization is romantic in character. He could write of himself most realistically, and the contrast provided by the combination of romantic and realistic elements adds greatly to the interest of his familiar essays.

At the basis of Hazlitt's realism is his love of truth, the touchstone by which he tested and judged both people and things. "Where the pursuit of truth has been the habitual study of any man's life, the love of truth will be his ruling passion," [225] Hazlitt wrote, and this is the key to his philosophy of life. He also says that "to prefer the truth to all other things, it requires that the mind shall have been at some pains in finding it out." [226] He spent his life in seeking the truth, and if at times he seems pessimistic, this is the result of his effort to see things as they are. Like Carlyle, he wished to strip off the outer garments to seek the reality within. Therefore he spared neither himself nor others in his desire to reveal man as he is, and did not flinch if the portrait was unflattering.

One of the outstanding traits of Hazlitt's character is the steadfastness of his opinions. Once having made up his mind, he seldom changed it. "I pretend," he says, "to be master of my own mind. . . . I am not to be brow-beat or wheedled out of any of my settled convictions. Opinion to opinion, I will face any man." [227] He says he sympathized *beforehand* with different views and feelings that might be entertained on a subject, and was thus prevented from flinging himself into contrary extremes *afterwards*. [228] This accounts for his consistent attitude toward the French Revolution, and his dissatisfaction with Wordsworth and others, whom he considered turncoats.

Hazlitt speaks with the greatest frankness of his friends. Few

---

[224] "On Great and Little Things," *Works*, vol. VI, p. 236.
[225] "On Consistency of Opinion," Ibid., vol. XI, p. 509.
[226] "On Poetical Versatility," Ibid., vol. I, pp. 152-53.
[227] "On Consistency of Opinion," Ibid., vol. XI, pp. 508-09.
[228] Ibid., p. 509.

of those whom he has known intimately "continue on the same friendly footing, or combine the steadiness with the warmth of attachment." He confesses that he has quarreled with nearly all of them. "Old friends are like meats served up repeatedly, cold, comfortless and distasteful." [229] "There is no one," he says with regard to Wordsworth, "in whom I have been more disappointed . . . nor with whom I am more disposed on certain points to quarrel: but the love of truth and justice which obliges me to do this, will not suffer me to blench his merits." [230]

Hazlitt writes without disguise of his attitude toward the world. He is a good hater and he glories in it: "Without something to hate, we should lose the very spring of thought and action." "Hatred alone is immortal." "Pure good," he believes, "soon grows insipid" and "wants variety and spirit." [231] He speaks without reserve of the failure of his own life: "My public and private hopes have been left a ruin, or remain only to mock me." [232] When he contemplates the end of life, he reflects that if he had indeed lived, he would not care to die, but he does not like "a contract of pleasure broken off unfulfilled, a marriage with joy unconsummated, a promise of happiness rescinded." [233] He is courageous enough to express the bitterness toward life which he feels, but his zest for life, and his joy in the many things he found to like are an antidote to his bitterness.

It would be possible from Hazlitt's essays to make a reasonably long list of the things he enjoyed. Some of his chief interests in life he has expressed in a sentence: "So have I loitered my life away, reading books, looking at pictures, going to plays, hearing, thinking, writing on what pleased me best." [234] If we add to this his love of good conversation, of traveling, of taking long walks, and his enjoyment of nature, the list will be fairly complete. Some of the happiest hours of his life were spent in viewing his favorite paintings and in attending the theatre, pastimes of which he has

---

[229] "On the Pleasure of Hating," *Works*, vol. VI, pp. 130-131.

[230] "On Genius and Common Sense," Ibid., p. 45.

[231] "On the Pleasure of Hating," Ibid., vol. VII, p. 128.

[232] "On Fear of Death," Ibid., vol. VI, p. 325.

[233] Ibid., p. 325.

[234] "My First Acquaintance with Poets," Ibid., vol. XII, p. 269.

written with great critical appreciation. Books brought him one of his keenest enjoyments. " . . . Books let us into their souls and lay open to us the secrets of our own. They are the first and last, the most home-felt, the most heart-felt of all our enjoyments." [235]

The biographer who would come as close as possible to the man Hazlitt will find much of the raw material of which biography is made in Hazlitt's familiar essays. His likes and dislikes, his hopes and fears, his joys and sorrows, his ideas upon many subjects, in short his philosophy of life, are set forth for him who reads with understanding. Some of this material is of great importance not only as biographical data, but as literary history, for example the account of the beginning of his acquaintance with Coleridge, his visit to the Wordsworths at All-Foxden, his reading of the *Lyrical Ballads* in manuscript,[236] and his first meeting with Lamb.

The realistic features of Hazlitt's self-revelation serve to enhance the romantic elements. Were the romantic strain too long continued it would grow insipid or degenerate into sentimentality. In this fact perhaps consists one of the great differences between prose and poetry. The poet by the loftiness of his thought and its fitting metrical accompaniment can sustain for a long period a train of imagination and fancy and romantic sentiment. The passion of his mind and the intensity of thought, together with the music of words, transport the reader into the realm of the imagination where the prosaic realities of life do not enter, and the illusion is complete. The medium of prose, even when the diction is poetic, and the ideas clothed in romantic sentiment does not bring the reader completely under the spell. It is next to impossible therefore for the prose-poet long to sustain the intensity of poetic imagination. Moreover he must be exceedingly skilful in his transition from his impassioned moods or the reader will be too conscious of the contrast presented between the realistic and romantic, and the effect will tend toward the ludicrous. Hazlitt and Lamb were masters of the art of transition from an impassioned to a less exalted mood. Hunt seldom shows equal skill. He either allows his sentiment to be

---

[235] "The Sick Chamber," *Works*, vol. XII, p. 130.
[236] "My First Acquaintance with Poets," Ibid., p. 269.

prolonged into sentimentality, or he so abruptly changes his mood that the reader cannot quickly enough make the necessary adjustment, and the effect is spoiled.

Lamb is one of the most self-revealing of essayists. Unlike Hazlitt, his primary interest in writing of himself is not to record his sensations and emotions, but to recall incidents in his life which he invests with humor, pathos and sentiment. His relationship with his friends and family reveal him as one of the most courageous, kind, tender and sympathetic of men, characteristics which he unconsciously transmits through the medium of his essays. Also in contrast to Hazlitt he suffered "the slings and arrows of outrageous fortune" without becoming misanthropic or viewing himself with self-pity. His humor seems to have acted as a saving-grace in keeping him sane and free from morbid self-analysis. There is no self-probing as with Hazlitt, but rather the revelation of a sensitive nature, capable of intense joy and sorrow.

Lamb's tendency to write of events in his own life is discernible in his early work, before he had found his medium in the familiar essay. *Rosamund Gray* (1789), Lamb's earliest known prose, written when he was between twenty-two and twenty-three, is in part autobiographical, as is also *Mrs. Leicester's School,* which contains incidents of Lamb's childhood. The autobiographical element thus early evidenced, continued to be a feature of Lamb's writing. The amount of such material contained in his familiar essays may be readily seen by referring to Mr. Lucas's *Life* of Lamb, and observing the frequent quotation from the essays. Lamb defends his writing of himself in the preface to the *Last Essays of Elia.* "Egotistical," he says, his essays "have been pronounced by some who did not know that what he tells us, as of himself, was often true only (historically) of another. . . . If it be egotism, to imply and twine with his own identity the griefs and affections of another—making himself many, or reducing many unto himself—then is the skillful novelist, who all along brings in his hero, or heroine, speaking of themselves, the greatest egoist of all; who yet has never, therefore, been accused of that narrowness. And how shall the intenser dramatist escape being faulty, who doubtless, under cover of passion uttered by another, oftentimes gives blameless vent to his most inward feelings, and expresses his own story modestly?" [237]

Thus Lamb claims for the essayist the same freedom of self-expression as is permitted to the novelist and the dramatist. The use of the first person, Lamb says, is but "a favorite figure" of the essayist, employed by him to shadow forth his thoughts, and he may or may not be expressing his own feelings and writing out of his own experience.

Lamb's self-revelation is infused with wit, humor, charm, gusto and a deep understanding of life. He draws a realistic picture of himself, tinged with imagination and fancy, elements which were so native to him that the picture is all the more truthful by reason of them. Lamb's sweet sanity and common sense never allowed him to be a hero in his own eyes; hence he selects the weaknesses and oddities of his character to present to the reader and enjoys a good laugh at his own expense. In the "Preface" to the *Last Essays of Elia,* he has written a short sketch of himself in which he sums up his foibles in a most engaging manner. The sketch is a sort of self-caricature which clearly reveals Lamb's individuality. In spite of his jesting, the Elia of the essays is made real to us, and the key to his own character furnished. Elia is, he says, too much the boy-man. "His manners lagged behind his years. The *toga virilis* never sate gracefully on his shoulders. The impressions of infancy had burnt into him, and he resented the impertinence of manhood." [238] This child-like spirit Lamb retained through life. His humor, his love of jokes and punning, his pleasure in the small happenings and ordinary details of daily living, his joy in life itself, are all expressions of his youthful spirit.

Lamb in his self-revelation is both a realist and a romanticist. His realism consists in his ability to see himself as he really was, to acquaint us with his likes and dislikes, and to present the world to us through his own eyes. In doing this, he employs a great deal of realistic detail, so cloaked in quaint language and whimsicalities, that he seems less of a realist than he is. But Lamb saw also with the eyes of a poet, and shared with the romantic poets of his

---

[237] "Last Essays of Elia," Preface, *Works*, vol. II, p. 151.
[238] Ibid., p. 153.

generation a love of the past, a desire to call forth again in recollection the things which had given him pleasure, and a deep sympathy for his fellow-men.   He reveals little of the love of nature
that was so characteristic of the nineteenth century romanticists,
but this does not imply a lack of imagination and fancy, but a
transfer of it to the scenes with which he was most familiar—
those of city life.   It might be said to require an even higher
imaginative faculty to invest the city with romantic fancy than
scenes of natural beauty.

Lamb, like Hazlitt, enjoys dwelling in the past, and suffusing
with sentiment scenes dear to him through association.   The atmosphere with which he envelops the scenes of his childhood and
other places held in affection is essentially a romantic one.   He, as
well as Hazlitt, seems to have come under the influence of Rousseau, although Lamb is so thoroughly original that the suggestion
of "influence" always seems to demand apology.   That Lamb had
great admiration for Rousseau's *Confessions,* we know from a
letter to Coleridge (Nov. 8, 1876) in which he says of some verses
which Coleridge had sent him: "I love them as I love the Confessions of Rousseau and for the same reason: the same frankness,
the same openness of heart, the same disclosure of all the most
hidden and delicate affections of the mind." [239]

In Lamb's essay "Blakesmoor in H——shire," he indulges in
impassioned recollection in the manner of Rousseau.   This essay,
in its brief whole, embodies some of the leading elements of
romanticism; the return to the past, impassioned recollection, sentimental attachment to well-loved scenes, sympathetic understanding
of childhood, and imaginative fancy.   Lamb, surveying the ruins
of the old house where he had spent so many happy hours of his
childhood, exclaims: "Had I seen these brick-and-mortar knaves
at their process of destruction, at the plucking of every panel I
should have felt the varlets at my heart.   I should have cried out
to them to spare a plank at least out of the cheerful storeroom, in
whose hot window-seat I used to sit and read Cowley, with the
grass-plot before, and the hum and flappings of that one solitary
wasp that ever haunted it about me—it is in mine ears now as oft

---

[239] *Life, Letters and Writings of Charles Lamb,* vol. I, pp. 339-40.

as summer returns. . . ." "Every plank and panel of that house . . . had magic in it," Lamb says, as he recalls his delight and fear in exercising his "tender courage" when a child, by stealing looks at the "sternbright visages" of the figures out of Ovid which adorned the tapestried walls. And the haunted room into which he crept "with a passion of fear, and a sneaking curiosity, terror-tainted, to hold communication with the past"—"*how,*" asks Lamb, "*shall they* build it up again?" [240]

In this old house and its garden, Lamb's imagination received its nurture. Such was his passion for the place that although he fancied "a romantic lake" only a few rods away, he never explored it because he could not break the spell which bound him to the house. "So far from a wish to roam, I would have drawn, methought, still closer the fences of my chosen prison; and have been hemmed in by a yet securer cincture of those excluding garden walls. . . . I was here as in a lonely temple." [241] "The solitude of childhood," he reflects, "is not so much the mother of thought, as it is the feeder of love, and silence, and admiration." [242]

"Blakesmoor" with its ample halls and ancestral treasures, gave Lamb an opportunity to glance beyond the humble confines of his own home at "the contrasting accidents of a great fortune." He pored over the mystic characters of the Blakesmoor scutcheon until, he says, "every dreg of peasantry purging off, I received into myself Very Gentility." "To have the feeling of gentility," he believes, "it is not necessary to have been born gentle . . . the claims of birth are ideal merely, and what herald shall go about to strip me of an idea? Is it trenchant to their swords? can it be hacked off as a spur can? or torn away like a tarnished garter?" [243] Lamb ends his musings with the thought that "as men, when they die, do not die all, so of their extinguished habitations there may be a hope—a germ to be revivified." [244]

In the Elia essay "New Year's Eve" he refers to the introspective tendency of his mind, and attempts to account for it. "That I am

---

[240] *Works*, vol. II, p. 155.
[241] Ibid.,
[242] Ibid.
[243] Ibid., p. 156.
[244] Op. cit., p. 157.

fond of indulging, beyond a hope of sympathy, in such introspection," he says, "may be the symptom of some sickly idiosyncracy. Or is it owing to another cause; simply, that being without wife or family, I have not learned to project myself enough out of myself; and having no offspring of my own to dally with, I turn back upon memory, and adopt my own early ideas, as my heir and favourite?" [245] As the letter-bell recalls to Hazlitt memories of the past, the peal of the bells ringing out the Old Year brings to Lamb's mind a train of recollections. "I have almost ceased to hope," he says, "and am sanguine only in the prospects of other (former) years. I plunge into forgone visions and conclusions. I encounter pellmell with past disappointments. I am armour-proof against old discouragements. I forgive, or overcome in fancy, old adversaries. I play over again *for love,* as the gamesters phrase it, games, for which I once paid so dear. I would scarce now have any of those untoward accidents and events of my life reversed. I would no more alter them than the incidents of some well-contrived novel. Methinks, it is better that I should have pined away seven of my goldenest years, when I was thrall to the fair hair, and fairer eyes, of Alice W——n, than that so passionate a love-adventure should be lost." [246]

This very much resembles the general strain in which Hazlitt writes in his essay "On the Feeling of Immortality in Youth." Both writers are, like Rousseau, distilling precious drops from the past. There is a similarity, too, in their recollection of romances whose memories they still cherish; and in the manner in which they recall their childhood. " . . . For the child Elia—that 'other me,'" Lamb says, " . . . I must take leave to cherish the remembrance of that young master. . . . I know how honest, how courageous (for a weakling) it was—how religious, how imaginative, how hopeful! From what have I fallen, if the child I remember was indeed myself,—and not some dissembling guardian, presenting a false identity, to give the rule to my unpracticed steps, and regulate the tone of my moral being?" [247] This idea of the high

---

[245] Ibid., pp. 28-29.
[246] Ibid., pp. 27-28.
[247] Ibid., p. 28.

instincts of childhood was a cornerstone of Wordsworth's philosophy, and although Lamb here gives the idea less exalted expression than either Wordsworth or Hazlitt, he is voicing essentially
the same thought.[248]

Lamb, like Hazlitt, contemplated the end of life. Counting the
probabilities of his "duration" he grudges "the expenditure of
moments and shortest periods like miser's farthings . . . I am not
content to pass away," he says, "like a weaver's shuttle." . . . I
would set up my tabernacle here. I am content to stand still at
the age to which I am arrived; I, and my friends: to be no younger,
no richer, no handsomer. I do not want to be weaned by age; or
drop, like mellow fruit, as they say, into the grave. Any altera-
tion on this earth of mine, in diet or in lodging, puzzles and dis-
composes me. My household gods plant a terrible fixed foot, and
are not rooted up without blood. They do not willingly seek
Lavinian shores. A new state of being staggers me." [249] The
disinclination to die is felt most strongly by Lamb in the winter
season. The blast that "nips and shrinks" arouses in him thoughts
of death. Then "all things allied to the unsubstantial, wait upon
that master feeling; cold, numbness, dreams, perplexity, moonlight
itself, with its shadowy and spectral appearances—that cold ghost
of the sun. . . . " [250] Hazlitt, writing on the same subject in his
essay "On the Fear of Death" also expresses a strong individual
attachment to life. "No young man," he says, "ever thinks he
shall die. He may believe that others will, or assent to the doctrine
that "all men are mortal" as an abstract proposition, but he is far
enough from bringing it home to himself individually." [251] This
closely parallels Lamb's thoughts on the same theme: "Not childhood alone, but the young man till thirty, never feels practically
that he is mortal. He knows it indeed, and if need were, he could
preach a homily on the fragility of life; but he brings it not home

---

[248] Lamb's essay, "New Year's Eve" appeared in the *London Magazine*,
January, 1821, and Hazlitt's paper "On the Feeling of Immortality in Youth"
was first published in the *Monthly Magazine*, March, 1827.

[249] *Works*, vol. II, p. 29.

[250] Ibid., p. 30.

[251] "On the Fear of Death," *Works*, vol. VI, p. 324. Originally published
in the *Round Table*, 1821-22.

to himself any more than in a hot June we can appropriate to our imagination the freezing days of December." [252]

The tender regard for children manifested by Wordsworth and Lamb may be considered one of the phases of the newly awakened sympathy for mankind which was a feature of the Romantic Revival. In Wordsworth, this sympathetic attitude toward childhood was accompanied by the belief that the child has enjoyed a pre-existence and has not yet shaken off the "clouds of glory" of his celestial home. Lamb's sympathetic understanding of children and his yearning affection for them had their source in his keen recollections of his own childhood, and in the survival in him of a child-like spirit. In his essay "Christ's Hospital Five-and-Thirty Years Ago" he recalls his school days with such poignancy, that sympathy is not only quickened for the joys and sorrows of Lamb's childhood, but for those of all children. Although he says that he writes of Coleridge and not of himself, Lamb is in part at least, recollecting his own youth. The manner in which he envelopes this playtime of his life with the romantic glamor of the past may be seen in his apostrophe to Coleridge: "Come back into memory, like as thou wert in the day-spring of thy fancies, with hope like a fiery column before thee—the dark pillar not yet turned—Samuel Taylor Coleridge—Logician, Metaphysician, Bard! How have I seen the casual passer through the Cloisters, stand still, entranced with admiration (while he weighed the disproportion between the *speech* and the *garb* of the young Mirandula), to hear thee unfold, in thy deep and sweet intonations, the mysteries of Jamblichus, or Plotinus . . . or reciting Homer in his Greek, or Pindar—while the walls of the old Grey Friars re-echoed to the accents of the *inspired charity-boy!*" [253]

In this same essay Lamb says that he was a "hypochondriac lad" and describes the vivid impressions made upon his sensitive mind by the rigorous school discipline. In "Witches and Other Night Fears" he speaks of the nervous fear he suffered as a child. "I never laid my head on my pillow," he says, "from the fourth to the seventh or eighth year of my life . . . without an assurance,

---

[252] "New Year's Eve," *Works*, vol. II, p. 29.
[253] "Christ's Hospital Five-and-Thirty Years Ago," *Works*, vol. II, p. 21.

which realized its own prophecy, of seeing some frightful spectre." [254] He is partially able to explain his fear by the pictures in Stackhouse's history of the Bible, over which he pored as a child, but how account, he asks, for dear little T. H., "that nurse-child of optimism," who starts at shapes, "unborrowed of tradition." Thus Lamb introduces the supernatural element into his musings on childhood. He does not, like Wordsworth, represent the child as bringing with him recollections of a heavenly sphere, but he attributes his childish terrors to some previous existence. He compares the effect of the fears of childhood to "the fear and dread" of Coleridge's Ancient Mariner, and concludes that the kind of fear depicted by Coleridge "is purely spiritual—that it is strong in proportion as it is objectless upon earth—that it predominates in the period of sinless infancy." [255] Could the problem of whence comes this fear be solved, it might, Lamb thinks, "afford some probable insight into our ante-mundane condition, and a peep at least into the shadow-land of pre-existence." [256] Addison in the *Spectator* (No. 12) has also written with sympathy of the fears of children. Observing the effect of ghost-stories upon a little boy, Addison remarks: . . . "I am mistaken if he ventures to go to Bed by himself this Twelve-month." [257] "Were I a Father, I should take a particular Care to preserve my Children from these little Horrors of Imagination, which they are apt to contract when they are young, and are not able to shake off when they are in Years." [258] Although Addison and Lamb are writing upon similar themes, it is only necessary to compare their essays to realize the difference not only in treatment of material but in outlook between the two essayists. Addison is concerned with the moral import of apparitions; and suggests "Reason and Religion" as a means of dealing with supernatural agencies. Lamb offers no solution. He only questions.

---

[254] "Witches and Other Night Fears," *Works,* vol. II, p. 67.
[255] Ibid., p. 68.
[256] Ibid.
[257] *The Spectator,* N. Y., 1907, pp. 47-48. (Everyman edition.)
[258] Ibid., p. 48.

The eighteenth century essayists frequently made use of the dream device in their papers. Lamb also clothes his thoughts in the form of dreams, and in "Dream Children: a Reverie" he imagines himself recounting to his two children the story of their great-grandmother Field. He recalls again the old house described in "Blakesmoor in H—shire" and his pleasure in roaming through its empty rooms and spacious gardens. Great pathos is lent this dream because the children Lamb pictures so vividly are but shadows. As they gradually grow fainter to his view, he fancies he hears them saying: "We are not of Alice, nor of thee, nor are we children at all. . . . We are nothing; less than nothing, and dreams. We are only what might have been, and must wait upon the tedious shores of Lethe millions of ages before we have existence, and a name." [259]   It would be difficult to imagine Rousseau or Hazlitt writing as follows of their "glowing image": "Suddenly turning to Alice, the soul of the first Alice looked out at her eyes with such a reality of re-presentment, that I became in doubt which of them stood there before me, or whose that bright hair was." [260]

Lamb enjoys putting his worst foot forward, and this is another phase of his self-revelation. He writes most frankly of his mental short-comings. . . . "My head," he says, "has not many mansions, nor spacious; and I have been obliged to fill it with such cabinet curiosities as it can hold without aching." [261]   In everything that relates to science, he is "a whole Encyclopedia behind the rest of the world"; [262] in figuring he has no skill; [263] *sentimentally* he is disposed to harmony, but *organically* he is incapable of a tune. [264] "I am entirely unacquainted," he confesses, "with the modern languages; and, like a better man than myself, have "small Latin and less Greek." I am a stranger to the shapes and texture of the commonest trees, herbs, flowers, . . . and am no less at a loss

---

[259] "Dream-Children; a Reverie," *Works*, vol. II, p. 103.
[260] Ibid.
[261] "The Old and New Schoolmaster," Ibid., p. 49.
[262] Ibid., p. 49.
[263] "South Sea House," Ibid., p. 2.
[264] "A Chapter on Ears," Ibid., p. 38.

among purely town objects, tools, engines, mechanic processes." [265]

His shortcomings, Lamb would have us believe, are not all intellectual ones. Under "culinary disappointments" he is "impatient and querulous." [266] Concerning his appetite for food and drink, he indulges in the exaggeration of which he was fond. He has a most inordinate appetite, he says, "not for wealth, not for vast possessions . . . not for glory, not for fame, not for applause, . . . nor yet for pleasure, properly so called, . . . but an appetite, in its coarsest and least metaphorical sense—an appetite for *food*." [267] Strong drink and tobacco are also set down by Lamb among his follies, and while his "Confessions of a Drunkard" should not be taken literally, there is a ring of truth in the essay, which is borne out by facts in Lamb's life. The following paragraph, the reader suspects, was written out of Lamb's experience. "To be an object of compassion to friends, of derision to foes; to be suspected by strangers, stared at by fools; to be esteemed dull when you cannot be witty, to be applauded for witty when you know that you have been dull; to be called upon for the extemporaneous exercise of that faculty which no premeditation can give; to be spurred on to efforts which end in contempt; to be set on to provoke mirth which procures the procurer hatred; to give pleasure and to be paid with squinting malice; to swallow draughts of life-destroying wine which are to be distilled into airy breath to tickle vain auditors; to mortgage miserable tomorrows for nights of madness; to waste whole seas of time upon those who pay it back in little inconsiderable drops of grudging applause—are the wages of buffoonery and death." [268]

In "The Wedding" Lamb writes amusingly of his inclination to laugh upon serious occasions: "I do not know what business I have to be present in solemn places. I cannot divest me of an unseasonable disposition to levity upon the most awful occasions." [269] This disposition of Lamb to perceive the ludicrous probably led him to say: "I love a *Fool*—as naturally, as if I were of kith and kin to

[265] "The Old and New Schoolmaster," *Works*, vol. II, p. 49.
[266] "Grace before Meat," Ibid., p. 95.
[267] "Edax on Appetite," Ibid., vol. I, p. 119.
[268] "Confessions of a Drunkard," Ibid., p. 135.
[269] "The Wedding," Ibid., vol. II, p. 241.

him." [270] "I have never," he says, "made an acquaintance . . . that lasted; or a friendship that answered; with any that had not some tincture of the absurd in their characters." [271]

But even more delightful than Lamb's revelation of his foibles, is his frank enthusiasm for the things he likes. He sighed not after riches, or the unobtainable, but extracted the deepest pleasure from simple things which are free to all or which his humble circumstances made it possible for him to afford. The very limitations of his poverty yielded him enjoyment. There was "pleasure in eating strawberries before they became quite common—in the first dish of peas, while they were yet dear—to have them for . . . a treat." [272] In his essay "Old China," Bridget Elia deplores the better state of hers and her brother's finances. "What treat can we have now?" she asks. "It is the very little more that we allow ourselves beyond what the actual poor can get at, that makes what I call a treat." [273] Lamb reveled in the things which can be enjoyed by all; he was in love with the green earth, the town and country, the "rural solitudes, and the sweet security of streets." [274] Musing, he inquires: "Sun, and sky, and breeze, and solitary walks, and summer holidays, and the greenness of fields, and the delicious juices of meats and fishes, and society, and the cheerful glass, and candle-light, and fireside conversations, and innocent vanities, and jests and *irony itself*—do these things go out with life?" [275] To this list of Lamb's enjoyments, should be added his love of books, and his fondness for people.

Lamb's books were among his dearest possessions. He not only writes of his favorite authors in his familiar essays, but the essays themselves are frequently a tissue of thoughts and fancies suggested by his reading. That which he read became a part of him, and, filtered through his sensitive imagination, lends a grace and flavor to his writing. His essays, like those of Hazlitt

---

[270] "All Fool's Day," *Works*, vol. II, p. 44.
[271] Ibid.
[272] "Old China," Ibid., p. 250.
[273] Ibid., pp. 250-51.
[274] "New Year's Eve," Ibid., p. 29.
[275] Ibid.

and Hunt, abound in allusions, quotations, recollections of books
read: of characters, scenes, situations, which are used by way of
illustration to give point to an idea, or as frequently happens, because the essayist wishes to share his pleasure with the reader.
Lamb's taste in reading was a catholic one. "I have no repugnances," he tells us. "Shaftesbury is not too genteel for me, nor
Jonathan Wild too low. I can read anything which I call a
book." [276] But he says there are things in that shape which he
cannot allow for such. Among the books which are no books he
includes scientific treatises, the writings of Hume, Gibbon, Robertson, Soame Jenyns, Paley's *Moral Philosophy,* and all those works
which "no gentleman's library should be without." [277] Hunt declared the backs of Lamb's books "a discipline of humanity. The
depths of philosophy and poetry are there, the innermost passages
of the human heart." But in spite of Lamb's breadth of taste in
reading he had certain preferences. In "Mackery End, in Hertfordshire," he compares his own and his sister's taste in reading,
and says that he has little concern in the progress of events, or in
"the fluctuations of fortune" in fiction.[278] Lamb poignantly expresses his affection for his books, when, musing on the shortness
of life he asks: "And you, my midnight darlings, my Folios! must
I part with the intense delight of having you (huge armfuls) in
my embraces? Must knowledge come to me, if it come at all, by
some awkward experiment of intuition, and no longer by this
familiar process of reading?" [279]

One of Lamb's pronounced likings was for people, and he had
the gift not only of attracting friends, but of keeping them.
He had certain antipathies, however, of which he humorously
writes. Though he liked Quaker ways and Quaker worship, he
couldn't like the Quakers—"to live with them." "I must have,"
he says, "books, pictures, theatres, chit-chat, scandal, jokes,
ambiguities and a thousand whim-whams, which their simpler taste
can do without." [280] Neither could he learn to like Scotchmen.

---

[276] "Detached Thoughts on Books and Reading," *Works*, vol. II, p. 172.
[277] Ibid.
[278] "Mackery End, in Hertfordshire," Ibid., p. 75.
[279] "New Year's Eve," *Ibid.*, p. 30.
[280] "Imperfect Sympathies," Ibid., p. 63.

In analyzing the difference in his own type of mind and that of a Scotchman, Lamb very cleverly describes his own characteristics, under the editorial "they": "The light that lights them is not steady and polar, but mutable and shifting: waxing, and again waning. Their conversation is accordingly. They will throw out a random word in or out of season, and be content to let it pass for what it is worth. They cannot speak always as if they were upon their oath—but must be understood, speaking or writing, with some abatement. They seldom wait to mature a proposition, but e'en bring it to market in the green ear. . . . Their minds . . . are suggestive merely." [281] As for Jews he has no disrespect for them "in the abstract," but old prejudices cling about him, and he cannot believe "that a few fine words, such as candour, liberality, the light of a nineteenth century, can close up the breaches of so deadly a disunion." [282] As to negroes, Lamb loves what Fuller calls these "images of God cut in ebony." But he admits, "I should not like to associate with them, to share my meals and my good-nights with them." [283] In his "Preface to the Last Essays" Lamb says that Elia "chose his companions for some individuality of character which they manifested. Hence, not many persons of science, and few professed *literati,* were of his councils. They were, for the most part, persons of an uncertain fortune. . . . His *intimados,* to confess a truth, were in the world's eye a ragged regiment. He found them floating on the surface of society; and the colour, or something else, in the weed pleased him." [284] Here Lamb is again engaging in that exaggeration which so much amused him. The friend of Coleridge, Wordsworth, Hazlitt, Leigh Hunt, Barry Cornwall, Crabb Robinson, Procter and Talfourd, could scarcely be said to have found his friends "floating on the surface of society."

Lamb has left in his familiar essays not only a record of his recreations and his social diversions, but of those long hours spent in a counting house, in that workaday world, where he earned his living. "Melancholy was the transition," he writes, "at fourteen

---

[281] Op. cit., p. 59.
[282] Ibid., pp. 61-62.
[283] Ibid., p. 62.
[284] "Last Essays of Elia," Preface, Ibid., p. 152.

from the abundant playtime, and the frequently intervening vacations of school days, to the eight, nine, and sometimes ten hours' a-day attendance at a counting house." Sundays, when he had the day to himself, he missed "the cheerful cries of London, the music, and the ballad-singers—the buzz and stirring murmur of the streets." He was shut out from prints and pictures, and all "the endless succession of knacks and gewgaws." There were no "book stalls deliciously to idle over. No busy faces to recreate the idle man." [285] In "The Superannuated Man" Lamb has left an affecting picture of himself arrived at the age of fifty, with no prospect of being emancipated from his labor. Then came a pension and liberty, and Lamb describes his reactions to his new freedom: "I could scarce trust myself with myself. It was like passing out of Time into Eternity—for it is a sort of Eternity for a man to have all his Time to himself." [286] "I am no longer, clerk to the Firm of etc. I am Retired Leisure." [287]

In spite of Lamb's fanciful and exaggerated manner of expressing himself, much of his self-revelation, as the foregoing shows, is of the most realistic kind. His frankness and his objective manner of writing of himself show his ability to view himself with such complete detachment that he could call attention to his own shortcomings and picture himself as he appeared to others. Lamb's self-revelation would, however, lose a great deal of its real charm and spiritual significance, were it not for the romantic elements which suffuse it.

Leigh Hunt has left the record of his personality in his *Autobiography* and in his familiar essays. His story of his life differs from the self-revelation of Hazlitt and Lamb in degree and kind. He does not possess a sense of the dramatic, which would enable him, like Hazlitt, to disclose the innermost workings of his heart; he has not, like Lamb, the kind of humor which would cause him to laugh good-naturedly at his own shortcomings. He has however in common with his fellow essayists certain characteristics that give vitality and interest to his story: a zest for life, a vivid recollection of the past, the power to observe closely, and a

---

[285] "The Superannuated Man," *Works*, vol. II, pp. 193, 194.
[286] Ibid., p. 195.
[287] Ibid., p. 198.

familiar, conversational manner of writing about himself and whatever interests him. He resembles Hazlitt in his passion for truth and justice, and is like Lamb in his sympathy with others.

Hunt's self-revelation is more objective than either Lamb's or Hazlitt's. At first glance it would seem to have fewer romantic elements, to be more matter-of-fact and commonplace than that of his fellow essayists. But a closer examination of Hunt's writing reveals that he is imaginative in a romantic sense, and that his very commonplaces are one phase of his romanticism. Hunt distinguishes between the world of fact and that of fancy; that is between the commonplace and the imaginative, or the material and the spiritual. He uses these terms interchangeably, and without philosophic nicety. He assures us that he knows nothing of metaphysics. "Our faculty," he says, "such as it is, is rather instinctive than reasoning; rather physical than metaphysical; rather sentient   because   it   loves   much,   than   because   it   knows much. . . ." [288]

Frequently in his essays Hunt is preoccupied with things, with the objects about him, with all the minutiae that constitute everyday living. We know the most intimate details of his daily life in a way that we do not know those of Lamb or Hazlitt. It is characteristic of Hunt, however, that he seldom describes objects as they are in themselves, unattended by the feeling which they call forth. His emotional responses to the commonplace things of life, and the associations which objects recall are the theme of many of his familiar essays. He tells us, for instance, that he likes a hard bed, because he was used to this kind at school, and he describes the delicious feeling of repose that he experiences in lying down at night; or how he feels on a cold morning when it is time to get up and the house begins to stir. The steaming kettle, the easy chair drawn up before the crackling fire, the drawn curtains, the kitten at play, the table set for breakfast, the boughs outside of his window, outlined against the sky, all these things he describes with such loving observation that his affection for the homely and domestic things of life is strongly revealed. . . . "Our secret passion," he says, "is for a homely room in a cottage, with perfect quiet, a book or two, and a sprig of rosemary in the win-

---

[288] "On the Realities of the Imagination," *Indicator*, pt. I, p. 173.

dow. . . . Add to this a watch-dog at a distance, and a moaning wind, no matter how "melancholy," provided it does not blow a tempest . . . and we drop to sleep in a transport of comfort." [289]

Imagination is the well-spring of Hunt's interest in the commonplace. "We are among those," he says, "who believe with the old romance of Heliodorus, that under circumstances which affect the earliest periods of existence, familiar objects are not without their influence upon the imagination." [290] His desire to invest the commonplace with imagination may be seen from his essay "Amiableness Superior to Intellect," in which he says that commonplaces "are the common clay of which human intercourse is made, and therefore are as respectable in our eyes as any other of the ordinary materials of our planet, however desirable we may be of warming them into flowers. Nay, flowers they have, provided the clay be pure and kindly." [291] Hunt also considered the commonplace romantic, and in "Romance of the Commonplace" writes, "Every sentiment . . . pushed to excess, bears, from that excess, a character of romance: even dulness may be romantic." [292] The power of common objects, through the association of ideas, to call forth imagination, is, of course, one of the tenets of nineteenth century romanticism. He expresses this idea when he says: "The beauty of this unlimited power of suggestion in writing is, that you may take up the driest and most commonplace of all possible subjects, and strike a light out of it to warm your intellect and your heart by. . . . It is the benevolent provision of Nature, that, in proportion as you feel the necessity of extracting interest from common things, you are enabled to do so." [293]

Hunt was keenly interested in the imaginative faculty of the mind, and in addition to his work "Imagination and Fancy" he frequently discusses imagination in his familiar essays. He conceived the universe in which he dwelt as consisting of two worlds: "the world that we can measure with line and rule, and the world that we feel with our hearts and imaginations. To be sensible to

---

[289] "Beds and Bedrooms," *Men, Women and Books*, p. 73.
[290] Ibid., p. 74.
[291] *The Seer*, vol. II, pp. 134-35.
[292] Ibid., p. 130.
[293] Ibid., pp. 160-61.

the truth of only one of these, is to know truth but by halves." [294]
He defines matter-of-fact as "our perception of the grosser and
more external shapes of truth." "Fiction represents the residuum
and the mystery. To love matter of fact is to have a lively sense
of the visible and immediate; to love fiction is to have as lively a
sense of the possible and the remote." Fiction is of course used
here in the sense of the imaginative. "These two senses," he continues, "if they exist at all, are of necessity as real, the one as the
other." [295] In his essay "A Novel Party" he plays with the idea
that the creations of the novelists have a reality. "Common
physical palpability," he says, "is only a proof of mortality." [296]
"But the immortal people in Pope and Fielding, the deathless
generations in Chaucer, in Shakespeare, in Goldsmith, in Sterne,
and Le Sage, and Cervantes, acquaintances and friends who remain for ever the same . . . —what is the amount of the actual
effective existence of millions of Jacksons and Tompkinses compared with theirs?" [297] Hunt has expressed a similar idea in his
essay "On the Realities of the Imagination," where he says: "The
advantage, nay even the test, of seeing and hearing, at any time,
is not in the seeing and hearing, but in the ideas we realize, and
the pleasure we derive. Intellectual objects, therefore, inasmuch as
they come home to us, are as true a part of the stock of nature,
as visible ones." [298] It is necessary to understand this attitude of
Hunt's toward what constituted reality for him in order to appreciate the romantic elements of his self-revelation.

It has been noted that Hunt said that to love fiction was to have
a sense of "the possible and the remote." This, of course, is just
another way of expressing the romantic glamor of the past. Hunt,
like Lamb and Hazlitt, found pleasure in turning to the past and
living over again in imagination events connected with his early
life. In his *Autobiography* he says: "Life often seems a dream;
but there are occasions when the sudden reappearance of early
objects, by the intensity of their presence, not only renders the

---

[294] "Fiction and Matter of Fact," *Men, Women, and Books*, p. 3.
[295] Ibid., pp. 3-4.
[296] Ibid., p. 57.
[297] Ibid., p. 58.
[298] *Indicator*, pt. I, p. 178.

interval less present to the consciousness than a very dream, but makes the portion of life which preceded it seem to have been the most real of all things, and our only undreaming time." [299]

In common with his fellow essayists, Hunt muses upon death and the necessity of giving up the good things of life. In his essay, "An Earth Upon Heaven," he turns in thought to a future state of existence, which he contemplates not in a tragic or disillusioned manner, but in a joyful one. "Frenchmen have died sitting in their chairs, full-dressed and powdered. I have a better taste in mortality than that; but I think I could drop off with a decent compromise between thought and forgetfulness, sitting with my pipe by a fireside in an old elbow chair." [300] He expresses the hope that he may become accustomed to heaven, by passing through other heavens of "a less superhuman nature." [301] "Familiar as we are," he says, "both with joy and sorrow, and accustomed to surprises and strange sights of imagination, it is difficult to fancy even the delight of suddenly emerging into a new and boundless state of existence, where everything is marvelous, and opposed to our experience. We could wish to take gently to it; to be loosed not entirely at once." [302]. Like Lamb, he would not lose the good things of this life: "Earth and its capabilities—are these nothing? And are they to come to nothing? Is there no beautiful realization of the fleeting type that is shown us? No body to this shadow? No quenching to this taught and continued thirst? No arrival at these natural homes and resting-places, which are so heavenly to our imaginations, even though they be built of clay, and are situate in the fields of our infancy?" [303] "To realize everything that we have justly desired on earth, will *be* heaven," Hunt believes, and he makes a list of the "items" that he would like to have in another world. They include a friend, "generous, just, entertaining," with whom he will read the poets, and renew an earthly evening "picked out of a dozen Christmases"; a mistress, "good-

---

[299] *Autobiography*, p. 41.

[300] "Coffee-Houses and Smoking," *Essays (Selected)* (Everyman Edition), pp. 43-44.

[301] *The Companion*, p. 170.

[302] Ibid.

[303] Ibid.

tempered, laughing, serious"; books—"Shakespeare and Spenser, he says, "should write us *new ones!*" [304] Hunt ends his musings upon a future life in humorous fashion, indulging in the fancy which he so much enjoyed. "For horses, we shall ride a Pegasus, or Ariosto's Hippogriff, or Sinbad's Roc. We mean, for our parts, to ride them all, having a passion for fabulous animals. . . . There will be enough cold in the winter to make a fire pleasant of an evening. The fire will be of sweet-smelling turf and sunbeams; but it will have a look of coal. If we choose, now and then we shall even have inconveniences." [305]

Hunt shares with Wordsworth and Lamb a deep understanding and love of childhood. Full of pathos is his essay on "Deaths of Little Children," a pathos similar to that with which Wordsworth has invested the graves of children in "We are Seven." "The remembered innocence and endearments of a child stand us instead of virtues that have died older," Hunt says.[306] It is characteristic of his philosophy that out of sorrow he extracts happiness, and in the loss of a child, he finds balm for his grief. His thought is that those who have lost a child are never without one. The memory of the child lives on in their hearts, while that of their other children is lost, as they grow older. Writing within sight of the grave of a loved one, he says: "It is the existence of that grave which doubles every charm of the spot; which links the pleasures of our childhood and manhood together; which puts a hushing tenderness in the winds, and a patient joy upon the landscape; which seems to unite heaven and earth, mortality and immortality, the grass of the tomb and the grass of the green field: and gives a more maternal aspect to the whole kindness of nature." [307]

Quite different in the sentiment it evokes is the incident Hunt relates in his essay "Twelfth Night," of the small urchin, "one of those equivocal animal-spirits of the streets." Standing with his nose against the window of a pastry cook's, the child views with interest another boy inside the shop trying to choose between two

---

[304] Op. cit., pp. 171-172.
[305] Ibid., p. 173.
[306] *Indicator*, pt. I, p. 183.
[307] Ibid.

buns. Hunt follows in imagination the emotions of the boy on the outside: "He shifts the expression of his mouth and the shrug of his body at every perilous approximation which the chooser makes to a second-rate bunn. (sic.) He is like a bowler following the nice inflections of the bias; for he wishes him nothing but success: the occasion is too great for envy. He feels all the generous sympathy of a knight of old, when he saw another within an ace of winning some glorious prize, and his arm doubtful of the blow." [308]   Hunt's description of the boy as "the nightingale of mud and cold," recalls Lamb's comparison of the young chimney-sweepers to the matin lark.[309]

Also very different in nature is Hunt's philosophizing on childhood in his "Thoughts on Human Nature." [310]   "Nature," he reflects, . . . "appears to succeed best in making childhood and youth. The symphony is a little perturbed; but in what a sprightly manner the air sets off! What purity! What grace! What touching simplicity! Then comes sin, or the notion of it, and 'breaks the fair music.' " [311]   Do men die, Hunt questions, in order that life may be renewed as often as possible, or do children grow old "that our consciousness may attain to some better mode of being through a rough path?" No answer is given by Nature, he says, but her "calm and resolute silence tells us at once to hope for the future and to do our best to enjoy the present." [312]

"Cruelty to Children," one of Hunt's essays in the *Companion*,[313] offers a strong contrast to his other essays on childhood in its practical wisdom and common-sense viewpoint, and shows he could be as didactic as any eighteenth century essayist when he chose. "The great art of being a good parent," he says, "consists in setting a good example, and in maintaining that union of dispassionate firmness with habitual good humor, which a child never *thinks* of treating with disrespect." [314]

---

[308] "Twelfth Night," *The Seer*, v. 2, p. 118.
[309] "The Praise of Chimney Sweepers," *Works*, vol. II.
[310] *Indicator*, pt. II, pp. 62-63.
[311] Ibid., p. 62.
[312] Ibid., pp. 62-63.
[313] *The Companion*, p. 217 ff.
[314] Ibid., pp. 219-20.

Much of Hunt's self-revelation is most realistic, especially in his *Autobiography*.[315] In the early chapters, he follows a chronological arrangement in telling of his ancestors, childhood, school days and youth. Thereafter he makes little attempt to date events in his life, but presents its chief interests and happenings in successive chapters, like separate essays in form. Chapter six, for example, is devoted to his recollection of famous singers, dancers and actors; chapter seven to an account of his favorite books and authors, and to his entrance into theatrical criticism; chapter nine to the *Examiner;* chapter ten to his literary acquaintances; chapter eleven to political characters. By thus arranging his material by subject, Hunt succeeds in giving a particularly vivid and interesting impression of his life. Moreover, he is writing from the vantage ground of ripe age, and he continually views his life in retrospect, commenting upon his decisions and actions, feelings and emotions, pointing out his mistakes, subjecting himself to an admirable self-criticism, free from sentimentality and self-pity. This objective manner of viewing himself constitutes one of the most realistic features of the *Autobiography*. Hunt's realistic method is further evidenced in a study of the characteristics of his ancestors, which he finds reproduced in himself—"a man is but his parents, or some other of his ancestors, drawn out." [316] Such genetic study, sometimes carried to extremes, was a feature of eighteenth century biography. Hunt does not overemphasize his inherited traits, but devotes sufficient attention to them to supply the key to his character. "I may call myself," he says, "in every sense of the word . . . a son of mirth and melancholy." [317] On his father's side he came from a line of "creoles and claret drinkers, very polite and clerical," and on the maternal side his forbears were "sailors and rough subjects, with a mitigation . . . of Quakerism." [318] His mother's timidity and melancholy strove in him with the gay, happy, carefree temperament and "animal spirits" inherited from his father.

---

[315] As has already been noted this work is included in a study of the familiar essay because of its essay-like character.
[316] *Autobiography*, p. 37.
[317] Ibid., p. 28.
[318] Ibid., p. 18.

Hunt does not, like Hazlitt, indulge in self-probing, or in minute analysis of his sensations and emotions. He states simply, certain facts concerning himself which are important indexes to his character, as when he says: "I never in my life had any personal ambition whatsoever, but that of adding to the list of authors, and doing some good as a cosmopolite." [319] In spite of hardships and disappointments which might have embittered another, he is able to write: "I am now in my seventy-fourth year, and I have seen a good deal of the world, the dark side as well as the light, and I say that human nature is a very good and kindly thing, and capable of all sorts of virtues. . . . To evils I have owed some of my greatest blessings." [320]

Like his fellow-essayists, Hunt reveals himself in writing of the things he liked best. In recalling them, he frequently mingles the romantic with the realistic. Books, music and the theatre were among his chief enjoyments, and his *Autobiography* and familiar essays are the richer in consequence. Books were his constant companions—"a never-ceasing consolation." As a schoolboy he developed a passion for reading which remained with him all his life. "How I loved," he says, "those little six-penny numbers containing whole poets! I doted on their size; I doted on their type, on their ornaments, on their wrappers containing lists of other poets, and on the engravings from Kirk. I bought them over and over again, and used to get up select sets which disappeared like buttered crumpets; for I could resist neither giving them away, nor possessing them." [321] Hunt's favorites in his youth, were Spenser, Collins, Gray and the *Arabian Nights,* and Spenser continued to be his life-long favorite.[322] He fell passionately in love, he says, with Collins and Gray, and wrote a poem called *Winter,* as a result of reading Thomson.[323] In later life he spent much of his time in his study surrounded by his favorite works; when he went to prison, his books accompanied him; when he sailed for Italy his favorite volumes went too, and were the solace of that ill-fated

---

[319] Op. cit., p. 133.
[320] Ibid., p. 220.
[321] *Ibid.,* pp. 69-70.
[322] Ibid., p. 71.
[323] Ibid., pp. 69-70.

journey. . . . "I can hardly be said to have ever been without a book," he writes, "for if not in my hand, it was at my side, or in my pocket." [324]   The magic that a book held for Hunt, he has well expressed in his essay "Breakfast in Summer." "We read, in old stories," he says, "of enchanters who drew gardens out of snow; and of tents no bigger than a nut-shell, which opened out over a whole army. Of like nature is the magic of a book,—a casket, from which you may draw out, at will, bowers to sit under, and affectionate beauties to sit by, and have trees, flowers, and an exquisite friend, all at one spell." [325]

The books he liked to have about him most were Chaucer, Spenser, the minor poems of Milton, the *Arabian Nights*, Theocritus, Ariosto, and "such old good-natured speculations as Plutarch's *Morals*." [326]   Hunt's favorite authors furnish the subject matter of several of his essays, and are the occasion for some of his best prose writing. "It is true," he says, "one forgets one's books while writing—at least they say so. For my part, I think I have them in a sort of sidelong mind's eye; like a second thought, which is more like a water-fall, or a whispering wind." [327]   Whatever his subject, it furnishes him an excuse to introduce some comment on his literary favorites. For instance the weather, the subject of his paper "Fine Days in January and February," makes him think of Chaucer, from whom he quotes, and after commenting upon him, he begs the reader's pardon for the digression, and says: "It is . . . an old fancy of ours to associate the ideas of Chaucer with that of an early and vigorous manifestation of light and pleasure." [328]

Hunt had, like Lamb, an affection not only for the authors of his books, but for the books themselves. "Sitting . . . among my books," he says, "walled round with all the comfort and protection which they and my fire-side could afford me . . . I began to consider how I loved the authors of those books: how I loved them, too, not only for the imaginative pleasures they afford me, but for

---

[324] *Autobiography*, p. 151.
[325] *The Seer*, vol. I, p. 84.
[326] "My Books," *Indicator*, pt. II, p. 141.
[327] Ibid., p. 138.
[328] *The Companion*, p. 181.

their making me love the very books themselves, and delight to be in contact with them." [329] That books were his solace is clear from many passages in his essays. "I entrench myself in my books," he writes, "equally against sorrow and the weather." . . . "If a melancholy thought is importunate, I give another glance at my *Spenser*. When I speak of being in contact with my books, I mean it literally. I like to lean my head against them." [330] In his love of "bookstall urbanity" Hunt says he yields to none. But he likes to see his favorite purchases neatly bound, for most of them "a plain good old binding," but for his *Arabian Nights* the binding should be "in as fine and flowery a style as possible," with "an engraving to every dozen pages." [331] "May I confess," he asks, "that the passage which I recollect with the greatest pleasure in Cicero, is where he says that books delight us at home, *and are no impediment abroad;* travel with us, ruralize with us . . . I am so much of this opinion, that I do not care to be anywhere without having a book or books at hand, and . . . stuff the coach or post-chaise with them whenever I travel." [332]

Hunt's reading covered a wider range than that of either Lamb or Hazlitt, and furnished him with a wealth of apt quotations which adorn and enrich his essays.

Hunt reveals his love of music in two of his essays, "The Piano-Forte" and in "Why Sweet Music Produces Sadness." He mentions his liking for old songs and other musical compositions in his *Autobiography* and in several of his familiar essays. He calls music "one of God's goods," and says, "if we do not avail ourselves of it . . . we turn not our hands, ears and souls to their just account, nor reap half the benefit we might from the very air that sounds it." [333] He deplores the fact that the poor in England have not the opportunity to enjoy music, and attributes it to the rich having monopolized music, and made it costly.[334] The greatest men, Hunt says, have been lovers of music, and in consequence

---

[329] "My Books," *Indicator*, pt. II, p. 136.
[330] Ibid., p. 136-37.
[331] Ibid., p. 141.
[332] Ibid., p. 143.
[333] "The Piano-Forte," *The Seer*, vol. II, p. 90.
[334] Ibid., p. 88.

have united both action and contemplation. His answer to the question "why sweet music produces sadness?" is, that "we have an instinctive sense of the fugitive and perishing nature of all sweet things,—of beauty, of youth, of life; of all those fair shows of the world, of which music seems to be the voice, and of whose transitory nature it reminds us most when it is most beautiful, because it is then that we most regret our mortality." [335]

In his *Autobiography,* Hunt recalls the songs that were popular when he was a boy; they abounded in Strephons and Delias, he says, and "the association of early ideas with that kind of commonplace" [336] gave him more than a tolerance for it. This kind of sophisticated sentiment which made it possible for men and women to play at being shepherds and shepherdesses, finds a responsive chord in him: "I think of the many heartfelt smiles that must have welcomed love letters and verses containing that sophisticate imagery, and of the no less genuine tears that were shed over the documents when faded; and criticism is swallowed up in those human drops." [337] He attributes to his sympathy with such sentiment his interest in the works of Shenstone, and in the correspondence of the countesses of Hertford and Pomfret, and of Lady Luxborough. "The feeling was true," he says, "though the expression was sophisticate and a fashion; and they who cannot see the feeling for the mode, do the very thing which they think they scorn; that is, sacrifice the greater consideration for the less." [338] He recalls his pleasure in finding on a bookstall two songs which were the only ones he remembered singing as a child. "I looked on them," he says, "with the accumulated tenderness of sixty-three years of age. . . . What a difference between the little smooth-faced boy at his mother's knee, encouraged to lift up his voice to the piano-forte, and the battered grey-headed senior, looking again, for the first time, on what he had sung at the distance of more than half a century! . . . There I stood; and Wardour Street, every street, all London, as it now exists, became to me as if it had never been." [339]

---

[335] "Why Sweet Music Produces Sadness," *The Seer,* vol. II, p. 103.
[336] *Autobiography,* p. 38.
[337] Ibid.
[338] Ibid.
[339] Ibid., pp. 40-41.

This brief summary will emphasize the fact that a great deal of the self-revelation of Hazlitt, Lamb and Hunt contains romantic elements. In the frankness and fulness with which they reveal themselves, as well as in the romantic coloring of their writing, they differ from the essayists of the eighteenth century. Addison and Steele often write in the first person, tell of their own experiences, and take the reader into their confidence, but they are not personal or intimate in the manner of the later familiar essayists, nor do they ever write of themselves with the passionate intensity which characterizes the self-revelation of Hazlitt, Lamb and Hunt. As one critic has well observed, the personal element in the essays of Addison and Steele "is no greater than that found in the most objective writers,—in dramatists, novelists, or short-story writers. . . . We see very clearly Steele's opinions on duelling, on women, on marriage; and in a sense we thus come to know his personality. But in the same sense we know Shakespeare in his dramas, or Thackeray in his novels." [340] Moreover the periodical essayists were hampered in their self-revelation by the use of fictitious mouthpieces. The "lucubrations" of Mr. Spectator or of Isaac Bickerstaff are not strongly individual, and at times it is difficult to determine who is behind the mask. On the contrary, the self-revelation of Lamb would never be mistaken for that of Hunt or Hazlitt. It is the strong individuality which stamps the work of these three essayists which makes their self-revelation different from what went before. This individuality expresses itself in both a romantic and realistic manner. The romantic coloring is particularly evident in the way past events are recalled, especially scenes and incidents remembered from childhood. In writing of the things which have given them pleasure, as well as of their sorrows and disappointments, Hazlitt, Lamb and Hunt have left highly individualized portraits of themselves. The realistic details mingled with the romantic elements of their self-revelation give the necessary contrast and lend verisimilitude. It is the blending of the romantic and realistic which constitutes the great charm of the self-revelation of these essayists.

---

[340] Prof. P. V. D. Shelly, "The Familiar Essay," *University of Pennsylvania. Public Lectures,* 1916-17, p. 245.

Chapter VI

IMAGINATION AND EXALTATION OF FEELING

Perhaps the greatest difference in the work of the early nineteenth century from what had gone before is that it contains elements which appeal to the emotions and the imagination in a manner new to the essay. The familiar essayists, like the Romantic poets, viewed the world afresh, and in their search for truth looked deep within their own hearts. Their lyrical cries represent not only a revolt against restraint, convention, imitation, and a narrow social order, but a delight in the free expression of their own personalities. And their self-revelation is not confined to conscious outpouring of spirit, but manifests itself in the individuality which stamps their work and colors the whole fabric of their thought. They write to a large extent out of their own experience, and spin their essays from the stuff of life itself. The individuality of their work is intensified by the imagination and fancy with which it is suffused. This is particularly true of Lamb's essays, in which the play of fancy continually reveals fresh aspects of his personality and gives added flavor to his writing. Hunt and Hazlitt also reveal themselves through the imaginative element of their work. Hunt creates for himself an ideal world in which he loves to dwell, surrounded by the pleasing images his mind calls forth. The way in which he invests the ordinary things of life with imagination serves to reveal the man. A pebble, a drop of rain upon the window, the sight of bricks and mortar on a hot day, are sufficient to start a train of recollection and imaginative reflection. By means of impassioned recollection Hazlitt unfolds his past life, revealing not only the things from which he has derived intense pleasure, but also his disappointments, and the unsatisfied yearning of his heart. His personality is further revealed in his search for truth. His uncompromising spirit goes unsatisfied in its search for the ideal, and hence the elements of struggle and revolt which characterize much of his work.

220

The familiar essays of these writers display a wide range of imagination, which runs the scale from light and entertaining fancy to passionate intensity. Lamb has a fanciful way of pressing home his subject which lends charm and freshness to his observations. His figures of speech are original and unexpected, but never far-fetched. He says, for example, that the garb and stillness of the Quakers "present a uniformity, tranquil and herd-like—as in a pasture—'forty feeding like one.' . . . Every Quakeress is a lily, and when they come up in bands to their Whitsun-conferences, whitening the easterly streets of the metropolis from all parts of the United Kingdom, they show like troops of the Shining Ones." [341] He frequently invests the most ordinary things with fancy, as when he writes of playing cards: "The pretty antic habits, like heralds in a procession—the gay triumph-assuring scarlets— the contrasting deadly-killing sables—the 'hoary majesty of spades' —Pam in all his glory!" The game might go on "pictureless," Lamb says, but "stripped of all that is imaginative" in it, it would "degenerate into mere gambling." [342] Lamb's figures of speech often are humorous, as when he speaks of himself as "a votary of the desk—a notched and cropped scrivener—one that sucks his sustenance . . . through a quill." He whimsically describes his "enfranchised quill, that has plodded all the morning among the cart-rucks of figures and ciphers," as it "frisks and curvets so at its ease over the flowery carpet-ground of a midnight dissertation." [343] No one would claim that such figurative writing is poetic, but it shows admirable fancy, a humorous dalliance with metaphor and simile, an original perception which hovers on the borderland of poetic imagination.

Lamb's imagination at times rises above the fanciful to the truly poetical. The imagery and figurative expressions and the rhythmic beauty of the language in many of the essays of Elia are more characteristic of poetry than of prose. Such, for example, is the passage on silence in "A Quakers' Meeting": "Dost thou love silence deep as that 'before the winds were made'? go not out into

---

[341] "A Quaker's Meeting," *Works*, vol. II, p. 48.
[342] "Mrs. Battle's Opinions on Whist," Ibid., pp. 34-35.
[343] "Oxford in the Vacation," Ibid., p. 8.

the wilderness, descend not into the profundities of the earth; shut
not thy casements; nor pour wax into the little cells of thy ears,
with little-faith'd self-mistrusting Ulysses. Retire with me into a
Quakers' Meeting." [344]   Lamb speaks of silence as—"eldest of
things, language of old Night, primitive Discourse." [345]   He often
gives his figurative description added beauty by weaving into it
some literary allusion, as when he writes: "Not so sweetly sang
Plumer, as thou sangest, mild, child-like, pastoral M—; a flute's
breathing less divinely whispering than thy Arcadian melodies,
when, in tones worthy of Arden, thou didst chant that song sung
by Amiens to the banished Duke, which proclaims the winter wind
more lenient than for a man to be ungrateful." [346]   He compares
the man of all work on the Margate Hoy to "another Ariel,
flaming at once about all parts of the deck, yet with kindlier minis-
trations—not to assist the tempest, but, as if touched with a
kindred sense of our infirmities, to soothe the qualms which that
untried motion might haply raise in our crude land-fancies." [347]

Lamb often draws upon classical mythology to give added
imaginative charm to his writing. In describing the garden where
he played as a child, he says of an antique statue which stood
there: "Child of Athens or old Rome paid never a sincerer worship to Pan or to Sylvanus in their native groves than I to that
fragmental mystery." [348]   In "Witches and Other Night Fears,"
he figures forth a dream he had, in images drawn from Greek
mythology: "Methought I was upon the ocean billows at some sea
nuptials, riding and mounted high, with the customary train sound-
ing their conchs before me (I myself, you may be sure, the *leading
god*), and jollily we went careering over the main, till just where
Ino Leucothea should have greeted me . . . with a white embrace,
the billows gradually subsiding, fell from a sea roughness to a sea
calm, and thence to a river motion. . . . " [349]

His apostrophe to the past in "The Old Benchers of the Inner

---

[344] *Works*, vol. II, p. 45.
[345] Ibid., p. 46.
[346] Ibid., p. 6.
[347] "The Old Margate Hoy," Ibid., p. 178.
[348] "Blakesmoor in H—shire," Ibid., p. 157.
[349] "Witches and Other Night Fears," Ibid., p. 69.

Temple" shows an intensity of feeling which rises to lyrical heights: "Fantastic forms, whither are ye fled? Or, if the like of you exist, why exist they no more for me? Ye inexplicable, half understood appearances, why comes in reason to tear away the preternatural mist, bright or gloomy, that surrounded you? Why make ye so sorry a figure in my relation; who made up to me—to my childish eyes—the mythology of the Temple? In those days I saw Gods, as 'old men covered with a mantle' walking upon the earth." [350]

Imagination will not wholly perish from the earth as long as there are children, Lamb believes: "Let the dreams of classic idolatry perish,—extinct be the fairies and fairy trumpery of legendary fabling,—in the heart of childhood, there will, forever, spring up a well of innocent or wholesome superstition—the seeds of exaggeration will be busy there, and vital. . . . While childhood, and while dreams, reducing childhood, shall be left, imagination shall not have spread her holy wings totally to fly the earth." [351]

Hazlitt's figures of speech, which seldom surprise by the unexpectedness of the analogy, but which continually please by their aptness, are less spontaneous, less sportive and less humorous than Lamb's, but they color and quicken the thought, and give it added meaning. Their function is frequently an interpretive one, as may be seen from Hazlitt's comment on John Buncle, one of his favorite characters: "He converts the thorns and briars of controversial divinity into a bed of roses. He leads the most refined and virtuous of their sex through the mazes of inextricable problems with the air of a man walking a minuet in a drawing-room; mixes up in the most natural and careless manner the academy of compliments with the rudiments of algebra." [352] His comments sometimes have the pith of an aphorism, as when he says: "Art is the microscope of the mind, which sharpens the wit as the other does the sight; and converts every object into a little universe in itself." [353] Or when he writes of Spenser, "His poetry was the

---

[350] "The Old Benchers of the Inner Temple," Op. cit., p. 90.
[351] Ibid.
[352] "On John Buncle," Ibid., vol. I, p. 52.
[353] "On Imitation," Ibid., p. 74.

essence of romance, a very halo round the bright orb of fancy." [354]

Hazlitt studied the art of investing thought with "the gossamer web of fancy." "The great art," he says, "is not to throw a glare of light upon all objects, or to lay the whole extended landscape bare at one view; but so to manage as to see the more amiable side of things, and through the narrow vistas and loop-holes of retreat, 'Catch glimpses that may make us less forlorn.' I hate to annihilate air and distance by the perpetual use of an opera-glass, to run everything into foreground, and to interpose no medium between the thought and the object. The breath of words stirs and plays idly with the gossamer web of fancy: the touch of things destroys it." [355] Hazlitt possessed the fine art of perceiving the elemental quality in a thing, and letting his imagination play around it, until he reveals the truth he sees. In his essay "On a Sun-Dial," in reflecting on the various ways of marking time, he makes this very illuminating comment: "Robinson Crusoe lost his reckoning in the monotony of his life and that bewildering dream of solitude, and was fain to have recourse to the notches on a piece of wood. What a diary was his! And how time must have spread its circuit round him, vast and pathless as the ocean." [356] The last sentence exactly conveys the passing of time in solitude, and the figure which expresses it is so fitting an analogy that it scarcely seems to be a figure. It is indeed "the gossamer web of fancy."

But more than this, Hazlitt's imagination frequently expresses itself in a poetic manner, and as it wings higher, its self-revelatory character becomes at times impassioned. Like Lamb, he shows the influence of classical mythology; he turns to an Arcadian past which holds for him visions of beauty, and invests its figures with the romantic veil of remoteness. When he imagines objects of nature, he can, he says, "easily form a mystic personification of the friendly power that inhabits them, Dryad or Naiad, offering its cool fountain or its tempting shade."[357] In his essay "On a Sun-

---

[354] "Of Persons One Would Wish to Have Seen," *Works*, vol. XII, p. 30.

[355] "On the Conversation of Lords," Ibid., pp. 42-43.

[356] "On a Sun-Dial," Ibid., p. 58.

[357] "On the Love of the Country," Ibid., vol. I, p. 19.

Dial," he again speaks of these fleeting glimpses of beauty: "Perhaps some thoughts I have set down float before me like motes before my half-shut eyes, or some vivid image of the past by forcible contrast rushes by me—'Diana and her fawn, and all the glories of the antique world'; and then I start away to prevent the iron entering my soul, and let fall some tears into the stream of time which separates me farther and farther from all I once loved." [358]

Hazlitt's imaginative faculty is strongly revealed in the glamor with which he invests the past. "All that strikes the imagination, or excites any interest in the mighty scene, is *what has been*," [359] he says. Some event in his own life usually serves to start a train of recollection accompanied with imaginative fervor which at times becomes lyrical. Passionate yearning, frustrated hopes, an intense desire for life lived to the fullest are in his heart cry, "Ye woods that crown the clear brow of Norman Court, why do I revisit ye so oft, and feel a soothing consciousness of your presence, but that your high tops waving in the wind recal (sic) to me the hours and years that are for ever fled, that ye renew in ceaseless murmurs the story of long-cherished hopes and bitter disappointment, that in your solitudes and tangled wilds I can wander and lose myself, as I wander on and am lost in the solitude of my own heart. . . . Without that face pale as the primrose with hyacinthine locks, forever shunning and forever haunting me, mocking my waking thoughts as in a dream. . . . Without that form gliding before me like Oread or Dryad in fabled groves, what should I do, how pass away the listless leaden-footed hours? Then wave, wave on, ye woods of Tuderley, and lift your high tops in the air; my sighs and vows uttered by your mystic voice breathe into me my former being, and enable me to bear the thing I am!" [360]

Hunt also enjoyed dwelling in an imaginative world, but it is a different world from Hazlitt's. Unlike Hazlitt, he does not seek to escape from life by dwelling upon past events and investing them with romantic fancy; he adds to the enjoyment and richness of his life by continually associating what he sees with fanciful and

---

[358] "On a Sun-Dial," *Works*, vol. XII, pp. 58-59.
[359] "The Love of Power or Action," Ibid., vol. XI, p. 266.
[360] "On the Past and Future," Ibid., vol. VI, pp. 24-25.

poetic ideas. The most commonplace things suggest to him beauty and set his imagination to work. The images he recalls are not usually connected with events in his past life, but result from his wide reading in imaginative literature. In his essay "On the Realities of the Imagination" he reveals the extent to which imagination has enriched his life, and emphasizes the reality of its pleasures. Let as many 'glad imaginations' throng the mind as possible, he pleads: "Read the magical works of the poets, and they will come. If you doubt their existence, ask yourself whether you feel pleasure at the idea of them; whether you are moved into delicious smiles, or tears as delicious. If you are, the result is the same to you, whether they exist or not." "Knowledge, sympathy, imagination," he says, "are all divining-rods" with which man discovers treasure. Hunt is more fanciful than imaginative in a poetic sense. The delicate fancy in which he sometimes indulges is well illustrated in his Introduction to the *Wishing-Cap Papers*, in which he imagines himself a spirit: "A spirit I certainly am, by universal acknowledgment; though what sort of one has been much contested. . . . Certainly I am not a malignant spirit, though I trifle now and then with a Caliban. Neither am I the devil on two sticks, confined to my bottle; nor the spirit, that according to the Italian poet, dwelt in the smoke of roast meat. But like certain spirits in poetry and romance, I have seen a good deal of the world, visible and invisible. Like them, I see knowledge. Like them I am fond of music, of the air, of the trees and flowers, and of liberty. . . . Like a spirit I can dilate myself, till mountains become mole-hills; or shrink into such diminutive compass, as to stand by the side of a brook, and live in imagination on the banks of it, with the little insects, as if it were some mighty river. Millions of times have I ridden on the bat's back, and gone to sleep in a buttercup. But my tears inform me that I am human, to say nothing of my frailties." [361]

Although Hunt emphasizes the part that imagination plays in life, and lived to a large extent in a world created by his fancy, he never rises in his essays to the lyrical heights of Lamb and Hazlitt. He does not recall the past in an impassioned manner,

---

[361] *Wishing-Cap Papers*, p. 18.

nor people it with fleeting shapes drawn from classical mythology; nor does he deeply stir our feelings or emotions. His imagination plays over the surface of things, and is more concerned with extracting pleasure from the commonplace, than in winging its way upward. The difference in the quality of Hunt's imagination as compared with Lamb's and Hazlitt's may be partially owing to the fact that he lived too much in a world of books. His experiences are vital to him in the degree that he can relate them to his reading. The continual association of incidents in his life with literary allusions shows his tendencey to view life through the medium of books. He is less original, less searching, and less often concerned with fundamentals than either Lamb or Hazlitt. His struggles, doubts, perplexities, fears are not given imaginative expression, but he reveals in a fanciful and sometimes poetic manner his love of nature and his delight in simple pleasures, which he would have all men share.

On the contrary Hazlitt pours forth his innermost thoughts in a flood-tide of self-revelation which is frequently highly imaginative in a poetic sense. He stirs us emotionally because of the intensity of his own feeling. Life disappoints and frustrates him, and he cries out against it or seeks solace in recalling happier days which he invests with the glamor of the past.

Of a yet different quality is Lamb's imagination. He is not concerned with giving voice to defeated hopes, like Hazlitt, nor is he interested in preaching a gospel of beauty, like Hunt, but he gives us the full flavor of his personality, by letting his mind play in an imaginative manner over whatever pleases his fancy. He sees deeply into life, but his observations are cloaked with so much humor and infused with such originality that the reader thinks of them not as a "criticism of life" but as a delight shared.

CHAPTER VII

CONCLUSION

In thus tracing the elements old and new which went into the making of the familiar essay in the early nineteenth century, it becomes clear that many elements from the essays of the seventeenth and eighteenth centuries came over into the nineteenth century familiar essay. It carries on the traditions of the Montaigne type of essay in its literary flavor, its self-revelation, its easy conversational style, its digressions, and in the choice of subject according to the whim of the author. It shows the influence of the seventeenth century in style, theme, and the use of the "character." It exhibits many of the characteristics of the eighteenth century periodical essay in its realistic description, humor, intimate style, anecdotes, incidents, and reported conversation. In theme also it shows the influence of the periodical essay. More specific influences are to be seen in the use of the "character," the character-sketch and the familiar letter. The character-sketch not only adds to the interest of the familiar essay, but definitely contributes to its development, through its wealth of excellent portraiture and its emphasis upon individuality and the revelation of fundamental human qualities. The letter likewise contributes to the interest of the familiar essay, and its use demonstrates the close union between the two forms. This union is effected by the introduction of letters into the essay, by the employing of a style characteristic of the familiar letter and by the use of material from actual letters, either as part of the essay, or to furnish a theme.

In spite of seventeenth and eighteenth century influence, however, the divergence of the early nineteenth century essay from the periodical essays of the Tatler-Spectator type is so marked as to demand explanation. The familiar essay not only flourished anew, but reached its highest development in the work of Hunt, Hazlitt and Lamb. The factors contributing to its development

228

were varied. The intellectual curiosity aroused by the French Revolution and the Industrial Revolution resulted in the establishment of literary periodicals which fostered the essay by the greater amount of space they afforded, by the emphasis they placed upon literature and the fine arts, and by the high standard of excellence in writing set by their editors. Increased wealth, extension of education, and improved methods in the printing and distributing of periodicals secured for them a wide circulation. The essayists were thus writing for a larger and more cosmopolitan public, and the essay took on greater variety of theme and a universality of interest that it had heretofore lacked.

But the most powerful influence in the shaping of the new essay was the Romantic Revival. In the essays of Hunt, Lamb and Hazlitt may be traced Romantic elements which parallel those found in the Romantic poets. This influence is the more pronounced because of the friendship that existed between the essayists and the poets. It manifests itself particularly in the romantic coloring given to the love of nature and the picturesque and to self-revelation in the familiar essay, and in the highly imaginative and poetic quality of many of the essays of Hunt, Lamb and Hazlitt. The poetic and cadenced prose of these writers was in part the result of their theories as to the legitimate relation between prose and poetry, but chiefly an expression of their romantic temperament.

A reawakened sense of the beauties of nature, which was a striking feature of the Romantic Revival, is found in the work of the familiar essayists as well as in the poetry of the period. The essayists not only describe nature and the picturesque, but discuss nature in its relation to art and life. Hazlitt's theory of man's attachment to natural objects, and the romantic sentiment with which he invests them, closely parallels Wordsworth's treatment of nature. The familiar essayists' love of nature and the picturesque expresses itself in charming natural description which frequently is poetic in expression; in description of the picturesque in towns and people; in a gospel of beauty elaborated by Hunt; in the romantic interest with which places are invested, evidenced particularly in Hunt's and Lamb's treatment of London life; and in the recollection of well-loved places and scenes connected with the essayists' childhood. In its treatment of nature as well as in its self-revelation, the familiar essay marks a definite divergence from the periodical essay. Even though the essays of the latter part of the eighteenth century show some romantic feeling in the treatment of the picturesque in nature and in city life, they contain nothing comparable, in amount or kind, to the romantic treatment of nature in the work of Hunt, Lamb and Hazlitt.

The impulse given to self-revelation comes largely from Rousseau, whose influence was especially strong upon Hazlitt. A parallel may be drawn also between Wordsworth and the familiar essayists—in the romantic elements of their self-expression, their impassioned recollection, their turning to the past, and their sympathy with lowly life. Mingled with these romantic elements are realistic features which provide contrast, lend verisimilitude, and give added charm to the essay. In the frankness and fulness with which Hunt, Lamb and Hazlitt reveal themselves, no less than in the romantic coloring of their writing, they differ from the essayists of the eighteenth century. The familiar essayists are not hampered by the use of fictitious mouthpieces. They speak in their own persons and from the heart—confessing not only their "amiable weaknesses" but at times personal matters that other men would hug to their bosoms, and not infrequently breaking forth in lyric cry that has the poignancy of lyric poetry.

The most distinctive element in Hunt, Lamb and Hazlitt is the highly imaginative and individualistic quality of their work. This appears equally in their treatment of nature and their self-revelation. Their imaginative range is wide and runs the scale from light and entertaining fancy to passionate intensity. Hunt is more fanciful than imaginative in a poetic sense, and seldom shows exaltation of feeling. Hazlitt, on the contrary, frequently pours forth his emotions in a lyrical ecstacy. Lamb's imagination is the most original in the manner in which it plays over and illuminates whatever interests him. The way in which these essayists view life, muse upon its meaning, and discover truth and beauty in simple things makes their appeal comparable to that of the poet. They work in the spirit of the creative artist. They deal with the stuff of the imagination and the emotions, and in a manner to give full play to individuality and temperament. And it is this more than all else perhaps that raises these early nineteenth century essays, or at least a large proportion of them, to the rank of great literature and places them at the very summit of achievement in the essay form in England.

BIBLIOGRAPHY

Ainger, Alfred. *Charles Lamb.* N. Y., 1882.
Aitken, George Atherton. *The Life of Richard Steele.* 2 vols. Lond., 1889.
Aldington, Richard. *A Book of Characters.* Lond., and N. Y., 1924.
Ames, John Griffith, Jr. *The English Literary Periodical of Morals and Manners.* Mt. Vernon, Ohio, 1904.
Ashton, John. *Social Life in the Reign of Queen Anne, taken from Original Sources.* London, 1919.
Babbitt, Irving. *Rousseau and Romanticism.* Bost., 1919.
Bacon, Francis. *Essays,* edited with Introduction and Notes by F. G. Selby. Lond., 1902.
Baker, Harry T. "Lamb and the Periodical Essay." *North American Review,* ccxv, 519 ff.
Baldwin, Edward Chauncey. "La Bruyère's Influence upon Addison." *P.M.L.A.,* xix, 1904, 479 ff.
Baldwin, Edward Chauncey. "The Relation of the Seventeenth Century Character to the Periodical Essay." *P.M.L.A.,* xix, 1904, 75 ff.
Bee (The). In Goldsmith, Oliver. *Miscellaneous Works, with Biographical Introduction by Prof. Masson.* Lond., 1928, pp. 353 ff.
Beers, Thomas. *A History of English Romanticism in the Eighteenth Century.* N. Y., 1899.
Beers, Thomas. *A History of English Romanticism in the Nineteenth Century.* N. Y., 1901.
Binkley, Harold C. "Essays and Letter-writing." *P.M.L.A.,* xli, 1926, 342 ff.
Birrell, Augustine. *William Hazlitt.* N. Y., 1902. (English Men of Letters.)
Blunden, Edmund. *Leigh Hunt and His Circle.* N. Y., 1930.
Blunden, Edmund. *Leigh Hunt's "Examiner" Examined.* Lond., 1928.
Breton, Nicholas. *Works in Verse and Prose,* collected and edited by A. B. Grosart. 2 vols. Edinburgh, 1879.
Brinton, Clare. *The Political Ideas of the English Romanticists.* Oxford, 1926.
British Essayists: With Prefaces, Historical and Biographical, edited by A. Chalmers. 45v. in-28. Lond., 1817.
Reprints of the leading essay periodicals of the eighteenth century.
Browne, Sir Thomas. *Works . . .* edited by Geoffrey Keynes. 6 vols. Lond., and N. Y., 1928-31.
Burton, Robert. *Anatomy of Melancholy,* edited by A. R. Shillets, with an Introduction by A. H. Bullen. 3 vols. Lond., 1893.
Butcher, S. H. *Aristotle's Theory of Poetry and Fine Art, with a Critical Text and a Translation of the Poetics.* Lond., 1895.
Cambridge History of English Literature, edited by Sir A. W. Ward and A. R. Waller, vol. XII, N. Y., 1916.
Coleridge, Samuel Taylor. *Biographia Literaria,* edited with an Introduction by John Calvin Metcalf. N. Y., 1926.
Coleridge, Samuel Taylor. *Coleridge's Literary Criticism,* with an Introduction by J. W. Mackail. Lond., 1921.

233

Companion (*The*), by Leigh Hunt. N. Y., 1845. (Bound with the *Indicator*).
Cooper, Anthony Ashley, third Earl of Shaftesbury. *Characteristicks of Men, Manners, Opinions, Times,* 3 vols. Birmingham, 1773.
Cross, Launcelot, *i.e.,* Frank Carr. *Characteristics of Leigh Hunt as exhibited in . . . Leigh Hunt's London Journal.* Lond., 1878.
Dawson, William J. and Dawson, Coningsby W. *The Great English Letter-writers,* 2 vols. Lond., 1919.
Dobell, Bertram. *Sidelights on Charles Lamb.* Lond., 1903.
Drake, Nathan. *Essays, Biographical, Critical, and Historical,* illustrative of the *Rambler, Adventurer,* and *Idler,* and of the Various Periodical Papers which, in imitation of the Writings of Steele and Addison, have been published between the Close of the eighth volume of the *Spectator,* and the Commencement of the year 1809. 2 vols. Lond., 1809-10.
Drake, Nathan. *Essays, Biographical, Critical, and Historical,* illustrative of the *Tatler, Spectator, and Guardian.* 3 vols. Lond., 1805.
Drake, Nathan. *The Gleaner:* a Series of Periodical Essays; selected and arranged from Scarce or Neglected Volumes, with an Introduction and Notes, by Nathan Drake . . . 4 vols. Lond., 1811.
Earle, John. *Microcosmography or Piece of the World discovered in Essays and Characters.* 1628. (Arber, Edward, ed. English Reprints, 1869-71. vol. 4, no. 2.)
Elliot, Arthur R. D. "Reviews and Magazines in the Early Years of the Nineteenth Century." *Cambridge History of English Literature,* vol. XII, 154 ff.
Examiner (*The*), a Weekly Paper on Politics, Literature, Music, and the Fine Arts. Lond., 1808-1881.
Field, James T. *Old Acquaintance: Barry Cornwall and Some of his Friends.* Bost., 1876.
Fielding, Henry. *The Covent Garden Journal,* by Sir Alexander Drawcansir, knt. censor of Great Britain (Henry Fielding), ed. by Gerard Edward Jensen. 2 vols. New Haven, 1915.
Forster, John. *Historical and Biographical Essays.* vol. 2, Lond., 1858.
Fuller, Thomas. *The Holy State and the Profane State,* with notes by James Nichols. Lond., 1841.
Gilpin, William. *Observations on the River Wye and Several Parts of South Wales,* etc., relative chiefly to Picturesque Beauty Made in the Summer of the Year, 1770. Third edition. Lond., 1792.
Gilpin, William. *Remarks on Forest Scenery and other Woodland Views* (relative chiefly to Picturesque Beauty), illustrated by the Scenes of New Forest in Hampshire. 3 vols. Second edition. Lond., 1794.
Goldsmith, Oliver. *Miscellaneous Works,* with Biographical Introduction by Professor Masson. Lond., 1928.
Gosse, Edmund. *Aspects and Impressions.* N. Y., 1922.
Grabo, Carl H. *Romantic Prose of the Early Nineteenth Century.* N. Y., 1927.
Graham, Walter. *The Beginnings of English Literary Periodicals; a Study of Periodical Literature,* 1665-1715. N. Y., 1926.
Graham, Walter. *English Literary Periodicals.* N. Y., 1930.
Greenough, C. N. "The Development of the *Tatler* particularly in Regard to News." *P.M.L.A.,* xxxi, 633 ff.
Grierson, H. J. C. *Classical and Romantic.* Cambridge (Eng.), 1923.
Hansche, Maude Bingham. *The Formative Period of English Familiar Letter-writers and their Contribution to the English Essay.* Phila., 1902. (Univ. of Penna. diss.)

Hazlitt, W. C. *Lamb and Hazlitt.* N. Y., 1899.
Hazlitt, W. C. *Four Generations of a Literary Family.* Lond., and N. Y., 1897.
* Hazlitt, William. *The Collected Works of William Hazlitt,* edited by A. R. Waller and Arnold Glover. 12 vols. Lond., 1903.
Hazlitt, William. *New Writings,* collected by P. P. Howe. N. Y., 1925.
Hazlitt, William. *New Writings;* Second Series collected by P. P. Howe. N. Y., 1927.
Hazlitt, William. *The Round Table; A Collection of Essays on Literature, Men and Manners.* 2 v. in 1. Edinburgh, 1817.
Hood, Thomas. *Memorials of Thomas Hood,* collected, arranged and edited by his Daughter; with a Preface and Notes by his Son. 2 vols. Lond., 1860.
Hone's Table Book, Lond., 1827.
Howe, P. P. *The Life of William Hazlitt.* Lond., n.d.
Howe, W. D. "Hazlitt." *Cambridge History of English Literature,* xii, 181 ff.
Howell, James. *Epistolae Ho-Elianae; The Familiar Letters of James Howell,* edited, annotated and indexed by Joseph Jacobs. 2 vols. Lond., 1892.
Hunt, Leigh. *The Autobiography of Leigh Hunt.* Lond., 1891.
Hunt, Leigh. *A Book for a Corner,* or Selections in Prose and Verse from Authors the best suited to that Mood of Enjoyment, with Comments on each, and a General Introduction by Leigh Hunt. Second Series, N. Y., 1859.
Hunt, Leigh. *The Correspondence of Leigh Hunt,* edited by his Eldest Son. 2 vols. Lond., 1862.
Hunt, Leigh. *Essays,* selected and edited by Reginald Brinley Johnson. Lond., 1891.
Hunt, Leigh. *Essays* (Selected), with an Introduction by J. B. Priestley. N. Y., 1929.
Hunt, Leigh. *Essays,* edited with Introduction and Notes, by Arthur Symons. Lond., n.d.
Hunt, Leigh. *Imagination and Fancy, or Selections from the English Poets.* Lond., 1891.
Hunt, Leigh. *Leigh Hunt as Poet and Essayist,* being Choicest Passages from his Works, selected and edited with a Biographical Introduction by Charles Kent. Lond., n.d.
Hunt, Leigh. *Men, Women and Books,* a selection of Sketches, Essays and Critical Memoirs, from his uncollected Prose Writings. Lond., 1891.
Hunt, Leigh. *The Months,* descriptive of the Successive Beauties of the Year. Lond., 1821.
Hunt, Leigh. *The Old Court Suburb: or Memorials of Kensington, Regal, Critical and Anecdotal.* 2 vols. Phila., n.d.
Hunt, Leigh. *A Saunter through the West End.* Lond., 1861.
Hunt, Leigh. *The Seer, or Common-Places Refreshed.* 2 vols. Bost., 1864.
Hunt, Leigh. *Table-talk to which are added Imaginary Conversations of Pope and Swift.* Lond., 1851.
Hunt, Leigh. *The Town; its Memorable Characters and Events.* Lond., 1889.
Hunt, Leigh. *Wishing-Cap Papers.* Bost., 1888.
Hunt, Leigh. *Wit and Humour, Selected from the English Poets.* Lond., 1890.

* Note : The definitive edition of the *Works* of Hazlitt, edited by P. P. Howe has not been used, owing to its still being incomplete.

Indicator (The), and the *Companion*; a Miscellany for the Fields and the *Fire-Side*. By Leigh Hunt. In Two Parts. Parts I-II, Lond., 1840. Original periodical.

Indicator (The). A Miscellany for the Fields and the Fireside. By Leigh Hunt. In Two Parts. Parts I-II. N. Y., 1845. Reprint in book form. Also contains the *Companion*.

Jensen, Gerald E. "Fashionable Society in Fielding's Time." *P.M.L.A.*, xxxi, 79 ff.

Johnson, R. Brinley, ed. *Shelley-Leigh Hunt; how friendship made history, extending the bounds of human freedom and thought*. 2nd ed., Lond., 1929.

Johnson, Samuel. *A Journey to the Western Islands of Scotland*. Bost., n.d.

Johnson, Samuel. *Works:* with an Essay on his Life and Genius, by Arthur Murphy, Esq. 12 vols. Lond., 1823.

Knox, Vicesimus. *Winter Evenings, or Lucubrations on Life and Letters*. 2 vols. Lond., 1823.

La Bruyère, Jean de. *Works . . . to which is added the Characters of Theophrastus*. 2 vols. Lond., 1776.

Lake, Bernard. *A General Introduction to Charles Lamb*. Together with a Special Study of his Relation to Robert Burton, the author of the "Anatomy of Melancholy." Leipzig, 1903. (Doctoral diss.)

Lamb, Charles, *Eliana:* being the hitherto Uncollected Writings of Charles Lamb. N. Y., 1865.

Lamb, Charles. *Life, Letters and Writings of Charles Lamb*, ed. by Percy Fitzgerald, 6 vols. Lond., 1886.

Lamb, Charles, and Lamb, Mary. *The Works of Charles and Mary Lamb*, edited by E. V. Lucas. 6 vols. Lond., 1905.

Leigh Hunt's London Journal and The Printing Machine. To assist the inquiring, animate the struggling, and sympathize with all. 2 vols. Lond., 1834-1835.

Liberal (The). Verse and Prose from the South. 2 vols. Lond., 1822.

London Magazine (The). 10 vols. Lond., 1820-24. New series. 9 vols. Lond., 1825-27.

Lucas, E. V., ed. *Charles Lamb and the Lloyds*. Phila., 1898.

Lucas, E. V. *The Life of Charles Lamb*. 2 vols. N. Y., 1905.

Maar, Harks G. de. *A History of Modern English Romanticism*. Vol. 1. Oxford, 1924.

MacClintock, W. D. *Some Paradoxes of the English Romantic Movement of the Eighteenth Century*. Univ. of Chicago Decennial Publications. First Series, vol. VII, Chicago, 1903.

MacDonald, W. L. "The Beginnings of the English Essay." *Univ. of Toronto Studies*, No. 3, 1914.

Marr, George S. *Periodical Essayists of the Eighteenth Century*. N. Y., 1924.

Monkhouse, W. Cosmo. *Life of Leigh Hunt*. Lond., 1893.

Montaigne, Michael. *The Essayes of Michael, Lord of Montaigne*, translated by John Florio. 3 vols. Lond., 1910.

Morley, Edith J., ed. *Blake, Coleridge, Wordsworth, Lamb*, etc., being selections from the Remains of Henry Crabb Robinson. Manchester University Press, 1922.

Morley, Edith J., ed. *The Correspondence of Henry Crabb Robinson with the Wordsworth Circle* (1808-1866). 2 vols. Oxford, 1927.

Murphy, Gwendolen. *Bibliography of English Character-books*, 1608-1700. Oxford, 1925.

Murphy, Gwendolen. *A Cabinet of Characters*. Oxford, 1925.

Overbury, Sir Thomas. *Miscellaneous Works in Prose and Verse,* edited with Notes and a Biographical Account of the Author by E. F. Rimbault. Lond., 1856.

Pater, Walter. *Appreciations, with an Essay on Style.* N. Y., 1906.

Phelps, William Lyon. *The Beginnings of the English Romantic Movement.* Bost., 1893.

Pierce, Federick E. *Currents and Eddies in the English Romantic Generation.* New Haven, 1918.

Procter, Bryan Waller. *Bryan Waller Procter*; an Autobiographical Fragment and Biographical Notes. Lond., 1877.

Rambler (The), by Dr. Samuel Johnson. Lond., 1793. Vol. III-IV. (paged separately). (Leigh Hunt's own copy, with marginal annotations. In Cornell University Library.)

Rannie, David Watson. *Wordsworth and His Circle.* Lond., 1907.

Reflector (The), a Quarterly Magazine on Subjects of Philosophy, Politics and the Liberal Arts, conducted by the Editor of the *Examiner,* vols. I-II. Oct., 1810-Dec., 1811. Lond., 1811.

Robertson, J. G. *Studies in the Genesis of Romantic Theory in the Eighteenth Century.* Cambridge (Eng.).

Robinson, Crabb. *Blake, Coleridge, Wordsworth and Lamb.* Manchester, 1922.

Roscoe, E. S. *The English Scene in the Eighteenth Century.* N. Y., 1912.

Rousseau, Jean-Jacques. *Confessions, translated from the French.* With a preface by Edmund Wilson. 2 vols. N. Y., 1928.

Saintsbury, George. "The Antiquaries." *Cambridge History of English Literature,* vol. XII, 264 ff.

Saintsburg, George. "The Landors, Leigh Hunt, De Quincey." *Cambridge History of English Literature,* vol. XII, 226 ff.

Shelley, Percy Bysshe. *Complete Poetical Works.* Bost., 1901. (Cambridge Edition.)

Shelley, Percy Bysshe. *Prose Works,* edited by H. B. Forman. 4 vols. Lond., 1880.

Shelly, Percy Van Dyke. "The Familiar Essay." *University of Pennsylvania Public Lectures,* 1916-17. Phila., 1917.

Smith, Hamilton Jewett. *Oliver Goldsmith's The Citizen of the World, a Study.* New Haven, 1916.

Smollett, Tobias. "Travels through France and Italy." *Works,* vol. XI. N. Y., 1900.

Spectator (The). N. Y., 1907. (Everyman ed.)

Stephen, Leslie. *English Literature and Society in the Eighteenth Century.* N. Y., 1904.

Stephen, Leslie. *Hours in a Library.* Vol. II. Lond., 1892.

Stephen, Leslie. *The Playground of Europe.* Lond., 1910.

Sterne, Laurence. "A Sentimental Journey through France and Italy." *Works,* vol. II. Lond., 1873.

Swift, Jonathan. *Works,* with Memoir of the Author by Thomas Roscoe. Vol. II. Lond., 1848.

Symons, Arthur. *The Romantic Movement in English Poetry.* N. Y., 1909.

Talfourd, Thomas Noon. *A Sketch of the Life of Charles Lamb with Final Memorials,* to which are added notes and illustrations by Percy Fitzgerald. Lond., 1876.

Tatler (The), a Daily Journal of Literature and the Stage. Lond., v. 1-4, 1830-32.

Taylor, Hedley V. *Letters of Great Writers, from the Time of Spenser to the Time of Wordsworth.* Glasgow, 1912.

Taylor, Jeremy. *Rule and Exercises of Holy Living.* Lond., 1682. Contains also *Rule and Exercises of Holy Dying.*
Thompson, A. Hamilton. "Lamb." *Cambridge History of English Literature,* vol. VIII, 199 ff.
Thomson, J. C., comp. *Bibliography of the Writings of Charles and Mary Lamb: a Literary History.* Hull, 1908.
Thompson, Elbert N. S. "The Seventeenth-century English Essay." (*University of Iowa Humanistic Studies,* III.)
Thorndike, Ashley H. *Literature in a Changing Age.* N. Y., 1920.
Vaughan, C. E., ed. *English Literary Criticism.* Lond., 1896.
Walker, Hugh. *The English Essay and Essayists.* Lond., 1928.
Wheatley, Henry B. "Letter-Writers." *Cambridge History of English Literature,* vol. X, 274-306.
Whitmore, Charles E. "The Field of the Essay." *P.M.L.A.,* xxxvi, 551 ff.
Withington, Robert. "The Romantic Essay." *So. Atlantic Quarterly,* xxiii, 269-76.
Wordsworth, William. *Poems,* ed. by Matthew Arnold. Lond., 1903.
Wordsworth, William. *Poems dedicated to National Independence and Liberty,* ed. by Hutchinson. Oxford, 1895.
Wordsworth, William, and Coleridge, S. T. *Lyrical Ballads by William Wordsworth and S. T. Coleridge,* 1798, edited with an Introduction and Notes by Thomas Hutchinson. Lond., 1907.
Wylie, Laura Johnson. "Social Studies in English Literature." Bost., 1916. (*Vassar Semi-Centennial Series.*)
Zeitlin, Jacob, ed. *Seventeenth Century Essays from Bacon to Clarendon.* N. Y., 1926.